# THE GIRL ON THE BRIDGE: A MEMOIR

## TRACEY HIGGINS

*To all sufferers who are still struggling to find a way out of schizophrenia—may my story bring you hope and inspire your healing.*

*A special mention to Morgan Geyser, a twelve-year-old girl diagnosed with schizophrenia and sentenced to forty years in a mental health facility for a crime. Children with mental health conditions should never be behind bars. We must fight against this, for the only answer should be rehabilitation and healing.*

# Contents

# INTRODUCTION

"When confronted with a disturbing realization that you're not mentally equipped to handle, your mind creates a new reality (world) to live in."

— Tracey Higgins

First, the word *crazy* is problematic and pejorative and mostly about stigma and ridicule. Boiled down to its essence, for most people, it would mean someone who acts in ways that don't make sense. Well, schizophrenia makes sense. It is a desperate response to desperate circumstances. It is about survival, and survival makes sense. Survival is the most basic instinct there is. There are triggers that lead to schizophrenia, and those triggers can be examined and used as handholds to climb out of it again. It took me a long time to figure that out. Never underestimate the power of psychosis.

Second, approximately seventy million people suffer from schizophrenia worldwide. The stigma that stems from debunked brain-disease models of schizophrenia has been dissuading people from coming forward to seek the help they need for decades now.

There are many and diverse possible contributing factors to the onset of schizophrenia; just because my case involved extreme childhood abuse, it doesn't mean that is the case for others. Each case of schizophrenia is unique even though the resulting symptoms are more or less the same. Some suffers may exhibit all the symptoms, others only a few.

Schizophrenia is survival mechanism brought on by disturbing or traumatic circumstance. When the realization of a threat to self and its perceived implications overwhelms the individual, a survival mechanism within the brain is triggered, one which seeks to shield or protect the sufferer from confronting or apprehending the truth of the situation. In other words, schizophrenia exists as a last-ditch response to a direct threat to self—real or imagined—when the sufferer believes there is no way out.

The mind creates a whole new world for the sufferer to inhabit—albeit a terrifying one at times. The symptoms of schizophrenia are natural responses to the trauma. Symptoms present themselves to protect the sufferer from ever having to deal with the trauma. Memories are pushed back into the place where traumatic memories are stored in the brain. Feelings are suppressed. Perceptions are skewed. Each symptom lays hold to a piece of the schizophrenic puzzle and deliberately keeps them apart.

Healing requires nothing less than the reintegration of the self. The puzzle needs solving. But it is important to recognize that it is the self that needs healing, not the brain. The brain can heal on its own when the underlying circumstances have been set to right.

The brain is only responding to the traumatic stress acting upon it. Schizophrenia is not, therefore, a flaw nor a disorder so much as a strategy. It is a survival mechanism which co-opts feelings, memories, and perceptions to avoid what it perceives as an existential threat to the self. When activated, all five senses are conscripted.

I went into the world of schizophrenia and came out the same way—through disturbing realizations.

We must ask ourselves, is schizophrenia a natural response to trauma?

Biological psychiatry has made everything so complicated. Though the biological basis of schizophrenia has never been fully endorsed by the greater psychiatric establishment nor elevated to the status of recognized theory, that hasn't stopped hypotheses from flourishing, especially in the eighties and nineties, and skewing treatment approaches for decades. When you add in the vested interest of big pharma and their overly cozy (even insidious) relationship with all aspect of the medical establishment, not just psychiatry, what you end up with are generations of lost sufferers written off and relegated to lifelong prescriptions.

A drug might offset a symptom and alleviate some aspect of suffering, but it cannot heal trauma. In that respect, there is a place for medication. However, all pills come with side effects especially in the long term. Furthermore, it is possible that drugs and their side effects prolong, or inhibit altogether, the kind of work needed to address the underlying trauma.

My greatest fear is that drugs are damaging the part of the brain that stores traumatic memories. Those memories need retrieving. Those suppressed feelings need to be explored. For me, those memories were so disturbing that I responded by developing trauma amnesia. It wasn't until many years after the events in question that the repressed memories resurfaced by way of a disturbing realization. That epiphany was what allowed me to set the recovery process in motion, and it might not have occurred had I been drugged to the gills.

Schizophrenia is a personal journey. There are no two stories alike. There are many paths to recovery. Mine is just one. However, the human process in the development of schizophrenia is all the same. By the time the sufferer gets into see a psychiatrist, the only thing the doctor is seeing is the end state.

Too often, and for too long, the first line of treatment for practicing psychiatrists has been medication. The doctor gives little attention to anything else. There is an expedience to medication, and the effect on individual symptoms are obvious and cannot be denied. But addressing a symptom is not the same as affecting a recovery—that is Medicine 101. Still, little emphasis is given to the schizophrenic language of the patient, better known as word salad. Within that language there are clues to the onset of schizophrenia. However, many psychiatrists fail to listen to their patients. Treatment resolves around ten-minute appointments once a week, mostly to see how the medication is working.

If any psychotherapy is offered, it takes months to get in to see a therapist even though schizophrenia needs intervention immediately before it has the time to cement itself in the life of the sufferer. The longer recovery is prolonged or delayed, the longer it takes to recover. Furthermore, the medication regularly employed in the interim to suppress symptoms often makes the needed work more difficult by the time the sufferer is afforded therapy.

The most upsetting thing about this kind of drug-first treatment model is that the sufferer is stripped of their autonomy. The power imbalance between therapist and sufferer is too great for any meaningful dialogue. Equality never comes into play.

According to one sufferer who is in the self-discovery phase of her recovery: "Often hospitals operate by the one-size-fits-all approach. Personal history and family idiosyncrasies are rarely delved into, to tailor and tweak treatment. The sufferer is reduced to a cluster of symptoms that must be managed."

When does the sufferer even get to have a word in their treatment plan? Should it not be a collaborative effort? Some health professionals have no belief in the sufferer's ability to make sound decisions. Family meetings take place where the professional has excluded the input of the actual sufferer. My question is this: when will people with schizophrenia get the chance to tell their stories without someone running interference?

Not all people will recover from schizophrenia. But they do deserve half a chance. Should a lifetime of medication not be considered a last resort? It seems to me therapeutic options ought to be thoroughly explored before assuming someone's schizophrenia is set in stone.

For others, they choose to use medication because there are no other options for them. However, using medication does not constitute a full recovery, as psychiatry tends to say. Call it a partial recovery if anything. Using medication to suppress symptoms can never be considered a full recovery precisely because it is contingent on continued use of the medication; the schizophrenia is still there and sometimes those drugs can make their condition worse. Many mental health professionals say that medications were designed for short-term use only because of the threat of iatrogenic damage (which is to say illness caused by treatment itself). Some doctors are even over-prescribing them with little concern of the consequences. But my mission is not to attack the use of medication. I am just saying that they work for some and don't work for others. And we should always be aware of the harm they can cause. One must know the drugs they are on.

When I first found out I had paranoid schizophrenia, I was too sick to see it. One time I even went to the library to look it up, but I still didn't see it. That's the thing about schizophrenia—once I got it, the hallucinations blocked out anything in the real world. And the terrifying voices badgered me all day long. To cope with that, I imagined myself as a saviour of some kind; out to save the world from God knows what. All of this happened because I was trying to escape the reality of a terrifying incident that happened in my childhood. Schizophrenia is like being on the verge of death, but death never comes. The suffering is overwhelming and claws away at your will to live. You'd have to get close enough to understand it. Unfortunately, most people are afraid of it, including therapists. Everyone seems tends to dance around it.

As a child something unspeakable happened to me. It was so horrible that I checked out. I couldn't deal with it and needed an escape, so my brain automatically created a new world for me to live in. It wasn't a friendly world, though. I felt like I was walking through a minefield. I had to be careful—something sinister was out to get me. Strangers were plotting against me. It felt like I was playing a part in horror film. To onlookers, I appeared normal, but on the inside a war was being waged, I was fighting for my survival.

Some of the things I write of will be triggering for some. But if I am going to tell the whole story, I must include everything.

As a kid, when someone told me to lift three haystacks, I lifted six. I was training my brain to believe I could overcome anything. While deep in my psychosis, I searched for hope—I'd find it in something as mundane as a colour, the long grass I had laid in, a song, anything. I never let schizophrenia become my identity. I was on a mission to save myself, to overcome my insanity and become whole again.

Schizophrenia is the most stigmatizing, embarrassing, frightening, and misunderstood condition out there. It's no wonder therapists are having a hard time figuring it out. It's like a puzzle, and psychiatry seems to be focused on one piece of the puzzle, the brain. Though psychiatry has mastered the art of describing schizophrenic symptoms, psychiatrists can't see the forest for the trees.

As I've already said, too often the current treatment model revolves around pharmaceutical stopgaps. Patients are told—to justify this model—that they have an incurable brain disease, a chemical imbalance of some kind. That's a lie, and one that has never held up to scientific scrutiny. But that lie is an easy sell for medical practitioners who are unprepared or unqualified to lead the work needed to affect a recovery and loved ones desperate for something that will mitigate the legitimate suffering of those they care about. And big pharma, of course, is more than happy to oblige.

People are desperate for solutions, but desperation rarely leads to sound long-term decisions. When children as young as three are being medicated for things like ADHD, people should be concerned.

After my recovery, I moved on with my life. I had so many things I wanted to do. But in my quiet time, when nobody was around, I thought about all the people still suffering. I thought about all the mothers, fathers, sisters, brothers, uncles, and aunts who felt like they had lost their loved ones for good. For this reason alone, I present my story to you, hoping to provide some real hope for everyone affected by schizophrenia.

In the end, all I can say is this: people diagnosed with schizophrenia can fully recover and live perfectly productive lives. Finding the right therapist is half the battle. We can have careers, own homes, raise families—and we are resilient. There is so much hope. I know it looks dark, but if I can fully recover, so can you. There is nothing special about my case; anyone can do it with the proper tools and the right mindset. But we must acknowledge that many don't recover for many reasons. I am pro-medication for short-term symptom relief and crisis management. But I don't believe they should be used long-term. I don't advise that anyone simply go off their medication. That is a decision to be made with your doctor. I offer hope, nothing more, and nothing less. However, I don't believe anyone is beyond hope. What I have, I wish for others. A treatment model needs designing. New treatment centres need building. That is the only solution I see needed.

## About the book:

What you are about to read is true. The events are portrayed to the best of my memory. Names have been changed and some dates have been altered. Gaps in my memory have been filled in and inconsistencies reconciled. And of course, a great deal has been left out. But it is all true.

This is what happened to me.

The narrative presented here runs on two tracks. The life that started when I broke free of my family at fourteen and the years leading up to that point that made it necessary to do so. It switches back and forth, and the open circuit finally closes at the point when I am able to start healing after years of suffering.

This book has been decades in the making.

# ONE

# THE GIRL ON THE BRIDGE

It was a Sunday morning in late August of 1978, and I was fourteen years old. I stood halfway along a pedestrian footbridge over the Queen Elizabeth Way in Mississauga's Lakeview, watching sparse southbound traffic pass beneath me. I held a Garfield book bag by one strap—the other was broken, torn from the bottom corner, and hung uselessly from the back. The day was sunny, and the breeze coming off the QEW was already warm and arid.

I'd just fought with Martha, my older sister, when I left our place on South Service Road. She'd caught me trying to take our kid sister's bike, and I think, perhaps, she could tell I was not planning on coming back. I'd had to leave the bike. It didn't upset me though—the fight with Martha—for I felt emotionally disconnected from my family, from everyone. Locked away inside myself. I just knew I had to go.

I took no particular pleasure or shame knowing that the pocketful of loose change in my jeans was from Martha's jewellery box. When I took it, I just knew I was going to need it. But then again...

Maybe I wouldn't need it after all.

I just stood there for a few moments thinking about the shallow arch below my feet, perhaps in awe of the strength needed to hold up all that concrete and the passing of endless feet day after day, hour after hour. I felt broken, then, in comparison, and the urge to jump welled up inside of me. I put my hands on the railing and looked over, feeling the impulse churn. I envisioned my body plunging through the air and smacking violently on the pavement below and blood everywhere. The crush of truck tires. But none of this did anything to dispel the urge to jump. I had to reach down inside myself and find a tremendous source of strength to fight the suicidal urges. I took my hands back slowly and looked down and stared at my shoes. Then I started walking, counting my steps as I went and using them to keep myself calm and focused, like counting sheep to go to sleep. But the voices had intensified. They were loud now.

As I passed over North Service Road and reached the ramp at the end of the span, I felt like I was finally breaking free from my mother, my stepfather, and the world that had fractured me. There was one major problem, though; my head was a mess. I knew, even then, that no matter how far I ran, the demons would still be with me. I'd brought them along as sure as I brought the change in my pockets. Except I could *empty* my pockets.

The voices were not going away. They were me, weren't they? The dark impulses, the thoughts that kept me inside myself and made it impossible to connect with others. I needed distractions, fantasies so appealing and far-fetched that no one would understand my alternative world, no one could enter it and do me harm. So I was a pirate looking for hidden treasure, and that treasure was me, and I would somehow, someday, find me among all the rubble of the world. I pictured a hat on my head, one that sported a single white feather that reminded me of my innocence.

I descended the ramp, feeling empty inside, more than before. I didn't know where to look for myself, but I couldn't go home. I wasn't wanted there, and there was nothing there for me, anyway. A broad six-lane river of asphalt and traffic now lay between me and my family, and my only regret was having left Sarah to fend for herself there, but it was a distant regret, one that felt less real by the moment.

I remember sleepwalking through the parking lot of the Applewood Village Plaza in a mental fog, the queasy adrenaline of the bridge slow to settle. I can't remember where I went from there. I only remember walking in the gathering heat with my book bag slipping from my shoulder.

By early afternoon it was hot. I'd been walking for hours, and my clothes were sticking to me. I was tired and hungry, my feet were sore, and I was looking for a police station. I had asked for directions a couple of times but was having a hard time concentrating on what I was being told. I didn't want anyone to get too close to me. When people asked me questions, I lied to them, distrusting the looks I was getting.

At one point I'd stuffed the book bag in a trash can in case someone was looking for a girl with a Garfield backpack. It was empty anyway, except for some homework from the year before because I hadn't packed anything. After a few minutes, I'd turned and gone back and retrieved the homework and tore it into little pieces and threw that into the next trash can I came to.

I don't remember deciding to go to the police, that hadn't been the plan when I started walking. I didn't have a plan. I figured the police would know where I should go next. I would tell the officer at the front desk that I didn't want to go home, that I couldn't go home, because no one there wanted me. Hopefully that would be enough.

There was so much I wouldn't be able to say. Couldn't say. Like how, even then, after all that had happened, part of me was craving some of the things that had broken me in two. How could I explain what I didn't understand myself? I was confused and ashamed. I felt exhausted, unprotected, and alone.

I made my way to a police station on Bloor Street West deep in Islington City Centre. The door seemed to weigh a thousand pounds. I walked up to the front desk where an officer sat talking on the phone to someone in distress. He waved his index finger in the air as if to say just a moment, please. When he hung up the phone, he looked me straight in the eyes and asked how he could help.

My lips felt like rubber, and I worried that he might know I was crazy. I told him I didn't want to go home then hung my head and pushed my hair over my eyes. I imagined a cane in my hand and that I was blind. I chuckled nervously, but then remembered not to do that in front of people because my mother told me that people would think I was nuts and I would end up in an institution.

At fourteen, I was a thin freckle-faced kid with long knotted hair and no figure to speak of. I didn't like to meet other people's gaze, and I was wearing old jeans, sneakers, and my favourite T-shirt which was blue and had kittens on the front.

The police officer looked at me for a moment then asked my name. I told him, and he told me to have a seat and that he would get someone to talk to me. But instead of sitting down, I paced back and forth in front of the four chairs that were lined up against the wall. Every so often I'd look up at the plaques on the wall, admiring the men in their smart looking uniforms.

Soon a plainclothes officer came up to me and asked me to follow him. We went into a small room that I imagined was used to interrogate suspects. I felt like I was being interrogated for a crime I didn't commit.

Once I sat down, he took a seat and gave me a thin smile.

"Alright, Tracey, why is it you don't want to go home?" he asked.

I just shrugged my shoulders. What was I going to say?

He asked a few other questions, but I was having a hard time focussing—there in the interrogation room—so I was evasive, noncommittal.

Then he took some papers out of the desk and asked for some personal information. These questions I was able to answer. Age, address, telephone number.

When he asked about my father, I told him he was dead. My sisters and I lived with our mother and stepfather and our half-brother Billy, who was eight.

Then more questions but no more answers from me. I had crawled back inside myself.

After a few more minutes, he told me he was going to call my mother. My heart leaped, and suddenly I became paranoid. Was he going to lock me up, had I broken any laws? Still, I felt safe there in the room. I knew that even if they called her and she came down to the station, she couldn't barge in and start making demands on me. She couldn't slam me to the floor and beat me for running away.

I knew it was my opportunity to tell on her, but I didn't. I knew I would be in big trouble if they sent me back home. I didn't want to think about all that and didn't know what to do. Again, I felt trapped…

So I was a Russian spy, and the reason I was at the police station was that the officer was grilling me about being a traitor to my country. I pictured him slamming his fists on his desk in a rage to pressure me into breaking my silence.

I watched as the officer dial my mother's telephone number. He spoke for a few minutes, but because I was Russian, my English wasn't very good, and I didn't follow what was being said.

Eventually, he hung up the phone, collected himself, and told me she didn't want me back. I don't remember how he put it, but I could tell he was in shock by the flat expression on his face as he tried to play it cool. Who knows what my own expression betrayed at that moment?

He told me he would make a few calls to the Children Aid's Society to find a temporary placement for me and asked if I wanted something to eat or drink.

# Two

# My Mother

If the officer who'd called my mother was shaken by her response, that made only one of us. Though she was unpredictable and irrational, nothing my mother chose to do at that point would have surprised me. She was unwell. Even I knew that at fourteen, and I was unwell myself.

My mother, Mary, was a beautiful woman, like a model, but too petite to be one. She married in 1962 and was twenty-three when she had Martha, twenty-four when she had me, and twenty-seven when she had Sarah. And yet even after she had three kids she could pass for a teenager. A wild teenager.

Regardless of her age, she was married too young and had us girls too young. She wasn't ready to raise a family and would rather be out kicking up her heels with the bad boys at some seedy bar in and around town.

When she dressed up, the way she loved to do, she was stunning, with fine features, and a way about her that could catch the eye of any man. Her smile could radiate through an entire room and touch anyone she wanted it to. She had a childlike quality that drew men to her—and she knew it. It felt like power to her. It didn't matter what she was saying, when she was speaking to a man, her voice held the whispered promise of sexual possibility.

However, she didn't realize what an easy target she was for the wrong man. Her neediness and desperation for love made her easy to manipulate.

She was the picture of perfection. And her house was perfect too. On her hands and knees, she would scrub the floors spotless, move the furniture constantly as she searched for the perfect arrangement, and the way she made the beds would keep a draft sergeant happy.

In the beginning, my parents' marriage had seemed perfect. Parker was tall and handsome, born with a permanent tan, long lashes on big brown shiny eyes, and a body that would knock the socks off any woman. They made a very handsome couple back then—not that that counted for much.

I felt safe with my daddy. I liked his long eyelashes and the way he would play with me when he was home. He would bounce me off his knee, throw me high in the air, and then catch me easily in his arms. He would take me for a walk to the candy store around the corner. At times like those, I felt safe. He would make funny faces while telling a story that would make me laugh, and his eyes would sparkle with mystery. He knew everything there was to know, and I loved him. I loved the very sound of his voice; it caressed me in a way that made me believe in the kind of dream that could come true.

He had a way of telling a story that was smooth as peanut butter, so natural, as though he believed it himself. He was bigger than life. He was my world, and he was magnificent, like an actor on a world stage—self-assured and confident in his lines. He fascinated me as he did everyone around him. But he made promises he had no intention of keeping. Life was just one big game for him, and the word responsibility was not a part of his vocabulary. I laughed and giggled at the funny faces he made to entertain me, but sometimes I wanted to reach right through him with my tiny little hand to see if he was real, to see if the magic would disappear. Even when he would come home drunk with empty pockets, it didn't affect me; I still saw him as the magic man, the love of my life. I didn't see him stagger in with booze on his breath, but I heard the arguments. I'd eventually drift off to sleep, and in the morning, he was my daddy again going off to work.

But if he'd been out the night before, my mother would stay in her room all day and leave us kids to fend for ourselves, climbing up on the countertops to open the cupboards and get at Captain Crunch, and then watch TV. She was just too depressed worrying about where Daddy had been, whom he'd been with, and all the money he'd spent to bother getting up and facing the day. She knew that chasing women was, for him, a quick ego fix, but it drove her nuts. Half the time, she didn't know where he was and, panic-stricken, would telephone all around town to track him down.

Back when they were single, they flew together like Tinker Bell and Peter Pan. But now the responsibility of a family was tying her down more than it was tying him down. She would sulk in her room for hours because Peter Pan no longer wanted her on his adventures, and when he was home, he was not willing to share the responsibility of raising his daughters in a meaningful way. He would come and go as he pleased, apparently bored with family life.

The fights they had on nights when he'd been out were as vicious as they were predictable. My mother accusing him of sleeping with other women whom she referred to as sluts, whores, and bimbos. My father accusing her of fabricating things in her head and calling her crazy and delusional and paranoid. There was never any attempt on my mother's part to keep her voice down, and so my sisters and I heard this play out between them again and again. A strange vulgar vocabulary of terms and slurs we didn't understand.

One of my earliest coherent memories dates from when I was maybe three, probably four.

My parents were fighting. My sisters were in the kitchen, I think, but I was hiding in the corner of the dining room, behind the dining room table, listening to the temperature the argument rising, waiting for it all to end. An ache sat heavy in the pit of my stomach, twisting and turning, tensing muscles as I tried to hide, to protect myself from the violence, from the loud words were like steel. Then there were thudding sounds and a scuffling noise as my mother fell to the floor.

Tears sprang from my eyes, and my mind had gone numb. I was too little to comprehend the impact of what was happening around me, but my body responded by going cold, as though the air was passing through me, and I was afraid my bones would shatter.

The loud words rang and reverberated in my head, playing like a slow-motion film looping over and over.

Finally, I heard my father leave and my mother sobbing and muttering about how much she hated him—she was too self-absorbed to notice what it was doing to us kids.

Eventually Martha came out of the kitchen and went to attend our mother's needs. My little sister Sarah was there, too, but I didn't see her, she'd have been a toddler at the time. Martha was around five years old, but she had already understood our mother's limitations, so she put her arms around her, arms that didn't quite reach, and gave her a tiny kiss on the cheek, and then they sat together in silence until the storm was all gone.

I remained in my place of safety, watching tearfully as the same old play unfolded. I remained because I couldn't connect with my mother the same way my sisters did. I was terrified of her. Also, I didn't like to be touched, *especially* by her.

Finally, my tears began to dry up, and the only thing that was left was a little black spot no bigger than an inkblot all curled up on the floor. At times, I wondered if I was even there at all.

My father hadn't been looking for a wife or a committed relationship of any kind when he met my mother. He was looking for a good time, the golden cup of eternal youth. He might have thought of that before getting her, his half-wild girlfriend, pregnant.

Then again, he wasn't known for his brains, just for his playful personality. Besides, he didn't want daughters, anyway. He'd wanted sons—or so my mother would tell me time after time.

The wall between them was about to come down. They were destined eventually to go their separate ways. It was just a matter of time. One of them was bound to throw in the towel and call it quits from the game of love. As the fighting steadily worsened, my world grew dark. It was obvious they couldn't get along, obvious that someone would leave, and I was afraid it would be my father. But it would hurt too much to let go. My anxiety jumped up to a near unbearable pitch. Was he going to be leaving, or was he going to stay?

I began to deny my very existence. I would pinch my arms and legs to see if I still hurt, to check if I was real. I hoped I wasn't. If I believed that I wasn't real then maybe my world wasn't real, and if my world weren't real, then he would stay, and he'd continue to be my Magic Man—my anchor who made the world seem safer.

With each successive fight, the uncertainty of the family's future became overwhelming, and just thinking about the final split kept my mother off balance too. Absorbed in her fears, she grew even more distant from me. And, for me, there was no time to do the things I loved to do, such as searching for shiny things to touch.

Then another argument would take place and the slamming of the door. Sometimes my father would go away for a day, maybe three, but his last word was always the slamming of the door. And while he was away, my mother's mood would pitch back and forth—dark moods when the house would be shut up with curtains closed against the sun, and then a mood swing, and the curtains would be thrown open, and the sun would shine.

I remember this one time when my father left for few days—by now I was four. My mother was pacing back and forth in front of the couch, too upset to stop moving. She was like a caged animal. She glanced at a half-full cup of coffee on the coffee table, and something about it set her off. She picked it up and threw it with all her strength. It hit the wall with a great loud crash, splashing coffee everywhere, and broken pieces scattered all over the floor.

She whirled around and saw me sitting on the floor with my hair in every which way. At first, she laughed. I looked so funny sitting there with my hair like that. Then, her anger and frustration got the better of her again, and she started yelling.

"Stupid… ugly… I hate you!"

She whirled around and stomped up to her bedroom and slammed the door (finally, *she* had the last word).

To me, sitting on the floor in front of the couch, she seemed like a giant. She was only five two, but in my eyes, she appeared monstrous. Her feet pounding on the floor made a slapping noise that hurt my ears. I never knew when her foot might suddenly kick out at me in anger. I was never sure what might trigger her next bout of rage, whether it was a spilled glass of milk, a coffee cup on a table, messy hair, or just a sudden movement. So all I could think of to do was hide and keep quiet, just the way my mother liked it.

Beneath the dining room table was my hiding place, where I felt safe. It comforted me to think my mother might not notice me there. "Twinkle, twinkle, little star, How I wonder where you are." I would sit there for hours in a dreamlike state, a place empty of sight and sound. Sometimes cartoons would pop into my mind. It was like watching a TV screen.

My mind would become crowded with action figures as I planned my escape and dreamed of pink ribbons, bogeymen, rocking horses, hiding places, broken toys, tables hugging, curtains swishing back and forth, and a sun that winked down before darkness settled in.

My favourite cartoon character was Ralph Phillips from Looney Tunes, a young boy who daydreamed about heroic deeds all day long. The way he would fantasize about being what he was not, always the hero, out to save the world in his overblown role of self-importance. I was him, and he was me. But I couldn't laugh aloud. No laughing in the house! But the boy in the cartoon was there too. I could even be with him sometimes. I only wished that I could stay in my mind forever and dream.

My mother finally came out of her bedroom. She came down the stairs and noticed me under the dining room table. It was well past dinnertime, but she had no intention of making dinner for us kids or herself. We had already eaten anyway—having climbed up on the counters to get our food. And my mother wasn't hungry, so she made nothing. Something about the sight of me under the table annoyed her.

"Oh, God. Get the hell out of there, Tracey! And I mean now."

But I was afraid to move, and I trembled in fear as she got down on her hands and knees and clawed at me to get me out. She was angry with me for being so clumsy and difficult to get at, even at such a young age. Finally, I was out and yanking at my arm as she pulled me into the bathroom and savagely removed my clothes. She couldn't get them off fast enough. She stared at my nakedness with hatred in her eyes. With disgust.

"You're so ugly. Nobody wants you, you know that?"

Forcing me into the tub, she viciously scrubbed. She couldn't wait to get the job over with, for there were things she would much rather do than bathing a kid. She flinched when she got to my private parts! She cringed and threw the soap down and stomped out of the bathroom, leaving me stunned, not sure what to do next, not knowing if she would come back in to finish up or what. Mechanically, I reached for the soap and then stopped. I didn't want to touch those private parts either. If my own mother couldn't do it, then how could I? I figured there must be something very wrong. So I just sat motionless, wondering, confused.

Time stood still as I wondered where she could be. A sick feeling washed over me, paralyzing me, freezing me in time. I felt trapped. The bathroom seemed so small. It felt as though the walls were caving in and devouring me. I could feel them breathe, and it made me gasp. At that moment, it was so quiet in the house, yet so loud in my mind. The water had gone cold, and it felt sharp on my skin, like imaginary knives teasing.

If only she would come back and hold me just for one moment, just one moment of her time, just one loving hug. I think that would have made me feel better.

An eternity passed before she reappeared.

"Have you finished?" she said and waited impatiently for a reply.

I couldn't talk. She became frustrated, and pulling me by the arms, she shook me until tears welled up in my eyes. Taking up the soap and rubbing it vigorously between her hands to make suds, my mother rammed her finger inside me to get the job done. Then she stood and screamed.

"You can get out now, you slut!" ...and left in a rage.

Tears streamed down my cheeks unchecked. I hurt inside and out. I could not imagine what just happened. How could she hurt me like that? My mind raced around in circles, my chest heaved violently, I was hyperventilating, and I was out of control. But I would have to get out before she came back, so I yanked the towel off the rack on the wall to hide my nakedness and tiptoed to my bedroom. Then I hid under the bed and remained there for the rest of the night, nude, and curled up in a ball to disappear into the darkness. I felt so small, smaller than a speck of dirt, and now there was a hole in my body.

I had a newfound awareness of my body, but it seemed draped in dirtiness now. For the first time in my life, I felt shame, shame at the very core of my existence. Now every part of my body seemed tainted with ugliness. I just wanted to go to sleep, to forget the terror, but the visions returned in flashes, my mother's hand creeping in and out of my consciousness. How could I ever go to the bathroom again? It was too unbearable to think about. Better to avoid it at all costs. It hurt too much to remember. I prayed that, in time, I would forget. Eventually, I fell asleep, but my sleep was filled with dark figures, probing hands, enormous hands reaching deep inside me.

In the morning, I was terrified to leave my room, but I knew, if I didn't, there would be trouble. The smell of breakfast sausage was in the air, and I could hear my mother cheerfully humming a tune as if nothing had happened the night before. I couldn't bear the thought of looking her in the eyes. But she was singing. Was it just my imagination playing tricks on me? No, it had to be real. I couldn't possibly make up something like that. But what could I do? I could push the incident into the back of my mind and, like my mother, pretend it didn't occur. It was no big deal. She was smiling down at me. She was in one of her playful moods with a voice that sounded soft. But I knew I'd have to be careful. She could change in a flash; she was a clown. I couldn't help but wonder when she would turn evil again.

I couldn't help but admire her beauty at the same time. When she wasn't looking, I would take a quick look and pretend I was Ralph on one of his adventures and that my mother was a princess with gorgeous gowns and sparkling jewelry. And she lived in a castle on the hill, and when she went to see her prince charming, she rode in a beautiful carriage with four white horses, with red plumes on their heads.

I knew my mother had a heart full of black. The inside of her was ugly, just like the inside of me. But I had to believe that some part of her loved me. And when I made her a princess, she was perfect, with a perfect daughter, with a perfect life. My mother's beauty represented love.

Beauty represented love. And when I was admiring my mother's beauty, when I made her a fairy princess, when even the sound of her voice was soft, it was my chance for love. I so badly needed love. How could someone so beautiful on the outside be so ugly on the inside?

I knew she sensed my desperate need for love, but she could not give it. I even knew she saw my need for love as a weakness. And slowly the smile and the soft voice disappeared. Her face changed—the corners of her mouth turned up, and she ground her teeth. Her eyes turned dark with hatred. I knew there had to be someone else in there. I shivered in fear as I watched her eyes instantly shift from a dull green to a deep dark grey. It was as if tiny demons raced across their surface, halting to pace back and forth, as they anxiously awaited their release. Through my mother, for one brief moment, I could see evil. And the demons danced to the rhythm of my heart.

I felt lost and out of control. I'd done it then! I'd done number two in my pants. The words wouldn't roll off my tongue, but as a whisper in my mind I thought, *Please Momma, don't hurt me again.*

But it was too late. Like a predator, she smelled the odour, and her nostrils flared, her body became stiff, and she pounced on me with her fists.

"You stupid bitch!"

The sound of bones cracking rippled through the house. She dragged me along the floor and up the stairs, and it was as though the steps were alive. When we reached the top, she dragged me to the bathroom. The terror silenced me. She ripped my clothes from me, then picked up my underwear and shoved them into my mouth.

"Eat it, you bitch!"

Something exploded in my head. I had to leave, to get away. But how could I get free? Where was there to go? I heard the clanging sound of heavy steel slamming against cement, and it scattered my thoughts into a million pieces. My entire world was breaking up. My sense of smell and taste went suddenly dead. I visualized my hands frantically picking up pieces of flesh and bone from the floor and putting them in neat little piles. Each pile had to go into its separate compartment.

Knock, Knock. The lights were on. But no one was home.

My mother had already left, but the shadow of evil remained. I just lay on the floor, rolled up in a ball, holding my knees tight to protect myself. The house was quiet. The only sound I could hear was my heavy breathing. Where was everybody? Had they left me there to die? Suddenly I realized my nakedness and felt an overwhelming humiliation. I felt ugly. I felt dirty. I felt worthless. I had become nothing. No wonder my mother could not love me.

Eventually, out of the silence, came my older sister Martha—three and a half feet tall with big brown eyes like our daddy's and the prettiest auburn hair. It was always Martha to the rescue. She climbed up onto the bathroom counter with a cloth. She scraped her knee on the corner, looked down at it and saw the blood, then just wiped it away with her hand and got a cloth to clean up what my mother couldn't. She was the golden girl, Mother's little helper, always looking after me, in good times and bad. She smiled as she gently wiped my face. After getting me cleaned up the best she could, we tiptoed to the bedroom together, lay on the bed and I fell asleep in Martha's loving embrace.

It was one of the few times I wanted someone to touch me.

## THREE

# AUGUST 1978

At the police station, I ate a tuna sandwich that had come wrapped in cellophane and had a can of Pepsi. There was very little small talk from the officer in charge of me between phone calls. I sat there in my own head as the sugar worked its way through my system. It seemed like I sat there for hours.

Then a different officer arrived, and she drove me to a place in Port Credit just off Lakeshore Boulevard in southern Mississauga. I had the window open and could smell the water as we drove up.

An older woman came out and walked toward the car. She appeared to be in her early sixties. When I got out of the car, she threw an arm around me, but I only squirmed in discomfort. Being touched threatened to call things up from below the surface, dark shapes in my murky subconscious. I figured the only thing to do was to keep my distance from everyone, including her.

I vowed not to disclose any information about my family or myself. At that point, most of it had already been buried anyway, so that task wasn't all that hard. I'd learned that people were not to be trusted, especially the ones who claimed to be helping me. I thought everyone was out to get me. My mother and stepfather had tricked me one too many times, and now no one was going to have the chance to get close to me. Underneath that protective veneer, I felt vulnerable. But I wanted people to know. I wanted to trust them. I was human. And I only wanted what they wanted. I didn't know how to get it or even if it was available for someone like me.

The woman's name was Mrs. Johnson. She took me into her home and showed me around. The kitchen was bright with yellow paint, checkered curtains on a single window, and small plants on the sill. It all reminded me of home-cooked meals and a house that I would like to have lived in. There were no dirty dishes. The place seemed very organized. Mrs. Johnson showed me where I'd be sleeping, which was in her room. The room had two single beds and a nightstand with an alarm clock on it. There was a long dresser against the wall with a bunch of little trinkets lined up on it and a wooden jewelry box on a doily. I couldn't wait for the opportunity to rummage through them later.

"Are you hungry, dear?"

"Yeah."

"Let's do something about that."

I followed her back up to the kitchen where she made me a peanut butter and jelly sandwich. As I ate my sandwich, Mrs. Johnson sat across from me and stared as though she could see into my sad life and then tried to console me and tell me everything would be okay. I didn't understand. Why was she trying to fix things when no one else ever cared? I rolled my eyes and shrugged my shoulders. I detested people trying to connect with me, attempting the impossible.

Suddenly I just shut down emotionally. I could see Mrs. Johnson's lips move and that she knew I had lost interest because she changed the subject to something mundane, like the rules of the house. She told me she expected me to vacuum the rugs and do all the dishes every day. The chores seemed like monumental tasks.

*I'm just a maid service,* I thought, *and a way for the old lady to make some extra cash.*

When I finished my sandwich, she showed me where the vacuum cleaner was and the tea towels and left. I watched the back of her legs as she left the room and imagined cutting them off with an axe.

That night when I had the opportunity, I went through Mrs. Johnson's stuff but found nothing worth taking. So I put the radio on and listened to my favourite music and lay in my new bed staring up at the ceiling. I was afraid. I couldn't close my eyes because I was afraid that my mother or Robert would come and get me. But it was the devil I was concerned about because they didn't want me anymore. I felt like a helpless sheep waiting to be slaughtered in a pen. I decided I'd better monitor the door just in case the devil came in to eat my soul.

Mrs. Johnson had told me that I would be going to an assessment centre to meet with a psychologist. My family would be there too. Great! Then I would have a thousand eyes on me. Everybody was going to analyze me, pick me apart and try to figure out why I was tearing the family apart. My mother was deceptive. She could tell lies in such a way as to make others think that she was the victim. But I knew she was playing the pretend game again. I knew she would break down and cry and tell them how I was ruining her life. She'd fool everyone, and I would be the rotten apple.

The next morning Mrs. Johnson greeted me at the kitchen table where she was sipping hot tea with a slice of lemon. I liked the way she held her pinky finger, and I made a mental note to do the same. It made her look sophisticated. After breakfast, I was to go to meet with my mother and the psychologist.

As soon as Mrs. Johnson drove into the parking lot at the assessment centre, I saw my mother standing at the front door, cigarette dangling from her tiny fingers, and her body looking like a rag doll. She looked small. She'd always looked larger than life to me, but now she looked small. She gave me a dirty look and then quickly turned away. She was neatly dressed to make a good impression of sensibility with black nylons, a black dress, black pumps, and her hair pulled back in a no-nonsense look.

When Mrs. Johnson greeted her, my mother reacted coldly as though Mrs. Johnson were the enemy. I think she feared being found out, feared the thought of our family secrets being aired in public. I followed, cowardly, behind Mrs. Johnson. We went into the front lobby where Martha and Sarah were sitting on uncomfortable-looking chairs. It surprised me. Sarah's big brown eyes looked especially sad, and she was wearing a dress that hung well below her knees and a pair of shiny shoes.

Martha sat cross-legged with hands folded in her lap and looked very grown-up. I didn't want to make eye contact with her because by then I saw her as a silent accomplice, like a mechanical toy, and I knew she would probably give me the evil eye that she'd learned from our mother.

The chairs had been arranged in a circle, but no one made eye contact. I suspected my mother was staring at me, trying to get my attention so she could warn me to keep my mouth shut. I looked past everyone and stared at the wall. I noticed how clinical the room was, painted in that boring but common off-white with not a single picture to break the boredom. I didn't quite understand why we were there, and to make things worse, the psychologist turned her attention on me as soon as she introduced herself.

She asked me questions about how I felt about individual family members. I told her the truth, that my mother was mean, and that she hit me, and that she hated me. Everyone in the room became fixated on my mother. Of course, Martha interjected, saying that I was the real problem, and that our mother was only working hard to provide for all of us. She was right on cue, Martha always coming to her defence. In return, our mother gave her money and bought her new clothes. And doing my mother's bidding probably saved her from being abused like me. Martha had a good deal, and she wasn't about to let it go sour. In the middle of all the commotion, I lost my train of thought, and the next thing I knew my mother was storming out of the room. It pissed me off because, even there, she had the last word.

Mrs. Johnson tapped me on the shoulder and told me it was time to go. She told me we would have to come back in two weeks because the psychologist wanted to run a series of psychological tests on me and check my mental capacity. I felt vulnerable and defeated. Everything was a lie. My life was a lie, and now my mother had me scheduled for psychological evaluation. I wanted her to simply disappear, even though I felt that, on some level, I was to blame for what was happening.

# FOUR

# NOVEMBER 1968

It was a few months since my mother had degraded me by shoving my soiled underwear in my mouth, and I had not recovered from that. Sitting beneath the dining room table, my hands moved the blocks, but inside I felt nothing at all. I was pretending I didn't exist, and although my eyes could see, they revealed nothing. I could feel my emotions slide down in my belly until they found a secret place in my stomach where I could protect them.

My parents' relationship was unravelling fast, and though I suppose I shared that trauma with my sisters, I felt alone, adrift. I would dissociate and withdraw inside myself, drawing no comfort from anyone. Then one evening, through the familiar bickering and recriminations came words that cut through the haze and jolted me back to reality.

"You know what, Parker? It's over. I'm leaving. I want a divorce… You can take Tracey!"

There was more—a lot more—but I was so stunned it all just washed over me. I knew it would be my father who left… he'd been leaving a bit at a time my entire life. I loved him, but I think I knew, even then, some of the hard truths that so infuriated my mother.

My father would rather be out chasing dreams, fresh faces, a better lifestyle—would rather escape growing responsibility of raising a family. He had no desire to quench his thirst for exploring. It never occurred to him to look at himself for answers. He was always searching for something outside himself. To me, although he was the only love in my life, he was the mystery man, the crayon man, the make-believe Santa Claus, dishing out boxes of empty promises. Even I knew that beneath his glorious lies he was just an empty shell.

A few days went by, and things were in motion. I don't remember talking with Martha or Sarah. I don't know if my parents bothered to explain anything. My father was barely there, and my mother was a tight knot of hurt and fury.

Then, suddenly, there was my father. My mother threw a few of my things—only one outfit really—into a paper bag, and I knew that this was the day I was going to live with my father. There were no warm embraces or sad goodbyes, just walking out the door to the car holding my father's hand. Where were Martha and Sarah? My mother closed the door behind us, and when I heard the click, I imagined the door kicking me in the ass as I went down the steps. I felt like the paper bag I was holding, used, not worth much, not much inside. My father held the car door open for me to climb in, but everything was happening so fast. Why couldn't I stay and be a good little girl like my sisters?

This was early December about a month before my fifth birthday.

A chilly wind blew through the hole in my body, and my face remained expressionless like always. In the car, I sat still, feeling caught up in a whirlpool. Around and around and around I flew, where I'd land nobody knew.

Except I was about to find out.

The car came to a stop in front of a gloomy grey building. I felt frightened, but I didn't know why. There were large black letters printed on the top of the building and though I could not read the letters at the time—I know now that they spelled out CHILDREN'S AID SOCIETY—I knew it was not like any home I'd ever seen before.

My father grabbed the brown bag from the back seat, then came around and took me out of the car. We trudged up the big chunky grey steps, a tiny little girl holding onto the hand of a giant. We walked down the long corridor with my father's shiny brown dress shoes echoing off the walls. Eventually, we came to a relatively small desk at the end of the hall. Behind it sat a pleasantly plump older woman with a big smile—a smile that was inviting.

Mrs. Holland introduced herself as a social worker and told me this was where I would stay for a while. My father bent down and looked into my eyes.

"This is only temporary, Tracey. I'll be back for you when I have some money and a place where we can live, okay?"

Was it okay? It didn't feel like it.

He gave me a bear hug, then told me he loved me and turned to leave. I watched his legs sway in rhythm with his stride as he made his way out the door. I wanted to call after him. I wanted to say something, but the words wouldn't come. I couldn't spit them out in time.

Mrs. Holland tried to comfort me with soft words, but as with all the other kids at the orphanage, my sadness was inconsolable. She tried her best to reassure me that my father would come back as we climbed the stairs to the second floor. It was a lie she'd had to tell all of us as they came one by one, a necessary lie because she could think of no other way to make things better for us. She guided me into a vast room with dozens of small cots with clean, crisp sheets and took me over to the one that would be mine. Then she dropped my bag on the bed, turned, and walked away.

The sun was shining through the large windows, making the room bright and warm, giving it a feeling of life. But with all the brightness I felt dark and dirty and was afraid the others might see, so I tried to hide by hunching my shoulders and holding my stomach with my hands, to hide the secrets. The atmosphere in the gigantic room was one of overwhelming sadness. I sensed that all of us children had one thing in common: we were all unwanted, left behind to survive on our own, and we all knew it. We also shared the same feelings of pain and fear of the unknown. Our hearts bled for just one act of genuine kindness. In all our eyes, there was deep sorrow. To me, the other children all looked like dozens of worn-out boots lined up, side by side, in the back of a closet—the boots that were not good enough for anyone.

At the orphanage, we got three meals a day, a warm bed to sleep on, and activities to keep us busy and out of trouble. But what we needed, what we all longed for, was love. I watched the other children play from a distance. It helped me not to feel so alone. I dared not play with them for fear my secrets would fall out, and everyone would find out about the ugliness. The days came and went, and no one said a word about my father or when he would come. They didn't mention my parents at all, yet every day, something stirred inside me, a feeble hope that maybe this would be the day.

Christmas came and went with little ceremony—then my birthday with even less. No one visited me.

At night time, as I lay restlessly on my cot, I tried to swallow the pain of knowing that no one cared. As I lay on my crisp white cot, listening to the sobbing of the other kids, I could smell the sweet fragrance of my father's cologne and remember all too well the way he used to hold me. Even though the room was full of children, the emptiness grew and lay on my chest like a heavy piece of clay. The entire room seemed lifeless, with no place for feelings to go. I felt trapped, memories stalking me, reminding me of all the things that had gone wrong.

Throughout the day, I pretended to be a normal little girl by copying the behaviour of other children. I coloured on a piece of paper and took part in all the games. It fascinated me how my arms and legs could function with so little effort. I could control them without focusing, as though they belonged to someone else. The limbs of a puppet. I could watch myself as though from a distance, looking at the shadows overlapping my body. The lines I drew with the crayons thrilled me. They were so straight, so perfect. It made me feel as if goodness surrounded me—first yellow, then red, then blue—and through it all I glimpsed the beauty inside me.

Then I shook my head and remembered the dirtiness and the badness of being who I knew I was and the helplessness of being open and unprotected. I felt scared, so I imagined being covered up with a mound of bricks, beneath which could ever break my silence.

Every night, around seven o'clock, all the kids would have to have a bath. Usually, they would go into the tub two or three at a time, but one night Mrs. Holland ended up bathing only me. The gentleness of her soft hands and the purity of her motives amazed me. It was as though she were in a dream. Mrs. Holland wore a white smock, the towel was bleached-white, and so were the cloth and the soap. Everything was just so pure. I was not afraid in the hands of this angel as Mrs. Holland sudsed her hands and rubbed them over my skin and made it tingle. I was a hungry child feeding off the kindness, lapping up every ounce of affection I could, not unlike a stray cat that wraps itself around the leg of anyone who'll stand still long enough. But the weakness of wanting love made me sick to my stomach. The desire for love was my secret shame. Every thought, every action, reminded me of my mother's teachings, and there was no escaping what I had learned. Besides that fact, I didn't like people, just things.

# FIVE

# SEPTEMBER 1978

After two uneventful weeks of eating and sleeping and cleaning at Mrs. Johnson's place in Port Credit, I was again sitting in front of the psychologist. This time it was just the two of us. She had me look at inkblots and tell her what I saw. I told her I saw a woman holding a baby and that she was torn up inside that she had to abandon the child. After I completed numerous tests, she told me she would send in her report to my physician. Mrs. Johnson drove me back to her place. Life went on.

A few weeks after that, I got in to see the psychologist, and she told me I had paranoid schizophrenia. I remember the words, but at the time I had no clue what it all meant. I didn't know it was a serious mental health condition, one that mental health professionals considered hopeless, and no one bothered to tell me much of anything. I just remember the psychologist saying that I was bright so I would be okay.

The fact that I was *bright* seemed to make the psychologist feel better, but it didn't mean much to me. And there was no mention of therapy or even a follow-up visit to the psychologist. She told me I was gifted, but I didn't know what that meant either. Was she been trying to tell me I was smart? Because I couldn't even understand basic math or English. What good was smart if it didn't translate to simple things like that? I looked into her eyes—they seemed soft and thoughtful—and I thought I detected compassion in her voice, at least I was hoping I did, but she never got to know me, never asked the right questions, never looked any deeper into what made me tick. So what was the point? She might as well have been saying, "Yes, you have leukemia. Next?"

I left that meeting with Mrs. Johnson, but there was a part of me that longed to open up, to reach out to the psychologist who was the only one at the time that could help me. Unfortunately, I couldn't speak her language, and I guess she didn't understand mine. In fact, I could barely hear her because every time I started to speak, the sound of my voice would startle me to such a degree that I could not concentrate on what others were saying.

When I got back to Mrs. Johnson's, I told her I was going for a walk by the lake. The lake was just a short distance from her house, so I headed down there, chose a big rock to sit on, and gazed out over the water. I loved the sound of the water as it gently lapped the shore. The peaceful atmosphere had a calming effect, and I became fascinated with the trees and bushes that circled it and lined the pathway. They intrigued me somehow. I had a great love for natural things. I even loved the smell. But when I looked down at my hands, they were shaking and looked like dead branches. My mind was filled with thoughts and images of the devil that overshadowed any attempt to figure out the meaning of life. I looked behind me constantly, fearing that the devil was sneaking up on me. I didn't want to be caught unaware.

My mind was in a constant state of terror. To counter-act it, I raised my arms toward the sky as though reaching out to Jesus. I hoped that he would notice me, and perhaps his love would cure me. I wanted him to cast a magic spell upon me so I could be released from all my pain. I imagined being engulfed in a beam of miraculous white light. It was nuts, but I wasn't hurting anyone. Besides, everyone else had their coping mechanisms; mine was just a little more extreme. Sometimes I even felt like I was Jesus Christ, in search of the true meaning of life, and I honestly thought that I would be saved. I prayed often and asked God to kill me, and I promised to do good if he did. It all served to make me feel important, that I mattered, and I found great relief in those false beliefs. It was a way to get away from the constant state of terror in my mind. A way to flee from the devil.

In mid-October Mrs. Johnson enrolled me in Grade 8 at a local high school. It couldn't possibly have worked, though, because I'd stopped learning at about Grade 3. Perhaps I had coasted along by "being smart," or per-haps no one had paid much attention to me, and everyone was just happy to move me along.

I sat at the back of the class, mostly fantasizing about my real purpose in life, saving the world from destruction. Sometimes, though, I'd also watch the other students, the way they sat or held a pencil, and then I would try to mimic their behaviours. I tried hard not to be noticed. But when I was, and the teacher asked me a question, I'd squirm with embarrassment and tell her I didn't know. She'd call me a dreamer and tell me that, statistically, I'd be a dropout before the end of the year. The kids would laugh, and I'd turn red. I'd shuffle my feet nervously under my desk and eventually drift off into some fantasy, imagining myself with magical powers and superhuman strength—capable of overpowering everyone around me. This was my feeble attempt at having the last word.

Between classes, when we were supposed to be changing rooms, I quickly slipped into the washroom, hid in one stall, put my feet up on the toilet seat so that no one would know I was there, and listened to the kids talk as they came and went. Sometimes I'd think they were mocking me, calling me a slut, or whispering what an idiot I was. I'd wait for everyone to leave before going to my next class.

One day, on my way out, when I thought it was safe, I walked past the mirror and turned to catch a glimpse of myself—or so I hoped—but all I saw was the haunting image of a demon. I could see all my secrets pasted right there on my tongue. It was too ugly, too terrifying, so I turned and ran to the door. But I was losing my focus and couldn't tell if the door was real or not. I pushed it, and to my surprise, it opened, but when I got out into the hallway, it was like I'd run into a ghost town. The halls were empty. Even though I was just in the hallway, I felt lost and started gasping for air. I could feel my mother's hands on my throat. She squeezed so hard I couldn't breathe. She wasn't really there, of course, but to my mind she was. That's the way it was, reliving the trauma repeatedly. I hated it.

By the time I got back to my classroom, I had to knock on the door to get in. I felt like an intruder interrupting the teacher like that. I'd lost track of time while I was having my episode. The teacher was angry, so I headed sheepishly for my seat in the back row. Because she was mad at me, I sat down and obsessed about killing her. I imagined kicking the shit out of her, and then, as she lay on the ground, yelling at her not to fuck with me. I picked up my pencil and doodled. It was all I could think of to pass the time because I certainly couldn't concentrate on what I was supposed to be doing. I looked at the teacher again, and she was a plastic doll with dark eyes staring back. I hated looking into people's eyes because I believed that, by doing so, they could read my mind.

There were a lot of popular girls in my class, but I wasn't one of them. They had perfect faces on perfect bodies. I was skinny as a rail and had a flat chest and wore baggy clothes to cover what little I had. In warm weather, I would sweat rather than dress differently. In cold weather, I would sweat because I was so antsy. My hairstyle was the same as when I was little, stringy and knotted. Sometimes I'd try to mimic the way the popular girls walked, but usually, I'd just end up looking awkward and out of place. The girls said I walked like I had a pickle up my ass. I tried so hard not to draw attention to myself, but rarely succeeded. They noticed me for my awkwardness and strange behaviour. They sensed my poor self-esteem and took advantage of it. They made fun of me and showed no mercy.

At the same time, some girls called me a cockteaser because they thought I walked in a kind of sexual way. I had been aware of sex from a very young age and was probably unconsciously copying my mother. Having sex, though, was the farthest thing from my mind. I considered it disgusting, and the idea never aroused sexual feelings. Even looking at boys upset my stomach. I admired the boy's youthful bodies, their strong backs, and the muscular curves of their shoulders. But that was about it. Boys were unsafe because when boys and girls got together, they did things I didn't even want to picture in my mind. Even if I developed an attraction to the opposite sex, I'd have had to keep my thoughts and feelings out of it to avoid any closeness, any chance of revealing the secrets.

I was attracted, however, to the misfits and oddballs, the ones who stuck out like sore thumbs and dressed funny like me. I liked them, felt comfortable around them, and yet, I saw them as a threat to my delusional world. I knew that anyone could bust a hole in my imaginary world, and I couldn't allow that to happen.

I liked a girl named Eleanor who wore striped scarves in the warm weather and long Pippi socks. She reminded me of a witch who possessed her own worldly secrets, and soon I was invited into her world. She had an interesting story. Her mother and father had died in a car crash, and her uncle was now her guardian. I don't know how much of her story was true—I suspected she lied, like me, to cover up her own pain. I didn't develop long-lasting relationships with anyone, but I enjoyed fantasizing about rescuing the misfits, about being their saviour. What was so bad about that?

# Six

# June 1969

For six long months at the Children's Aid Society, I enjoyed the freedom of not having to think about my mother, just hoping and waiting for my father to come back. I lived every day with a room full of kids, but I made no friends. It would be dangerous to have friends because friends could find out I was different, a horrible little girl, dirty and ugly. But mimicking was easy now. I could do anything the other kids could do—eat, play, sleep—my mind didn't have to be there. I could pretend. Going through the motions was easy as was fooling the other kids and the lady with the smile.

Then one day the lady with the smile said, "Your mother is coming today."

I got dizzy. My stomach felt sick, and I thought I would faint. The sun was scorching, and I felt the burn while sitting on a chair waiting with great apprehension for her to arrive.

Amazingly, I felt as though a weight had been lifted off me. I knew where I belonged. I belonged to my mother. But I also felt a deep sadness. Where was my father? I had waited a long time for him to return, and now I knew my dream was not coming true. A bad little girl belonged with her mother.

I didn't deserve to be where I wanted to be.

The lady with the smile sat behind the desk as I sat in my chair beside it. My legs couldn't touch the floor, and I enjoyed the freedom of swinging them back and forth. Then they just stopped. My beautiful mother, with her beautiful phony smile, was walking down the long corridor toward me. Our eyes met, and it felt like knives piercing my soul.

The silly inconvenience annoyed her. She hurriedly signed the release forms as though it was the fault of the lady with the smile. Then she grabbed me, throwing in a little pinch, and marched me straight for the exit. Once outside, the smile disappeared, and the air turned cold despite the early summer sun. Throwing me into the car, she quickly slammed the door, missing me by inches.

Back to the little house of horrors we went.

Back at the house, my grandma—my mother's mother—had been waiting with Martha and Sarah. She looked like the typical grandmother with an apron, appearing as though she had freshly baked bread in the oven. But she wasn't typical any more than my mother was. She was short and stocky with a sharp sounding voice. She acted like a man. Quick-witted and filled with bitter sarcasm, she'd bite the head of a snake off if challenged. Her hands were all wrinkled, veins popping out, and her eyebrow hairs looked like a dead tree. She was right out of "Little Red Riding Hood," which is to say the wolf dressed as a grandmother. But that damn apron always gave off a distinct impression.

"It's about time you got home," she said. "Do you realize what a mess this house was until I got here? What would you do without me? The girls' hair needed combing. No wonder your kids get taken away. You don't know how to take care of them. You're a terrible mother. You should have never had kids. You can't do anything right, so how can you possibly look after kids? Good thing I brought groceries, or you'd be starving."

My mother broke out in tears. My grandmother left without so much as a second glance for me.

Once my grandmother's car pulled away, my mother pulled me aside.

"The only reason I let your father take you there is that you're not mine. Now get away. You make me sick."

It wasn't the first time she'd claimed I was adopted. I knew it wasn't true because I was the spit and image of her (my father had told me so), but it stung all the same because I knew it was said to hurt me. Her face was becoming distorted now and twisted. The sound of her voice seemed to throw a blanket of evil over the house. A creepy feeling entered my subconscious, and I felt scared because I knew deep down that she didn't want me.

I wasn't sure why she came and got me, but it wasn't out of love or even maternal responsibility.

In my mind, I was taking a walk to the candy store. I suspected, now, that my father wasn't coming back, but I enjoyed the memories of him carrying me there, the smell of his cologne, and no one could take the memories away. I believed *he* loved me at least. He must have loved me. When he got together enough money, I told myself, he would prove that he loved me.

Then the phone rang.

Maybe it was him. With each ring of the phone, butterflies would swarm. My breath stopped, and my heart skipped a beat. Could it be my father? Had he come to rescue me from the bitch squad?

My mother answered the phone. "Oh, hi Simon. How are you?"

She was going out. I'd just come home, but that didn't matter, in fact it helped. Martha too was just recently home; she'd been staying with my grandmother for a while. With me and Martha home, my mother felt she could go out to a bar (with a guy who wasn't my father). We were five and six after all, old enough in her mind to watch over Sarah who was two and a half.

Fishnet stockings, a black miniskirt, and a blouse that showed off her boobs—the perfect trap to catch the wrong man, using sex to get his attention. With stardust in her eyes, she would do anything for love and admiration, whispering promises of sex into his ear for nothing.

It was time—dark outside—and my sisters and I had had our bath and been put to bed. Cinderella was off to the ball with a man she barely knew. My mother had dreams, the kind that never worked out. She thought maybe she had found the man of her dreams. She was always pretending!

I felt lonely in my bed. The room was dark with the moon's shadow preying on me. The moon seemed so close. It was close enough to touch with my little hands. If only I could reach out and take a little part of its magic. The stars in the sky were blinking too. Maybe they had some secrets to tell, good ones, the ones little girls could imagine. The possibilities were endless. My imagination allowed me to see something unlike myself. I could be bigger, important and beautiful, so I hung onto the hope of being seen. That little girl who lay in the bed could grow up to be something. My eyes were sleepy, detached from my needs. I just wanted to dream a little about who I could be as I tried to keep awake. In the back of my mind, I worried about my mother. Something could happen to her. Something bad. If she didn't come back, who would feed me, make sure I didn't fall asleep forever. I had to stay awake because something bad might happen. I dreamt about the moon and the stars for a while longer until a noise woke me.

It was well after midnight, and she wasn't alone. I'd been waiting up all night long for her to come home and now she was giggling like a schoolgirl. A drunk schoolgirl.

"Shhhh!" More giggles. "Don't wake the kids."

Coming down the stairs the next morning, I could smell the familiar odour of stale beer and cigarettes in the air. She had passed out on the couch and was still wearing her fishnet nylons, now torn, and very little else. Her clothes were stained and strewn about the floor. Even at five I knew what the evidence of the night before meant. I looked for a stranger but found no one. I watched her from a safe distance, my eyes roaming her naked body, feeling the shame and trying to ignore what I saw—and ready to run if she caught me there.

Eventually, she woke up and headed straight for the fridge, just like I knew she would. She opened the fridge and took out a bottle of Coke to wash away the terrible taste in her mouth. Then she picked up the aspirin bottle sitting on the counter and popped a few into her mouth to get rid of a headache that was rumbling in her skull. The events of the night before appeared to have gone with the wind. Blackout! She couldn't remember what she had done or where she'd been. She'd made it home, and that was all that mattered.

The house was a messy and dark. A creepy feeling passed over it. Another secret to store away. However, for my sisters and me, it was a time of freedom. We knew we could do what we wanted because we were unsupervised. We took care of ourselves while our mother wallowed in self-pity.

She staggered around the house, unable to think straight. There was dust on the furniture, dishes piled high on the counters, and we kids were a mess. She stomped her feet in anger and yelled at us to get out of her way. With dirty-knotted hair and last night's dinner still on our faces, we were all too glad to run and hide.

The aching feeling in my belly grew, and the hunger pangs made funny growling noises in my stomach. Yesterday's peanut butter swished around inside, and yesterday's toast floated. My mother was still half corked, so there was no way she would cook anything that day. The day's special turned out to be sandwiches. Besides, we couldn't possibly be hungry—she wasn't hungry, how could we be? Whatever she felt, we had to feel. Why wouldn't we? To speak up as a distinct person was to attract punishment.

As the hangover wore off, she felt the shame, and then, to justify her behaviour, she had to clean the house, make things perfect again. Her spirit lifted as she shifted into her role as the perfect mother. A routine that was boringly consistent and easy to follow. She had to drink, didn't she? Life had dealt her a bad hand, and all she could do was to play it the best way she knew how.

She would make a plate of sandwiches. Afterward, she'd throw them on the table, and it would be every-one for themselves. I remember one incident when she used a knife first to cut a sandwich and then, looking at me out of the corner of her eye, she held the knife in the air and twisted it diabolically. I could hear it swish like it would in my belly. It amused her to see the fear in my eyes. The blade flashed as the light bounced off its steel surface and then, as a shadow crossed it, I felt as though it would turn and enter my stomach. The light in her eye matched the glare of the blade as she viciously sliced the sandwich in two. She handed a piece to me.

"Now get lost and don't get any crumbs on the table," she said, as though what she'd just done was normal.

I slowly walked away with the sandwich in my hand and the monsters following close behind me. I wished they would stop stalking me and leave me alone. Sitting at the dining room table, quietly eating my sandwich, I felt a presence, something that kept warning me to be aware. The fear I felt created visions of demons. I was on a Ferris wheel and didn't know when it would stop. A shadow waited in the darkness below with a fire that I would fall into and disintegrate. I saw the edges of a grave and something was telling me to jump in and embrace the terror. Suddenly, I was not afraid anymore. I had become part of it. I got down off the chair and hid under the table. Sitting there, I felt the stillness, as though I'd been under there forever.

My mother walked by and thumped on the table with a damp cloth.

"Fucking kids!" she muttered.

I imagined there must be a hundred people living inside her. One moment, she was an innocent child, and then I would get pulled into a web of deceit. The next she created fear, then she would be my most beautiful mother, leaving me feeling guilty for ever thinking she was evil. How could I think such thoughts about such a kind and beautiful woman?

# SEVEN

# NOVEMBER 1978

Soon it was time for me to leave Mrs. Johnson's house. It was only ever supposed to be a temporary placement anyway, and so, in late November, they were moving me to a town about fifty miles away, a place in Muskoka called Severn Bridge, a small farming community south of Gravenhurst. I put my only change of clothes in a plastic bag and nervously waited at the front door for my new social worker to arrive. It felt familiar, like ten years earlier when my mother shoved my clothes into a brown paper bag and sent me off to the CAS orphanage.

As soon as the social worker arrived, she rushed me into the car and got onto the highway. She started her talk about how wonderful my new home would be for me and how good it would be to make a fresh start. I listened half-heartedly. I wanted to stick my sock in her mouth, the one I had been wearing for about a week. She said that my new foster parent was nice. There was no doubt in my mind that she was, considering the fact that the government was footing the bill for my stay. I had learned early in life that nothing came for free and that people usually had their own best interests at heart, not anyone else's.

"Wait and see," she said. "You're really going to like your new home. Most of the children that live there are about your age. I'm sure you'll like them."

She sounded an awful lot like my mother whenever she was trying to convince herself of something.

I didn't like how the social worker sugar-coated things. She should have known I knew the truth, but she talked as though it didn't matter if I were there or not. I stared at her and listened to her ramble. She reminded me of a stranger lurking in the dark. Something came over me, and I had the impulse to grab the steering wheel and cause an accident. Instead, I just sat there and imagined the car swerving off the road, the smell of rubber burning, and the car smashing into the guardrail. I figured that if I had any luck, I'd get killed, but I knew I couldn't be that lucky. So I pretended to be lying on a hospital bed, a vegetable hooked up to a bunch of tubes and wires designed to keep a body alive, never mind the rest. I chuckled.

I stared at her again and noticed that her nose was much too big, probably because she was paid to snoop into everyone else's life. I guess she felt the heat of my gaze because she started talking faster. Sensing her discomfort, I turned away and tried to tune her out by listening to the voices in my head. I looked out the window and enjoyed watching the trees speed by. That's my genuine passion, I thought, nature. I watched the traffic racing by too and wondered why everyone was in such a hurry. It was unnatural. I didn't like mechanical things. They reminded me of humans. I thought everything humans got their hands on would eventually turn to shit. I saw nothing but deception and chaos. My anger bubbled up inside of me. My palms were sweating and when I put them on the leather seat, it made me think of a dragon's tongue. My mind raced. I felt like I was in mid-air. My feet felt like they were floating. I pinched my legs hard with my fingers to bring me back to reality.

Eventually, we drove into the driveway of my new home and I met my new foster parent, Lynda. I felt somewhat at ease because she was unfamiliar, meaning there was nothing about her to trigger anger, sadness, or despair. She was short and chubby with freckled skin and long flimsy golden blonde hair. She was so different from my mother that it comforted me.

As my social worker had predicted, I enjoyed my new home. I enjoyed the freedom of walking up and down the stairs to the second-floor washroom without a worry. No one followed me, except for those mysterious figures hiding in the shadows and hands reaching out from the walls. I knew I would never be free from them, but in my new environment, my fears seemed to be under control and lessen.

It was there that I met a girl named, Lisa. She was built like a man, dressed like a tomboy, and wore black horn-rimmed glasses that seemed to take the shine from her eyes. She wore the most unattractive faded brown turtleneck sweater that reminded me of shit. The thought gave me a nasty taste in my mouth, although I did not understand why.

She told me about her medications, how many she had to take and the name and dosage of each one of them. She spoke highly of her psychiatrist as if he were some kind of God. Every morning at eight, though, Lynda had to remind her to take her meds. It seemed unnatural to me to be taking so many pills, no matter what they were for. I decided I'd rather not take any pills ever. Besides, I could see how Lisa was slurring her words and spending a lot of time in bed. She even told me once that her medications meant she didn't feel like herself.

I turned my attention to my chores. I had to do the vacuuming, wash the dishes, wipe the counters, make the beds, and clean the bathroom. That kept me busy enough. It was also a good excuse to avoid people. I felt like a machine going through the motions of domestic chores, and I suppose I must have appeared mechanical to those around me because they thought I had no emotions and that I was unaffected by being moved around from place to place.

But I knew all about Lisa.

I could see into her soul—or at least I thought I could. I saw the same desperation in her eyes that I felt. The difference between us was that she had given up the fight. She tried to live up to everybody else's expectations. She wasn't stupid. In fact, I thought she was dazzling. She was just too desperate for approval. Most of her days were spent practically begging for permission to live. Like me, all she needed was direction, someone who cared, and someone to talk to. But there was no one to talk to. It wasn't in the schedule. The professionals, the know-it-alls believed that all we needed was structure and education, so we had to do our chores and go to school. I was glad I met Lisa, though, because she taught me the kind of person not to be.

Sometimes Lisa and I sat at the kitchen table and listened to Lynda sugar-coat our situation by telling us that all we needed was a good education and that we could eventually get our own places. They sounded like impossible tasks at that stage in my life. I didn't feel I was capable of such lofty goals. It was a pressure I didn't need. I wanted to talk about what brought me to that place. I knew I would have to confront the past before I'd be able to move on with the future. I was stuck in time. And I didn't understand why they didn't understand that.

Lynda had a little boy, a two-year-old called Michael. They had nicknamed him She-She, though, because he made funny little noises as if he were blowing his nose. He bounced around all day long with a hanky hanging out of his back pocket. He liked to bring the vacuum cleaner out and then put it back in the closet. He often mimicked his mother's actions, and he was the centre of her universe. She watched him lovingly. It was hard not to admire his blond curly hair and big blue eyes. He was just so cute. He couldn't sit still though, not even at the dinner table, and he never stopped asking questions. I tried to play with him sometimes, but he was shy and ran away, so I'd just sit and watch him. It was a good way to fill up the time when there was nothing else to do.

I'd arrived there on a Sunday, and Lynda's husband Mike came home the following Saturday. He was in the Canadian Armed Forces, and Lynda was going to drive out and pick him up at the airport. Before she left, she did the laundry and tidied up the house. She looked a little panicky to me. Until then, it didn't seem that important to her if the dishes were piled in the sink, sofa cushions were on the floor, and the beds were unmade. I didn't mind because it made me feel I didn't need to be perfect like I'd had to be at my mother's.

When Mike arrived, Lynda draped her arms around him, kissed him on the lips, and chatted for hours until, exhausted, they headed up to bed. I didn't like Mike right off. He was too tall and too loud. And he had jet-black hair and tanned skin like Robert. Just the sight of him turned my stomach. I felt my anxiety level go way up and started to sweat like a racehorse. Just when I was feeling more or less comfortable in a foster home, Mike had to come along and ruin it. I imagined him as the devil—watching me, waiting for the opportunity to move in for the kill. The voices got loud and then began threatening me with death. Instinctively I wanted to run and hide, but there was nowhere to go. I was forced to accept solace in the familiarity of the voices.

A few days later, I was sitting in the living room watching TV, and Mike walked by. I hadn't seen or heard him coming, and it startled me. His presence unnerved me. I jumped up and ran into the kitchen and took a knife out of the top drawer, the sharpest one I could find in a hurry, and went back into the living room. I stood in front of him with the knife in my hand, daring him to touch me. I felt my body swaying back and forth. I was in a fog. I must have looked to him like a rabid dog.

He sprang from the sofa and hit my hand before I had time to react. The knife dropped to the floor. Then he knocked me to the ground with some kind of military move. He yelled for Lynda to come right away, and she ran down the stairs with her housecoat wide and her hair flying out behind her. She'd been in a deep sleep.

He told her to call the hospital, and before long three men and a woman were holding me down. The knee in my chest hurt like hell. The woman put leather restraints on my hands and feet, and it was then that I noticed they were tingling. They carried me from the house and lifted me into the back of a long brown van. The door slammed shut. It seemed like an eternity before we reached the hospital in Brantford, where I was put into a room with nothing but a bed and a nightstand. I don't remember what happened after that.

## EIGHT

# JULY 1969

The moving truck slowly pulled away from the only home I'd ever known, away from the home I once shared with my father. I hadn't seen him since the day he dropped me off at the CAS orphanage. It felt like it was time to say goodbye to the man with the dancing eyes. Holding onto the memory of my father, I placed it in my secret garden. From the back of the car, I watched the house disappear behind me as tears fell and I said goodbye. I wondered why he had to leave, as the clouds grew dark over the back seat. I longed to see him again and ask him why. Then a voice from inside whispered in my ear.

*It is okay, sweet child, one day you'll meet in heaven.*

And I relaxed in the comfort of that secret, silent promise.

The sun was beating through the window of the car, and I was getting hot. I could see my reflection in the window, but I saw the face of a tired old lady in the eyes of a child. There was a weight on my shoulders, and I felt deep shame at the knowledge I had been unwanted. I felt an undertow drawing me under the surface, and I saw a child drowning in my mind. As my mother drove, I imagined someone throwing a life preserver for me. It was my daddy, saving me from the bottomless pit of hell.

Finally, the car turned onto a long street where all the houses were the same, all the lawns were the same height, and all the bushes neatly trimmed. All the cars were shiny and in mint condition. This was the suburbs of Burlington, and it looked unreal to me. I hoped it wasn't. As we pulled up to a white house with green trim, my mother honked the horn three times, and by the time we pulled into the driveway a tall, thin, smiling woman was waiting at the front of the house to greet us. She was followed by six children and a man with a shiny nose.

My mother quickly got out of the car, eager to start her new life. She opened the car door to let us kids out of the back. When it was just me in the back seat, she leaned in and gave me a cold, intimidating look.

"Get the hell out of there, and you'd better be good, or I will kill you."

She turned slowly then and put on a big smile and walked up to her sister Barb and Barb's husband, Don, to give them a warm hug.

I stepped out of the car and saw all the perfect people. I gasped for air because I felt like I was being strangled—as though my mother had me by the throat. I couldn't wait to get out of my perfect blue dress, let my hair hang down around my face, my ugly, imperfect face. I wanted desperately to get the dress off. It was drawing too much attention. I wanted, also, to rip the elastic band from my hair because it too was making me suffocate. I wanted to run and hide, but I had to follow my mother and the rest of the gang into the house, up the stairs and into the kitchen where there was a buzz of excitement, talking, and laughing.

"Diana," said Aunt Barb, "take Tracey and show her where she will sleep, will you?"

I liked Barb right away. She was safe. She seemed born to take care of others, eager to please, patient. Her features were fine, and her clothes were casual yet perfectly pressed, not even a speck of lint. She had not a hair out of place, and her nails were polished and even.

Perfect people living in perfect houses.

Diana took me by the hand, and I tried to pull away because I didn't like people touching me. We headed up the stairs and found Rebecca, one of Diana's younger sisters, already in the room where I was to sleep. She was organizing and getting things ready for me. All the stuff in the room stunned me. Toys were everywhere, stuffed animals all over the twin beds, a desk for homework, and beautiful dresses hanging neatly in the closet, everything smelled so clean. I couldn't believe people lived there. The sun, the spotlight, poured through an open window making me feel its invading presence.

The girls were excitedly showing me all the stuff and telling me I would sleep there with Diana and Rebecca and that I could play with any of the toys. But I did not know what to do. I just stood there holding my stomach, protecting it, so that my secrets wouldn't fall out, and hoping the girls would not touch me. I didn't want them to get the ugly disease. I wanted desperately to leave. The girls were talking to me, and I was getting dizzy like I was about to vomit.

I ran downstairs to my mother, to stand beside her where my secrets would be safe, where they wouldn't fall out in the wrong place. Sarah and Martha were off with Connie upstairs, they would be sleeping with her because Martha and Connie were already friends. The dizziness and the sick feeling in my stomach remained—the secrets were trying to surface again, and everyone around me was talking. I could hear their voices, although they seemed very far away. If I could only stand there long enough, still enough, calmly enough, the secrets would settle back to their place in my stomach, and all would be well.

Eventually, everything settled down with the secrets back in place, and so I wandered outside. I did not want to go upstairs because I knew I was different. I wasn't one of them. I didn't belong. I checked all around and felt crowded by their things. I did not want to touch any of it, did not want a connection to them. Did not want to infect anything.

I walked out to the centre of the lawn and sat down. I noticed all the cars parked so neatly in all the driveways. But I was sitting on the lawn, the perfect lawn.

Then I worried I might kill the grass, poison it somehow, and thought I'd better get off it or get into big trouble. No. I decided to stay and then check it later to see if it died. If it wasn't dead in the morning, then everything would be okay.

The next few hours went by mechanically, eating dinner, jumping on and off the mattress in the basement, and finally going to bed. I worried about the beautiful green grass. I couldn't wait to check it in the morning. I hoped that it would still be alive and green.

My sleep became broken because of the fits of uneasiness. I felt unbearably uncomfortable lying in a room with strangers. The room seemed too organized, too perfect, like my perfect cousins.

And so *unlike* me.

Even in the dark, I was afraid to move for fear my face would crack and it would reveal the ugliness. I imagined blotches of ugliness on my eyes, eyes that didn't want to see anything strange, eyes that preferred the familiarity of ugliness. I moved slowly, quietly, as I wiped the sweat from my hands onto the sheets.

Before anyone else was up, I climbed carefully out of bed and crept down the stairs to the living room and to the big bay window that looked out over the lawn. The windowsill was wide enough for me to sit on. I was nervous. My hair was matted, yet it felt comfortable the way it knotted in the back of my head. I was just one big, knotted mess. With my eyes half-closed, afraid to know the truth, I finally got up the courage to look outside. The grass was still green. It wasn't dead. Oh, goody!

But it couldn't still be green. It wasn't possible. I sat on it yesterday. Something was wrong, it couldn't be true... my fault... it had to be that I was so bad I could even trick the grass into looking like it was alive.

But as I sat there staring at that wonderful live green grass, I thought that maybe there was something good about me. But it was too difficult to believe. My feelings were becoming mixed up like the knots in my hair—the aching need to be seen crackled on my lips with hope. I couldn't talk. I wouldn't talk. In the pit of my stomach, the grass was growing. A hole was opening. Soft pillows of comfort and timeless space floated inside and around me. The trees on the lawn were dancing. For the first time in my life, I felt a light breeze on my skin, and something seemed to stir, an awareness of the beauty inside me, an innocence touching my toes, a tingling that changed to sparkle-dust. I was alive. I was alone, but there was magic in the world.

Usually, before dinner, Uncle Don liked to sit in his favourite easy chair, the one that nobody else could sit on. He would read the newspaper and wait for dinner. A beer usually sat in front of him on a TV tray. One night, I watched him from the far end of the family room, from what I perceived as a safe distance. He had a look of importance. His slippers were dangling from his toes, and his tie was on the end table nearby. He had a funny red nose, eyes that looked like two pinholes, a fat belly, and short legs. To me, he appeared to be a tiny man but with a big role to play.

Connie came up to him with a picture she'd coloured. She was only seven and enjoyed colouring clowns, and she proudly showed it to her father, her face bright with anticipation.

"Look, Dad. Look what I did. Isn't it pretty?"

Uncle Don looked down at his young daughter, picked up a cigarette, lit it carefully, and took a puff, then exhaled slowly while scrutinizing Connie's work.

"Not bad," he said finally. "Not bad. But this isn't right over here. And look at that, you coloured way over the line. And whoever saw a clown with a mouth that colour? Can't you do better than that yet?"

Connie took her picture back from her father, hung her head, and walked away. Then he noticed me standing in the doorway.

"Come on over, Tracey. Come sit beside me," he said, patting his hand on the couch beside him.

At that moment, I didn't like him. The hair on the back of my neck stood up, warning me to run for cover. My stomach started turning. I was receiving bad vibes from him, but I knew I'd better play along—at least for now—because my mother had taught me to never say no to an adult. I walked over and jumped up onto the couch near his chair.

My mother was nowhere around, but in my mind, I could hear her hands claps loudly, demanding me to stay away, don't get close enough to tell the secrets. I had to obey her. My emotions were at such a high pitch that everything became a blur. Eventually I just got up and walked mechanically away from him and into the kitchen without remembering, without knowing what he had said.

The kitchen was perfect. Not one glass on the counter. Not one crumb on the floor. It gave me an uneasy feeling. I couldn't trust anyone. Why must I always pretend? On the surface, everything seemed normal, but underneath I knew things were not. Scanning the kitchen, I searched for a clue to suggest that I was normal, but I was not a perfect glass, a perfect floor, and a perfect child. My smile was lopsided, and I had crooked teeth.

I could hear Martha and my cousins playing in the basement. I wanted to join them, but I felt frozen in time, afraid to move. Silently, I found the courage to join them. They were jumping on the mattress and having a lot of fun. Diana invited me to try it. I knew I had to try to fit it in, but interacting with others didn't come easy. It took every ounce of my energy to mimic my cousins' behaviour as I sunk into my disguise and pretended to have fun. I jumped a few times, and it felt good. A smile escaped me. It was fun. I could fly like a bumblebee, but I'd better watch out, or I might get stung. Up and down. Up and down. My arms tingled with life. Excitement sizzled delightedly in my hot stomach.

I forgot about my mother.

I was on an adventure. I sat on the lawn, which was still alive and green. I was alone. I was Ralph Phillips. It was time to roam. There were treasures to find, places to see. My excitement grew. I was a crusader. I went up on the sidewalk, and it was beautiful, grey, and smooth. I liked the sound of my feet on the pavement. It was the sound of a tap dancer. I wanted to dance, to move to the rhythm of life and flap my arms while shouting out that I was alive. My legs were on fire. Everything around me was singing and buzzing with life, and there was a feeling in the air that I was about to stumble onto something magnificent.

I was soon a long way from home, but I had found the treasure. Lots of toys. A truck, a shovel, a doll, building blocks, and shiny red, green- and blue-coloured rings. I picked up the shiny rings and quickly put them on my arm, then grabbed the toys, as many as I could carry, and with them tucked under my arms and in my hands, I walked back to my aunt's and threw them all on the lawn. Ralph had succeeded. I sat cross-legged on the live green grass and examined each toy with a keen eye. The truck was red and made of plastic. I caressed it with my hand, marveling at its hard smoothness. I admired the rings on my arms, how they sparkled and shone so perfectly round. I especially liked the green one because it reminded me of the grass I didn't kill. From then on green became my favourite colour—the colour of hope.

I played there by myself for a very long time. Then I heard a voice. It was my Aunt Barb.

"Where did you get all those toys?"

I didn't answer. Trouble would follow. As my aunt walked away, I noticed her legs, her long beautiful legs. That's it, I thought, trouble is on its way. A sinking feeling grabbed me by the ankles. I knew I'd be forced to give up my happiness. Someone would point an accusing finger in my direction, and everything would end.

Minutes later my mother came out to where I was sitting on the lawn. Her face became distorted with anger.

"Tracey, put those back, you hear me?"

I got confused because my freedom was being taken away almost as soon as I got it. My mother's voice gave me goosebumps, the kind that takes an eternity to go away. Why did big people always have to ruin such grand adventures? Despondently, I picked up all the toys and took them back to their rightful owner a few blocks down the street. The hardest part was taking the rings off my arm and letting them fall onto the grass. But it was okay. I knew I'd soon get the chance to do it all over again.

When I finally came home without the toys, I expected punishment. But something strange was going on. My mother should have been freaking out. She should have been bursting at the seams. But then she was a great pretender, two-faced, bent out of shape with a smile as plastic as the coloured rings I'd just worn. It was just a game. But I didn't want to play games with her. I wanted my mother to be like Aunt Barb: caring, loving, and affectionate. But that was the good thing about living at Aunt Barb's—my mother could not do the things she wanted with others around. I wanted to tell her she was ugly and nothing like Aunt Barb.

What was strange was that her appearance had changed. She started looking more like Aunt Barb every day. She bought a long white skirt and a blouse that fit just right. It threw me off guard, gave me hope that maybe she was going to act like an actual mother. Maybe she was pretending to fit in so she could get what she wanted. I'd seen her mirroring the behaviour of others before to get her needs met, but I could see through her. And I would not let her trick me again. Aunt Barb was a picture of perfection, but it was just that she had this job to do—all the chores around the house—and she did it so well. It was as though she thought herself a queen and everyone else her pawns.

My uncle's favourite word for Aunt Barb was *distinguished*. Everything she did was impeccable. She had a way of doing things that made people think she had done such a perfect job because of the air in which she did it. My mother was a perfectionist too, in her way, but there was peacefulness at Aunt Barb's house. So Aunt Barb's perfectionism, although it was probably a little phony, was okay by me because it gave me a chance to explore my environment, which was all that mattered then. Perhaps she needed to be perfect because she was a people pleaser. But the charade, in this case, didn't bother me. In Aunt Barb's house, I slowly gained confidence in the sense of safety she provided, whether intentional or not.

Aunt Barb and my cousins had been virtual strangers to me when we first came to live with them, but it wasn't long before I was feeling the freedom to be a child for the first time in my life. Sarah too had started to brighten. For the first time I could remember, I had a semblance of friends. The horrors of my past were slowly fading, so they didn't seem so horrible anymore, almost as though the past had never happened.

The game of pretend, though, had its appeal. I was imagining my mother was not even real. Which gave me hope? It seemed like a magical time. Laughter rang throughout the house, toys were everywhere, and yesterday was dead.

# NINE

# DECEMBER 1978

The next morning I awoke disoriented in my Brantford hospital room. There was a nurse, and she told me I could go down the hall and have breakfast. I had two slices of toast with butter and jam and orange juice. It was just one big open room. I sat eating my toast and watching the other patients. They looked like zombies, walking slowly with expressionless faces and chatting obsessively to no one in particular while they ate.

I was sitting at a long table that had at least ten plates lined up on each side with plastic cutlery in case someone decided to slit their wrists or take out a staff member. At first, I chuckled at the thought, then I felt uneasy, like someone trapped me. I looked at all the sad faces around me and wondered why we were really there. Everything had a mechanical feel to it. And I sensed that everyone was afraid, lonely, and drugged.

A half-hour later, a nurse came in with a cart full of medications. She handed out small paper cups to all of us. Some said they didn't want any medication, and the nurse told them they had to take them, or they'd be given by injection. When she came to me, I took the pills like a good little girl and put them in my mouth and pretended to swallow them. Then I went to the bathroom and flushed them down the toilet, watching them swirl around the toilet bowl until they were out of sight. But I must have come back twenty times to make sure they were gone.

Finally convinced the pills were not coming back to tell on me, I started watching the patients and nurses closely. I copied the mannerisms of the nurses because I knew they were the normal ones. I saw some patients doing things like foaming at the mouth, walking around with their pants hanging real low, or wearing socks of two different colours. It would be stupid of me to mimic them. If I did, I'd never get out. So I mimicked the nurses. My mother had taught me a long time ago that acting normal would help in getting me out of trouble. She didn't say it in so many words, but I got the point.

Most of the staff, most of the time, sat behind a huge caramel desk near the exit, talking continuously. They didn't pay much attention to the patients other than making sure they couldn't escape and to hand out the meds. Watching one of the nurses, I got the impression she was talking about me, and when I watched her lips move, I swore she called me a whore. My face turned beet red, so I ducked behind one of the patients so the nurse couldn't see me. I felt as though I was being watched all the time and that my behaviour was being monitored somehow.

I watched a man in his late forties, a patient, walking up to the front desk and ask a nurse a question. He twitched a lot, his hands shook, and his hair was oily. The nurse, though, seemed to just brush him off. He went back to the table and sat down and put his head in his hands. All he needed was someone to talk to, but the nurse dismissed him as though he was unimportant, so I stayed clear of the staff. I'd had enough rejection in my life to allow it to happen in a hospital where they were supposed to help. Besides, if I avoided them, I could maintain control.

Another man, who was unshaven and bony as a model, was shouting at the nurses that he wanted to leave. Four big orderlies appeared out of nowhere, pinned him down on the floor, and injected something into him that stopped his screaming. Then they dragged him away, and we didn't see him for days. That was my cue to get with the program and keep quiet, or I would be next. I guessed that as long as I didn't express any emotion, especially anger, or make a fuss of any kind, they would leave me alone.

I guess it worked because a week passed, and no one approached me to talk about what had happened at Lynda's. I thought it rather odd that there were no real consequences for my actions except to be put into a hospital, especially when I had threatened someone with a knife.

Eventually, I was scheduled to see a psychiatrist. A nurse ushered me into a small room and told me the doctor would be in a few minutes. Shortly, the doctor came in and introduced himself, but I can't remember his name. I remember his shiny brown shoes because they were too perfect and recently waxed. When he extended his hand, I just looked down at the floor to avoid it and a most penetrating stare. When I finally shook his hand, mine felt cold. He told me to sit down, and I did.

He wanted to know if I heard voices. I did, and I told him so.

He wanted to know if I saw things that weren't real. I did, and I told him so.

He wanted to know if I thought people were trying to hurt me. I did, and I told him so.

Finally, I thought, someone who was interested, someone who would listen, but to my dismay, he only wanted to know if I was manifesting symptoms of schizophrenia and which ones they were. He then prescribed a cocktail of pharmaceuticals, and we parted. I don't drink cocktails.

Throughout the day I had nothing to do, so I just sat and listened to the patients relate their sad stories. Most of them had been sexually assaulted and beaten down emotionally, but they knew better than to talk about it to anyone other than another patient. The hospital staff perceived them all as chronic liars who couldn't tell the difference between reality and fiction. There was a great power imbalance between the patients and staff; they knew everything, and we were village idiots.

The psychiatric ward was just a babysitting facility. It was just a place to warehouse us and keep us out of society's way. It was a place where families could have their troublesome loved ones looked after, without anyone finding out why they were there. It was also a great place for abusers to have their victims warehoused because they never have to worry about them blowing the whistle on them because anything their victims remember is so disguised by the madness that no one will believe them.

The doctors just didn't get the language of schizophrenics, or they didn't want to. And the drugs played a part too. They made sure we couldn't remember anything at all. That was the beauty and the sadness of it.

Everyone had a story to tell, but nobody wanted to listen.

So I continued to follow the rules and sit quietly watching TV in the lounge. I waited to be called for another visit with a psychiatrist or staff member, but nothing happened. I tried to tempt them into my world by making jerky movements, even running up and down the hall and doing somersaults and cartwheels, but to no avail.

I was bored out of my skull with nothing to do but wait for my next meal and listen to the other patients' ramblings. Most of them told me their stories and how they got committed. It was usually just because they were acting strange or, sometimes, like me, had threatened someone else. There were also those that had attempted suicide. But I noticed how harmless everyone was. We just acted strangely because we were afraid. We spoke a distinct language because we couldn't trust the actual world any longer. Everyone had failed us, and now the docs were failing us.

The normal people, those who claimed to be helping us, had no desire to understand us, and I thought that was odd. The experts seemed to have no communication skills to use on us. They appeared to have no experience or training other than dishing out medications that didn't do any good. They got the nurses to monitor our behaviour to predict if we would hurt ourselves or others. The damn docs acted like gods. They discouraged any kind of therapeutic relationship only because they didn't know what they were doing. All they knew was that medications kept patients quiet, so they kept on giving them, regardless of possible long-term effects. I think it would have made a big difference if the staff could have been our friends and had some kind of therapeutic relationship with us.

Finally, a nurse approached me to tell me I had a visitor. I followed her to the waiting room and was surprised to find Lynda sitting there. She got up and gave me a hug. I pulled away. She told me I couldn't go back to her house because she was afraid I would hurt someone in her family. She brought with her a fresh shirt and pants for me. I thanked her and put them down on a chair. Lynda hugged me again and said goodbye. I left without the clothes. I wanted nothing that connected me to her. Also, I knew I had done something bad when I was there and wanted nothing around to remind me of it. I focused my attention on the light fixture on the wall and pretended it was a secret device designed to track my every movement. I imagined a big blue eye in the light bulb, and when I turned to walk away that eye was staring at my ass, so I turned around and walked backwards with my hands covering my breasts.

Christmas came and went—then my birthday. It felt like history repeating itself except this time there really was no one coming to get me. I was fifteen years old.

# TEN

# JULY 1969

That summer at Aunt Barb's place, my mother became involved with a new man. He was tall with jet-black hair and a prickly moustache. His nails were trimmed, but long and dirty; I could have sworn they were daggers. There were long creases down the middle of his pants, and his boots were black and shiny with not one scuff mark anywhere, suspiciously perfect. His name was Robert.

Though I didn't know it right away—at five years old—Robert would prove to be a pathological liar, and he had a knack when it came to persuading the pants off any street-smart woman. He had a pointy face with crow's feet and eyes that were as black and piercing as they were empty and distant, reflecting a soul that told a story of deception most people wouldn't notice or even understand. However, his mind was cunning and whip smart. He was worse than a bad boy. *Way* worse.

Even at five, I found him immediately unsettling and couldn't understand how my mother didn't have any misgivings. I don't know why, but from the first time I met him, I thought of him as *the dead man*. I didn't want to disrupt the delusional bubble my mother lived in. It felt as though she were deliberately trying to protect herself from the truth.

She was all giggles when he arrived, like a schoolgirl. She hung on his every word like he was some kind of superhero—but I didn't see any cape. It was like his words could reach out to her somehow, curl around her waist, and draw her ever closer to him. Even her posture seemed to slump timidly as she might have done when hiding her budding breasts at twelve. She probably thought she'd found the man of her dreams who would make her feel complete.

On that first day, he bent down in front of me, as adults do with little kids, to make eye contact, to get my full attention with some stupid wisecrack. His voice was loud yet distant, as though he were hollow. I stepped back quickly. I didn't trust him. I didn't want him to get too close because he gave me the creeps. I wanted to watch him from a distance, but he was right in my face, and I imagined I could read his mind and that he'd whispered, *Gotcha*.

I glimpsed at my mother standing over by her shiny red car in her high heels and her skirt with the long slit down the side. She was watching us with amusement. An icy chill ran up my spine because I already feared those bony fingers touching me. My mother was laughing in the background like a hyena. Just the sight of him created a sour taste in my mouth, and I wanted to hit him instinctively. I knew something was wrong. I just wasn't sure what, yet.

She'd insisted I say hello to him, but I could smell alcohol on his breath. I would choke on my words, but I finally whispered a feeble hello. I could sense the attraction between the two of them. They both had glazed over eyes. I suspected that it was because they were alike in their perversions. I think I had a built-in bullshit detector even then.

My mother was still standing by her car when she told me to kiss him goodbye. She was eager to get on with their date. And before I responded, the dead man had his mouth on my lips and had darted his tongue into my mouth with a quick jab. The texture of his tongue was like leather, old bumpy leather. His breath was hot and foul and made me think of a poisonous snake as he turned and left me standing in a puddle of venom. He looked back and shot me a sly, deadly smile that sent shivers down my back. I remember watching the bottom of his pants bobbing up and down as he walked away and noticing how his shiny black boots didn't make a sound.

As soon as they left, I ran into the house and down into Aunt Barb's basement. It was empty and lifeless, exactly the way I was feeling just then. I wanted to hide behind the drywall. I went down on my knees underneath the stairs, crouched on my heels, and rocked quietly back and forth, but in my mind, it was violent enough to tear my head clean off my shoulders. The stairs were my shelter, and hard—like my heart was becoming. I felt like a caged animal, trapped in a place that should have been home. I had shut down all my senses one by one. I didn't want to feel anything at all. I started to sing to myself.

"I've got the whole world in my hands. I've got the whole world in my hands."

Then I slowly reached out to touch the stairs, caress the wood. I needed to bond with something solid. I needed some way to stay in contact with reality. I felt like I could disappear into the lumber and that it would be safe because it was a part of the earth. Then I looked up, noticed the clouds outside the small window and pretended to drift away on the biggest, softest, fluffiest one. At first, it relaxed me. But then the terrible memories came back to me—visions of feces, tongues, fingers, hands, words like daggers, all swirling around and around and around in my head. All those ugly memories from my past I had so carefully stored away and tried to forget came rushing in at me all at once.

And I became undone.

I tried to stay focused, tried to ground myself in the present, tried to push my past away. My hands and feet were tingling, and my body felt like jelly. It made me think of peanut butter. All I would have needed was to plaster myself with peanut butter and I would have been one hell of a sandwich for some freak to eat on any day.

Time moved at a snail's pace, but at last I was slowly beginning to calm down. The tingling in my hands and feet gradually subsided. The whirlpool of disturbing images slowly stopped spinning around, and a deep sadness overcame me then. This was followed by complete exhaustion. I didn't cry. I felt dead at the very core of my existence. If I had just one wish at that moment, I would have used it to evaporate into thin air, to disappear forever. I had a strange aching need to disappear so I could survive. I was still curious about life, and I wanted so much to open up, but I was stretched tighter than a drum.

The basement was my place of safety, my refuge, and all I had to do to change focus and go somewhere else in my mind was to change the position of my body. If I wanted to focus on a different subject, a fresh perspective, all I had to do was put my legs out straight and sit like that for a while. So I did just that to think about Aunt Barb. She was perfect, like a well-carved statue. I liked her and yet she seemed odd to me, but maybe odd was normal. She was like a robot programmed to do the daily chores. It made me wonder if there was really a person inside her. I wanted her to be real, or my entire world would be just one big lie. It was funny the way I would base my entire identity on someone else's appearance. I constantly wondered about the surrounding people, wondered who they were, wondered why they didn't ask me questions, why they didn't talk to me. I had so many questions of my own, but no one to ask. Then I started thinking about my Uncle Don with his beady eyes. He was like a dour Santa because he was fat and had a red nose, but he wasn't jolly. I thought there was something strange about him. There seemed to be something wrong with everyone I knew—there *had* to be because I was all wrong too. I thought a lot about what might be wrong with them, and with me, because it was safer than thinking about my mother and her new boyfriend, the dead man.

Then I wanted to stop thinking about them, so I changed my sitting position again. I started thinking about the sky, another safe place for me. I enjoyed the peace that came from watching the countless twinkling stars in the night sky and thinking about how unreachable they were—and yet how I felt close to them, nonetheless. They were my friends. And I could watch them just by thinking about them, even way down in the basement under the stairs.

Then I heard the chiming of a bell, like a warning, or maybe it was just the buzzing in my ears. It seemed very far away, yet I knew something was there. I then visualized an open cut somewhere on my body. I didn't even know where it was, but I knew that death would befriend me one day. Eventually death would come knocking on my door.

Then I saw people around me, and they were all wearing masks. The sky was whispering its secrets—I felt a spiritual deadness—and then a tunnel opened and tried to pull me in. I knew I'd better be careful because something bad was about to happen. I desperately needed to find something good about life to hold on to. Clouds of courage swarmed around in my mind. I had to be brave or at least fake it like everyone else. My skin felt hot, baked, charred beyond recognition. I wasn't who I was.

I thought about the trees and how they had become twisted and tired—a knotted reflection of what I was becoming. I longed to go home, but I had none, not a real one, not one that was truly mine. I wanted to close my eyes and go to sleep forever. I wanted the sky to swallow me up because nothing mattered anymore. No one even knew that I existed. I felt so unbearably alone. My mind started playing games with me. I saw green rings jumping, yet all lined up in sequence, telling me to be silent. So there I sat under the stairs all alone, betrayed even by my mind. Images of words dripping like icicles were taking up too much space in my brain. Images of the bogeyman crowded inside me, but I placed them far away from the present by imagining boxes, many boxes to keep them in. I just closed the lids to silence the terror the memory of them would bring.

Then I heard the music. It was unfamiliar to me, but I also knew that only I could hear it. And with it came pretty colours that were moving in harmony to the beat of that unfamiliar tune. I felt a presence down there in that lonely basement, as though someone were watching over me. I didn't know who or what it was, but it took my loneliness away. It gave me hope. I felt a shadow of warmth that was fresher even than the taste of spring water. Something was pulling at me, enticing me into a secret garden where magical flowers bloomed, and self-creation dawned. It was a place where no one else could go, only me. No one could get in. And no one could take away my self-respect or my dignity when I was there.

My secret garden was my home back then. It was my most precious secret. A place where I dreamed of freedom and could believe those dreams might one day come true. I could not allow myself to forget what was on the outside of that precious secret garden. I knew all too well there was danger in it—dead leaves, rotten fruit, creepy hands, a garden of fools, and fingernails as sharp as razor blades.

My cousins eventually discovered me huddled there, under the stairs. They tried to get me to come out, but I wasn't ready. They tried to make a connection, to entice me to join them in their fun, but I stared at their fresh faces and cautious smiles. They made me feel smothered. I didn't want any involvement in their mindless, boring games, and I wasn't interested in jumping on that boring old mattress. I just wanted them to go away and leave me alone. I wasn't like them, and I knew it, but I did like to watch them play from a distance, I could feel their happiness second-hand by witnessing it. Listening to them laugh, I could take a little of their sunshine for myself. That's all I was worth, anyway, according to my mother. So I took on those second-hand feelings and tucked them away for later when I was by myself again. They were like happy bubbles that could fill my space when I needed them.

No one ever really knew how they'd end up inspiring me to come out of my shell one day. As my cousins went back to jumping on the mattress, I grabbed onto an imaginary golden rope that dangled above me. I swayed back and forth on it for a long time, grabbing at hidden treasures in the air. It was much more fun to play in my mind than with my cousins.

# ELEVEN

# JUNE 1979

One day in early June, when no one was paying attention, I slipped through the emergency back door and took off running down the street with one of the other patients. His name was Dave. He had walked up and invited me to take off with him—I guess because I was the only other young one there. I didn't like him, though, because he was good looking in a way that reminded me of my mother, but I wanted to get out of there, and I would never have left on my own, so we left. Dave decided we would hitchhike because he wanted to get to downtown Toronto. I didn't have a clue what to do, so I tagged along. About fifteen minutes later, a guy in a non-descript pickup truck picked us up. He was in his fifties, and I thought he was a pervert. He hardly said two words to us during the entire trip to town, which was all right by me.

He dropped us off in front of Sam the Record Man on Yonge Street where about a dozen street kids were hanging out. Dave introduced me to them and then took off to go see his girlfriend. Two kids were as young as twelve, and I think the oldest was twenty. I was only fifteen. They greeted me openly.

"Hey. How's it going?" one said.

One kid asked if I wanted to rip off a car. Another wanted to know if I'd like to smoke some hash and was eager to give advice on how to survive on the street. A kid named Bobby wore jeans, a T-shirt, and Hush Puppies that were almost, but not quite, unrecognizable beneath the filth.

I learned later they'd periodically steal new clothes and throw their old clothes away because they had no way to wash them. I was with them for the rest of that morning and most of the afternoon, hanging around the record store or laying on the grass in the park talking. All the kids had real chips on their shoulders and were full of anger—like me. None of them asked me where I was from or why I was on the street. They just accepted me as I was. It was a lot better than being at the hospital or even at home. By late afternoon, the cops pulled up, asked me my name, and told me to get in the car.

After a while, a social worker came and took me to a restaurant to get something to eat.

The social worker drove me to the juvenile detention centre on George Street. On the way there, she explained to me that the situation was only temporary and as soon as a proper placement came available, she'd have me moved. She figured it would only take two weeks, tops.

The centre looked more like a convent than a jail, except it didn't have any nuns roaming around. Down the street, there was a bathhouse for men to get a sauna or a quick shower. But over the years, it had turned into a place for men to go to get sexual favours. Some homeless boys would go there and turn tricks for a quick buck. A few doors down from the centre there was a women's homeless shelter (one where I would eventually stay for a couple of nights). The area was so run down that a few houses were condemned and had their windows boarded up.

As the social worker parked the car in the visitors' parking lot, I glanced across the street and noticed a young girl prancing around in three-inch heels on the corner. At first, I thought she was a beauty queen, but I found out later that she was only a prostitute on the lookout for Johns.

The social worker got out of the car, came around to my side, and opened the door. As I stepped out, she forcibly locked her arm in mine and marched me straight up the stairs to the entrance. As she rang the buzzer, I thought about running, but I had a funny feeling that the worker might outrun me because she was in exceptional shape, so I played it safe and stayed put.

Minutes later, a short, plump woman answered the door. Without hesitating, she grabbed me by the arm and rushed me in the doorway so fast that I almost lost my footing. Then she snapped at me to go take a seat in the lobby. I felt like I had just joined the navy. As I sat there, I listened to her and the social worker chat up a storm regarding my case at the front desk. But then I got distracted by a rack of pamphlets leaning up against a wall. Some headings read:

- Child Delinquency

- Youth in Action

- Youth Violence

- Serious and Violent Juvenile Offending

That's when I realized I was in serious trouble, so I sat there quietly and sized up the plump lady from a distance. I couldn't help but notice her box-shaped figure, too manly for my liking. While the worker signed the paperwork, I looked around the room. The floors were dirty, and I could see a buildup of dirt in the cracks of the floorboards. The walls had no pictures, just framed documents.

After they signed all the forms, the social worker nodded goodbye and left in a hurry as if she were Wonder Woman out to save the world. Then the plump lady took me into a small room down the hall. The room was bright—considering it had no windows—with blinding fluorescent lights. She told me to strip down to my underwear. I wasn't the least bit shocked. I didn't even flinch. I just stood there like a frozen Popsicle while she patted me down and checked through my hair for god knows what? She even looked inside my mouth with a small flashlight that she had picked up from a nearby table. I guess she was checking for cavities or something. I was just waiting for her to put duct tape over my mouth and shoot me with a gun. I imagined a bullet lodged in my head. The whole thing was absurd. It wasn't like I had committed a crime or anything.

Later on, another worker by the name of Jo—short for Joanna—came to see me. She wore a plain blue-collar shirt and blue slacks. A set of keys dangled from her belt buckle. She acted like she was in charge of the place, and that rubbed me the wrong way. I didn't like her military stance, her arrogance and no-nonsense attitude. Under my breath, I called her stony face and other things. When I zoomed in on her face, I could see two long chin hairs on her chin. I focused on them to avoid her icy stare. Besides, I didn't know how else to act around a woman who had more masculinity in her pinky finger than I had in my entire body.

After Jo finished with me, she took me down a long corridor and up two flights of stairs to my room where she had to use a key to get in. The room had two metal framed beds and two nightstands. In between the two beds, there was a beat-up dresser. To my surprise, there wasn't a lamp for reading. I guess they didn't want any loose cords lying around in case someone tried to hang themselves. I picked a bed and sat down on its edge. The bed was hard, and the mattress was thin, and it had a thick plastic covering that made a noise when I shifted my position.

I listened to Jo go over the rules. She handed me a sheet of paper to read as she continued to talk. I looked down at the sheet but couldn't focus because the words were moving around on the paper. But I processed some of what Jo had told me. However, there were things I didn't get, but I knew better not to ask questions because it would have put me in the spotlight. So I sat there, quiet as a mouse, even afraid to breathe. I didn't get why everyone was so bent on explaining the rules to me all the time. It wasn't like I was hard of hearing or brain dead. Besides, it wasn't rocket science that they locked me up and took all my freedom away. I knew well that I was nothing more than a puppet, and they were pulling my strings.

I couldn't wait for Jo to finish her spiel so I could get some rest. It felt like she was dragging things on forever, but then I finally she got to the end of what she had to say.

"Someone will come get you at dinnertime."

Then she left and I heard the door click tight.

Later, a worker by the name of Leanne came to get me. She was around five nine and had golden blonde hair. She was wearing a tight-fitted T-shirt and army pants, but not the proper kind. The plain green barrette in her hair matched her outfit. Her voice was soft, yet she was tough talking—the perfect balance. I followed her around the place like a puppy as she asked me light questions.

"Where you from?" –and– "What grade are you in?" –and– "Do you like sports?" –and– "What kind of music do you listen to?"

She made me feel like she was interested in me. I told her a pack of lies, and in between sentences, I flashed my white teeth like I was an up-and-coming movie star. I felt comfortable with her right off the bat. There was something genuine about her, the way she used her words carefully and didn't dig into my past. But as soon as I relaxed in her presence, my fear of being exposed kicked in. I imagined her trying to trick me into confessing my secrets, pouring out the ghosts that lay dormant in my soul.

With a snap of my wrist, I shut down, and I think she noticed because she stopped pressing me to talk and took me to the cafeteria right away.

The cafeteria was huge. It could hold at least a hundred people. The kitchen island must have been twenty feet long—perfect for prepping vegetables and sitting around talking nonsense. Big bowls of fresh fruit and canisters of plastic utensils sat at the far end of the counter. There were warming trays filled with food. One wall had hanging pots and pans. My eyes lit up when I saw the doubled-door fridge because I was starving. It felt like I hadn't eaten in ages. Once again, without missing a beat, Lee sensed a change in my demeanour and told me to have a look inside the fridge. When I popped it open, my jaw dropped, I couldn't believe how full it was, all kinds of goodies, just about anything my little heart desired. It felt like I had just hit the jackpot and won a raffle.

I got a large spoon and scooped out a serving of tuna casserole and then plopped myself down on a hard plastic chair in the back of the room. I sat in the corner so that nobody could sneak up behind me. Besides, when I let people stand behind me, I would have terrible visions of a faceless man trying to bash my head in with a bat.

On each floor in the building, there were at least three washrooms. Some had showers. Some only had sinks and a toilet. When I peeked into one bathroom, I could see green mould growing inside the shower stall.

There was a leisure room on the second floor. It had a TV and two old couches that looked in need of a cleaning. Down the hall, there was an activity room with a large built-in bookcase. Cans of pipe-cleaners and little plastic scissors, jars of buttons, glue bottles, and sketchbooks and paper products lined the shelves. Just the sight of all the stuff was enough to get my creative juices flowing.

A week later, Robert came to visit me. The dead man. (Though, at that point, I had stopped thinking of him that way. To me, he was just plain old Robert, my stepfather). A man I'd known since I was five years old. An inky impenetrable shadow that blacked out parts of my childhood.

I found Robert sitting on an oversized vinyl chair in the visitors' lounge. I remember the chair arm having little holes and white stuffing coming out. I took a seat across from him and watched him like a hawk. It'd been ten months since I'd seen him, and he was fidgeting with a pack of cigarettes, obviously at a loss for words, and his hands were shaking. The silence was killing me. Sweat was trickling down my armpits. He looked like weighed down with troubles, and his eyes were red like he'd been crying. He was thin too. He reminded me of a troll lurking under a bridge, waiting for small children to eat. I felt somewhat sorry for him. I suppose it was because of his appearance. He started talking, but I couldn't make out his words. I just stood there, stone-faced, and unable to comprehend a thing he was saying. It confused me. I couldn't understand why he was visiting me. I wondered if my mother knew.

I asked him for a cigarette, and he gave me three. As he handed them over, I noticed a shiny ring on his baby finger; it had a blue star in the middle of it. The sight of it brought up something deep inside me. Then his hand turned into a snake and began wiggling around in its place.

I was just about to leave when he stood up and shoved his telephone number into my hand. He told me if I needed anything to call him. On my way back upstairs to my room, I threw his number into a wastebasket.

And then I forgot about him. Out of sight, out of mind as the old saying goes.

When I got back to my room, I surprised to find a girl there. I guess they had just admitted her. I had only been in the room for two minutes, and she was already talking circles around me, asking a million questions that I had no intention to answering.

"Been here long?" –and– "How's the food?" –and– "What's your story?"

I just shrugged my shoulders, turned my back on her, and pretended she didn't exist. I guess she got the hint to leave me alone because she didn't say one word to me after that.

I had just started feeling comfortable, and the staff had to get me a roommate. I was fuming. I also couldn't believe that the girl had the gall to talk to me. Out of frustration and anger, I started rambling on about the staff and how they were monitoring my behaviour and spying on me. The girl then stopped talking to me.

Mission accomplished. I think she thought I was some kind of kook. She got that right!

Later on, I walked around and checked the place out. I didn't go into any of the rooms, though. I just poked my head in to have a quick look. I spotted three girls sitting at a round table in one room. An instructor was leaning over a girl's shoulder while checking out her work. It crossed my mind to join them, but after weighing the pros and cons, I decided against it. Besides, I had the attention span of a goldfish and didn't want to get into any lengthy conversations that would leave me exposed to criticism—although I would have liked to get my hands on those Popsicle sticks to build a log house.

In the morning, one of the staff told me I had to take part in a volleyball game at two o'clock in the afternoon. I wasn't pleased to hear that, so I tried to talk my way out of it, but she wasn't having it. She told me it was mandatory and then rambled on about how the exercise and the fresh air would do me some good. It seemed so unfair that I was being forced to do something against my will. But I knew better than to argue with staff because the administration called the shots.

I had giant sweat spots under my armpits, so I pinned the wet spots under my arms and held my arms in tight. I prayed to God that no one would see me sweating like a pig. I must have looked like a penguin walking around the courtyard.

The staff divided us into two teams and then flipped a coin to see who would serve first. My team lost the coin toss. Some girls had to sit out and wait their turns because we had too many players. At first, I was nervous about playing, especially in a crowd, but soon as I got to play, my nerves settled down, I began jumping around like a grasshopper, playing like a pro, and hogging the ball.

I was really getting into the game, but before I knew it, my fun came to a grinding halt. I had been so engrossed in the game that I didn't even hear the catcalls coming from over the concrete wall that separated the boys from the girls. I didn't even notice the two girls strut their stuff in the courtyard like they were peacocks. They were acting like sex goddesses, all primped up and rearing to go.

The administration had a policy in place that didn't permit the mixing of the sexes in the facility, just in case someone got knocked up or contracted a venereal disease. I remember feeling angry at the boys and girls for ruining my fun, especially since I had finally settled down and was enjoying myself.

After the game, I went to the bathroom, washed my hands and went downstairs to the cafeteria for dinner. I sat alone at a table closest to the wall and gobbled down a plate of meat and mashed potatoes, but I didn't touch the pudding because it had skin on top. I still felt hungry afterward. I don't know why, but I always felt hungry. It was like I was trying to fill a void in me or something. My stomach was a bottomless pit, the dead zone. My love tank was running on empty. Sometimes food seemed like the perfect companion, for food never let me down. Well, unless it was a can of sardines. I would stuff my face like there were no tomorrow. I suppose if it wasn't for all the exercise I got, I'd probably be as big as a cow. But I was thin.

My body was starting to change. I was losing my boyish figure. My breasts got big and hard like bullets. My body had curves in all the right places. I hardly had any fat on me. Even the lesbian girls were noticing me. I didn't notice them at first—it wasn't until one of the staff told me that the lesbians were hitting on me. She asked me I liked it and if I swung that way. As if I would notice anyone hitting on me. Besides, my sexual preferences were none of their business. Even if a girl found me attractive, there was nothing I could do about it. I wouldn't know how to fend off their advances or brush them off because I had no boundaries. I was just a sitting duck for anyone to take advantage of.

I didn't like boys. I didn't like girls. I just wanted everyone to leave me alone. The last thing on my mind was sex. I was too busy trying to survive.

Although I was aware of my sexuality, I wasn't comfortable with it. I wore baggy clothes to hide my body, and I had a hard time grasping the concept that anyone would find me attractive. I was still that unlovable kid that my mother accused me of being time after time.

I wasn't even aware that I was giving off any sexual vibes. I also wasn't aware that I was acting like my mother when she was in a sexual trance. On the outside, I purred like a little sex kitten, pouting my lips as if I were a model. It was easy for me to slip into that role without an identity, and since I was prone to copying, it came naturally to me.

I could almost hear people cheering as I stepped into any room. It felt like a million eyes were on me. And it was making me feel uncomfortable.

# TWELVE

# SEPTEMBER 1969

After a summer adapting to life at Aunt Barb's, September arrived. The leaves had started to change, and the air had cooled, especially in the evenings. Not only that, but it meant I would have to go to school. To kindergarten. It sounded spooky. I had to go on the school bus with Martha and my cousins, and it sounded like it must be far away. I was afraid that somehow, because of the distance, my secrets might somehow become exposed.

When the big day came, I remember gripping the guardrail at the top of the stairs in the front hall of Aunt Barb's house until my knuckles turned white. My hair felt sticky. The coat I was wearing felt like a ton of bricks. I couldn't breathe properly. I was frightened of a new experience that should have been one of delightful anticipation. I couldn't understand why my mother was throwing me out into the world without preparing me a little better for it. I felt like she had thrown me to the wolves.

And that thought brought with it visions of blood pouring down the stairs and dripping into deep dark puddles at the bottom. I smelled something foul that seemed to come from between my legs, and immediately I envisioned rotten flesh burning down a candlestick. I felt self-hate, and in a heated rush, a bouquet of dead daisies choked me into silence. A purple coffin floated by with velvet cushions in mid-air as they promised an escape. I thought the earth was going to open and swallow me whole. Goddammit, I couldn't go to school. Couldn't anyone see I was afraid of change? Stupid people!

I could hear my Aunt Barb faintly in the background. Her voice had a calming effect on me, it mesmerized. There was an angelic aura around her face, but it made me think she was a phony-baloney!

She bent down to make eye contact with me.

"School will be great. There'll be lots of things to do and lots of kids to play with."

There was no use arguing with her. Grown-ups always thought they knew what was best. She gently helped me on with my jacket and guided me outside and onto the sidewalk where we waited for the school bus. My cousins were eager to get to school. Martha and Connie were chatting and whispering. And Rebecca and Diana were bouncing around all over the place, full of smiles and laughter. I was off by myself. The next thing I knew, Barb was waving goodbye from the sidewalk.

I slumped down in the seat on the bus and imagined myself part of it. I held my jacket close to my chest so that no one could take it. I could feel sweat trickling down my face, and I was sure I could feel oil sliding down each strand of my hair. I looked out the window and became absorbed in the shapes of the clouds. I saw elves prancing around, playing on ladders, sliding down into a pool of laughter. I wanted to live in my imagination forever.

As I sat in the classroom on the first day of school, it all seemed so absurd to me. I remember the sound of the children's feet on the floor and the marvelous colours. It was a colourful place. There were numbers on the blackboard, building blocks piled up on a table, and a playhouse in the corner. All the other kids seemed to be in a hurry, yet they weren't going anywhere. They bounced around like yo-yos, but I felt like an oddball just sitting there like a piece of stale bread, untouched, waiting for vultures to come.

The teacher introduced herself, but I can't remember her name. She was a pleasant-looking woman in her early thirties. She had soft brown hair that caressed her shoulders and her perfectly straight teeth seemed too white. She wore a well-hemmed dress, and she had a good posture that was very noticeable. Her smile filled the entire lower part of her face but wasn't phony.

I pulled my bangs apart to inspect her and everything else that was happening. I'd put my jacket on by the time I got off the bus and was still wearing it in the classroom. It was my way of hiding. I was very curious about what was going on. Then the teacher started coming towards me.

"Tracey, please hang your coat up at the back of the classroom. There are plenty of hooks."

But there was no way I was going to take my jacket off. No way! I broke out in a sweat. No one had told me I would have to take off my jacket and leave it at the back of the classroom, which seemed like a million miles away.

For days, the teacher tried to get me to take my jacket off. Finally, Aunt Barb showed up and told me it would be okay to take it off, and the warmth of her smile just seemed to melt it off me. But I felt exposed and then terrified. I was afraid everyone was going to laugh and call me names and tease me for being such a weirdo. I imagined them holding hands and dancing in a circle around me, singing their chiding song about the weirdo in the middle of the ring.

# THIRTEEN

# JULY 1979

After about a month at the detention centre, I found out I was being transferred to a group home out of town. This time, though, I would be staying on a farm with another family in Severn Bridge. I got word that a social worker was coming to get me. I packed up my one bag of clothing and got ready to go.

The social worker arrived on time, and off we went down the highway in her blue car. I felt chatty that day, so I rambled on about the pleasant view, the trees, the weather, anything to settle down my anxiety. I guess I was talking too much because the social worker turned up the radio and drowned me out. I changed gears and sang along with the music instead. I didn't know the words. I just mouthed them while pretending to be a rock star. I then drummed my fingers on the dashboard. I was just about to take my singing career to a whole new level when the social worker turned off the radio. I wasn't pleased with that, so I cut my connection to her and sat there like a sack of rocks, stone cold.

About an hour and a half later, we were driving down a pebbled driveway where I could see a farmhouse. The scenery took my breath away. There were trees everywhere. I sat upright and took in my new surroundings, and all its glory. I couldn't believe my luck.

As soon as I got out of the car, Mr. and Mrs. Cameron and their two children, Amber and Martin, came over to greet me. Mrs. Cameron reminded me of Liz Taylor. She had a similar eye colour and the same hairstyle. She was wearing tight, dark blue jeans with a buttoned-up blouse that hid her cleavage. Mr. Cameron was tall, and I got a bad vibe about him from the get-go. He seemed unapproachable, like his shit didn't stink. I didn't like the smug look on his face as he sized me up like livestock. I knew he would be trouble for me in the long run.

There were animals everywhere: horses, rabbits, chickens, goats, dogs, and cats. I couldn't wait to get out there and explore my environment. There was only one problem. Before anything, I had to go over the rules with Mr. and Mrs. Cameron. They told me I had to get up at five AM to shovel the horseshit out of the stalls, sweep the barn, and lift seventy-five-pound bales of hay onto a tracker. I guess they thought hard labour would whip me into shape.

Mrs. Cameron spent most of her time doing household duties and running errands. She was in exceptional health. I couldn't see one ounce of body fat on her. If she had any, she sure knew how to hide it. She had wavy black hair, and it looked like she smothered it in beeswax because it was super shiny. There was another kid staying there. Her name was Elisha, and she was Mrs. Cameron's favourite sidekick. They'd busy themselves in the kitchen, baking pies and prepping for dinner. One evening, I found them in the living room painting each other's toes.

One time, when I was in the barn, Mr. Cameron told me to go get the shovel from against the wall and start clearing out the horseshit from the stalls. I didn't want to, so I protested. I told him no, and his response was I better get in there if I knew what was good for me. I didn't know what to say to that, so I went to work.

Doc, a two-thousand-pound horse beast of an animal, was scaring me. Every time I'd stand beside him, he'd move over, which left little room for me to get out. I swear he was doing it on purpose. As I worked away, sweat beads were rolling down my face. One wrong move, I'd be mincemeat. Dead. Gone.

Later, I got to know Mr. and Mrs. Cameron's teenaged children. I think they were two years apart in age. They looked like country bumpkins. Their plaid shirts and cowboy boots were a dead giveaway. Amber was Mr. Cameron's favourite. I could tell his eyes shone when he looked at her. Conversation between the two of them came easy. As for Martin, there seemed to be friction.

Martin had no interest in farm life. When we were alone together, he'd tell me that once he was old enough and found a good job, he was out of there. Most days, he'd be out in the bush driving a tracker, clearing land, and removing dead trees and branches that had fallen on the ground. I could sense his anger as it curved around the edge of his words. When we sat down at the kitchen table for dinner, he was silent as he listened to his father chat away about his plans.

One day, after two weeks of working on the farm, I couldn't get up in the morning because the work had exhausted me. My body ached. All that hard work had caught up to me, and I just wanted to sleep in. But Mr. Cameron would not have it, so he sent his wife into my room and she demanded that I get up at once. I ignored her words and rolled over and went back to sleep. Then Mr. Cameron came up and tried to coax me out of bed by towering over me and threatening to call my social worker if I didn't get up. He could threaten me all he wanted—I simply didn't have the strength to get out of bed. I was resenting him for using me as his farmhand. The only reason he wanted me up was to get me to do the work in the barn. It wasn't like I was getting paid or anything. I wasn't moving. His last words were, before he left my sight…

"She is hopeless. We can't help her."

While I was moseying around the farm, I came across a pen of goats. There must have been at least ten of them. I swear, when I looked into the eyes of one of them, it gave me the stink eye. I knew it was one of the devil's soldiers disguising itself as a goat. I wasn't about to let it trick me. I watched its eye turn gold with a hint of red. It reminded me of a bull's eye. I envisioned the seat of my pants being torn out by the goat's yellow and brown teeth. I laughed out loud nervously, so I put my hand over my mouth. I could have sworn someone was behind me, clawing at my back and pulling on my hair. But when I turned around, nobody was there.

Soon after, I went to the open field out behind the barn where the grass was short. I could see bundles of hay in the distance. I plopped down on the grass spread-eagle, took a piece of grass, and stuck it between my teeth and reminiscence about my beautiful ravine back home. Then I kicked my feet up in the air, rolled over twice and clapped my hands in anticipation of future experiences on the farm.

Suddenly, the sound of Mr. Cameron's voice interrupted me. He was calling me from the fence closest to the house. When I looked up, I could see him coming towards me. Before he could get to me, I got up and made my way back to the house. When I passed Mr. Cameron, I got the chills. His height alone was intimidating. When I looked into his eyes, they looked like black coals, so I blinked my eyes once and turned them into lit matchsticks and watched them burn down to the ground. Then I blinked my eyes a second time to shut out Mr. Cameron from talking to me.

Elisha and I were the same age, and she acted normal. She looked like the kid who always brought in apples for the teacher. I did not understand why she was in care. I figured she had a troubled home life, but she showed no signs of abuse or neglect. She was around five eight, and her natural blonde hair reached the small of her back. She had oval-shaped blue eyes that seemed too big for her face. She was my opposite and enjoyed doing her hair, ironing her clothes—she always seemed obsessed with her looks, as if that were the only thing that mattered. I was sitting in the living room, that day, admiring the braided brown and white oval rug when she came up to me in hopes of a brief conversation. I didn't want any part of that, so I got up and went to my bed.

My room was in the attic, which had been converted into a loft. It had four beds, small dressers, and a bookcase with a vase of fresh daisies sitting on top. The bookcase had all kinds of fiction books and a Bible. I took the Bible and opened it up. The thing I liked about the Bible is that it had metaphors in it, and I could guess what it meant. It was one big riddle. I thought the hands of God had planted it in the room for me. It contained secret messages for my eyes only. I can't count the times I flipped through the pages, looking for my missing self and looking for my secret mission in life. I felt that the Bible was my protection from the cruel realities of my life. I put the Bible under my pillow and tried to get some rest, but before doing that, I ran my hand over it, hoping it would soothe my broken mind.

The following morning, Mrs. Cameron woke me up at five o'clock. She told me to come downstairs for breakfast. Her beauty was mesmerizing, even first thing in the morning. Her hair was blue-black, and she had those violet Liz Taylor eyes. For her age, she was in terrific shape, not one bulge in her slender frame. She was almost forty years old.

I was sitting at the kitchen table eating a bowl of porridge. I put four big spoonfuls of brown sugar on top. I loved the texture of brown sugar in my mouth and the way porridge stuck to my gut. I was listening to Mrs. Cameron and Elisha going on about what they would do that day. I think they were trying out a new recipe. While they did that, I had to go out to the barn with Mr. Cameron and work.

Mr. Cameron was not a good-looking man. He was all work, no play. I could tell he was going bald even though he tried to hide it under a hat. His wardrobe comprised plaid shirts and dark blue jeans. He was plain to the eye, not worth a second glance.

When I got out to the barn, I still had sleep in my eyes. Mr. Cameron grabbed a shovel and put it in my hand and ordered me to get to work.

The longer I was at the farm, the more chores Mr. Cameron piled on me. I didn't have the words to express how I feared the horses, so I put the shovel down on the floor and just stood there with a dumb look on my face. When Mr. Cameron saw me not working, he demanded that I get to work, or he'd send me to my room with no dinner. I thought about that for a minute and got back to work because I needed food to survive.

Before Mr. Cameron left the barn, he told me to sweep it out and brush the horses down. I was standing in the walkway when I heard one horse talking to me. I could hardly make out the words, but the horse was saying something about killing me. I got terrified and dropped what I was doing and ran out of the barn, searching for a place to hide. I found a spot under a tracker alongside the barn to sit. I swear I was there for hours, and nobody came looking for me.

I used my telepathic powers and sent Mr. Cameron a message telling him I was one of God's chosen ones and cleaning out a barn was beneath me. A message came back saying that Mr. Cameron already knew.

# FOURTEEN

# OCTOBER 1969

Finally, we were going to move out of Aunt Barb's and be on our own. My mother had a job lined up, and it meant we were going to be able to afford a three-bedroom apartment in the Etobicoke neighbourhood of Rexdale, but it was on the wrong side of the tracks, a rough area with a lot of low-income housing. Our building was colourless, fifteen floors overlooking the city of Toronto. Cockroaches roamed freely through the cracks in the walls, and a bunch of them stopped in to say hello to us, the new tenants. The stench of urine seeped out from under the carpets in the hallways and stairwells, and dust was everywhere. Yellowed wallpaper was tattooed with graffiti. Cats meowed from behind closed doors, and angry words echoed down the hallways through the wee hours of the night. Everywhere the sound of families torn apart by poverty and alcohol and drugs, while children lay awake and listening in fear.

My mother organized the furniture and stuff as soon as it arrived. There was the old dark green couch with its uncomfortable flat cushions, flatware and dishes, linens, pillows, kitchen table and chairs, TV, coffee table, beds, and all odds and ends. She was so happy about being on her own. She always saw the potential in just about anything she put her mind to. And she had an exceptional talent for making something out of nothing. A badly scratched coffee table could become transformed with the simple addition of a table runner. Cracked walls were hid behind velvet paintings of clowns and a matador. It made her feel she had done a superb job for her family. My poor mother, always struggling along with the only life she knew.

I remember I had my own bedroom, while Martha and Sarah shared a bedroom. That way Martha could better look after Sarah who was turning three in December.

On the very first night in the new apartment, my mother wanted us all to have a bath before the dead man came over for the evening. As usual, she put my two sisters and me in the tub together, and then she told us she'd be back after we finished washing up. Later she came in and made sure all the shampoo was out of our hair by giving it a squeeze to remove most of the water then handed each of us a towel and reminded us to towel dry our hair and go to our room to dry off. She would do that one at a time, and I would always be last. I would sit on the bed with bathwater still in my ears, and my hair would stick out in every direction. I would wait for her to come in and fix it for me. She brushed my hair roughly and always ended the procedure with an intentional vicious tug that hurt. When the ordeal was over, she told us to watch TV, so we ran out and all lined up on the couch.

"When a Man Loves a Woman" started playing on the radio, and my mother immediately started swaying her hips to the beat of the music. I could see her in the kitchen. The apartment was small. It was like she was in a trance, and I knew that we no longer existed to her. It was her favourite fantasy—a life without us—she a love goddess with tremendous powers of seduction. A bottle of cheap wine and two chipped glasses sat on the kitchen table. The stage set for a passionate night of passion.

Finally, the dead man was standing at the door, finely dressed in black slacks and a light beige turtleneck. In his eyes, I glimpsed something sinister. I could tell that he was just as excited as my mother about being there. He handed her a yellow flower as they flirted behind a facade of small talk. Mother was looking as sexy as she could with her seductive smile and hips thrust forward like a little tramp.

In the kitchen, she poured two glasses of the cheap wine, and they gulped it down like beer. She sat with her legs spread just wide enough to tempt the dead man's lusty appetite. She acted as though there was no one else in the apartment, just the two of them studying each other's lips. She wet her lips in anticipation.

After a while, I wandered off to bed without my mother noticing me. But the dead man had noticed, and I was all too aware of the fact. He had special radar for neglected and needy little girls. As I strolled out of the room, I sensed that he knew how he was going to get me—like he knew my weaknesses, and it made me shudder.

In the morning, my mother called for me to come to her bedroom. When I got there, I stood reluctantly by the door and noticed the outlines of their flesh through the bed sheets. There was a funny odour in the room too.

...

"Get lost."

I left.

Somehow, I found my way out of the bedroom with my mother's laughter ringing in my ears. I was just introduced to a dirty little secret, and it made me sick to my stomach. I headed directly to the bathroom, light-headed and afraid, but got to the toilet bowl in time. I tried to vomit, but only a watery fluid came out, dripping warmly from my mouth, and in my mind, I saw the drops fall and turn into the shape of cut-out paper monsters. The bathroom became alive, the walls breathed, the tiles moved, and I saw tiny demons run across the floor. I thought they were trying to trap me. Then I realized it wasn't the tiles moving. It was my fear moving around and around and around inside me. It wasn't the room becoming alive.

It was me dying.

I ran from the bathroom and hurriedly put on some clothes and dashed out of the apartment into the hallway and finally through the exit door at the end of the hall. I was going to disappear without a trace. I raced down the steps with my demons following in single file. I knew they were trying to catch me. I jumped two steps at a time and hurried outside to the back of the apartment building. The sun was waiting for me, soothing my fears, and making me feel alive. Once I was outside, I felt safe because there were people around, and my mother couldn't hurt me then and neither could the demons. I slowed down and took my time to get to the field out back, but my mood was dark, foreboding.

Then, there it was, my magnificent long green grass—such a dependable symbol of hope for me. The sun was shining and warm. I searched for a favourable spot among the long green grass and weeds and sat down. I rocked back and forth while keeping an eye out for intruders who might stumble onto my private spot. If I'd had a shovel to dig my grave, I would have buried myself right there. But I just fell asleep.

I awoke to the humming of insects. A fence caught my eye, a fence that divided our property from a low-income housing development. I could see a grey cement government building that served the needy. The development took up a sizeable amount of land. Blankets hung like curtains on dirty windows. There were no flowers, no gardens, and no evidence of natural life, just a grey and lifeless area. I knew it to be a place where lost souls roamed without direction, and it was a sad reality of life. A dog barked, and I looked and saw an animal with bones starkly visible under a scruffy layer of fur. I felt like I was on the brink of some adventure. My interest awakened to the world of poverty—a world I knew reflected my own, of who and what I was. I became frozen in time, spellbound.

I realized that my hands now had a tight grip on the fence, and I was peering into the unknown. I just had to find out what was going on in there. I just had to. I backed up from the fence, though. Somehow, I couldn't quite bring myself to climb it. I sensed that I would need to wait for a time when I was more desperate, a time when the need would more clearly present itself. I was not ready. I knew that I was seeking to find my true self, but I was not prepared to find me. I knew the time was near for my glorious adventure of self-discovery to begin. However, for now, I would have to wait, and so I withdrew.

I made my way back to my apartment building and went in the back door. My feet felt heavy because I didn't want to go home, didn't want to be near my mother. I was acknowledging my resentment toward her, and I could feel the seeds of hatred beginning to sprout inside my stomach. The hate was becoming deep and growing at an alarming rate, and I would close my eyes to the burning fact that I was growing to despise my mother with a fearless passion. I had mixed feelings, though; one minute I would feel love for her and the next minute, hate. I didn't want to feel that way because it wasn't me.

As I went to open the door to the apartment, I heard her talking. Her voice was distant, but there was that laugh, twisted, deceptive, and psychotic.

# FIFTEEN

# AUGUST 1979

In August, an unfamiliar girl came to stay at the Cameron farm. Her name was Rebecca. She was a couple of years older than me and looked like a cave woman who was living a savage life. She had stringy brown hair and brownish teeth to match. She had a huge chip on her shoulder and swore like a trucker. She was someone I felt comfortable around. When no one was looking, she'd sneak behind the barn and light up a cigarette. I liked the way she talked with a cigarette dangling from her mouth. I loved to be around her. It was always a rush. I liked the way she talked circles around me.

Once Rebecca and I got to know each other better, she confided in me that Mr. Cameron was shooting pigeons off the barn roof and feeding them to us. I didn't see any evidence of that, but I knew I was eating rabbit meat. Amber would skin a rabbit on a wood table behind the barn. She tried to teach me how to do it, but I refused to learn. Instead, I stood a few feet back and watched her pull the skin off one rabbit's legs. My stomach got sick, so I turned my head.

Rebecca asked me if I wanted to run away with her. I didn't object. I couldn't wait to get the hell out of there.

I was growing tired of being made to do things against my will. The last thing I wanted to be was a farmhand, especially when I wasn't even being paid.

And so, one morning before anyone got up, Rebecca and I stuffed a bag full of clothes and then headed out. We had to go through the forest to avoid the watchful eye of Mr. Cameron. It seemed like he was always sneaking around, checking up on everyone and seeing what they were doing.

As I ran through the forest, I tried to defend myself against the giant black horseflies and mosquitoes that were landing on me. I tried to smack them off, but as fast as I got one off, another one would land on me. I swear the horseflies were as big as snapping turtles. I imagined the flies pointing machine guns at me and trying to mow me down.

As I weaved through the forest, I had to duck under tree branches—and jump over fallen ones—while making my way to the main road. By the time I got there, I must have looked like I had a severe case of chicken pox.

To my surprise, Mr. Cameron was already waiting for us when we came out of the forest. He was leaning against his truck with a smug look on his face. He looked pleased with himself, self-assured that he had beaten us at our own game. All I could think about was that I was wasting my time sweating and panting like a dog and working for someone who wasn't paying me a dime.

Without saying a word, I walked over to his truck, got in, and waited for Rebecca to jump in beside me.

Suddenly I broke out laughing because we looked like two fools covered in big red bite marks.

The following week, however, we ran away for good. This time Mr. Cameron wasn't waiting at the roadside to take us back to the farm. Rebecca and I hitchhiked back to the city where she introduced me to a man named Rocky. At least that's what he called himself. I think he was in his early fifties, too old to be hanging out with teenagers. His eyes had a dull look to them. His hair was light brown, and it hung just below his shoulders. He was dressed in a pair of jeans and a faded T-shirt. He worked in front of the CN Tower as a horse and buggy driver for tourists. I listened to him brag about having a third-degree black belt in karate. He had a reputation of taking young girls under his wing, mostly runaways. Once I saw him kiss a fourteen-year-old girl on the lips in the back of a horse carriage. I thought it was odd that she didn't resist.

One day, Rocky got into an argument with some stranger on the street. I can't remember how the fight started, but the next thing I knew, Rocky was standing there on one leg with his arms spread wide, eager to fight. I thought the whole thing was ridiculous, especially when Rocky constantly complained about a sore back. I didn't think Rocky had the strength to fight. He was all mouth, no action.

"Aw fuck it," the other guy said. "I won't hurt an old man."

And so the fight was over before it had even begun.

Rebecca took off on me, but Rocky promised me that, when he finished his shift at work, he'd rent a room in a motel and I could stay with him. I didn't want to go with him, but I had nowhere else to go. He got a motel room close to his work. It was a rundown three-storey brick building needing a paint job. The bathroom toilet bowl had a dark circle. The room only had one bed, so I realized I had to share the bed with Rocky. The thought of that made me sweat beads. A danger signal went off inside my head once I realized what he had in store for me.

I remember Rocky's creepy hands roaming all over my body. I tried to resist him, but he told me if I didn't put out, he'd make me sleep outside, so I gave in to his demand. He climbed on top of me and pushed a few times, and then it was over. Afterward, I went to the washroom. I had blood between my legs. I wiped myself up and went back to the bed, but I didn't close my eyes.

The following morning, I went with Rocky to his job site. I watched him get up on the carriage and grab the horse's reins. Then I got up on the carriage, but he told me to get down. He told me to go hang at a park until he finished his work shift. He gave me directions to get there—it was a short distance away from the detention centre. I told him goodbye without making eye contact. I was so ashamed of myself for being tricked into sleeping with an old man.

I hung out at the park and mingled with the other homeless kids, talking about our dreams and where we were heading in life. A lot of dead-end streets, I suspected. The other kids were friendly enough, and they didn't seem bothered by sleeping outside in the park on the damp grass. I guess, as long as they were together, they felt safe in numbers.

At night, young girls prostituted themselves while their pimps lurked nearby. Some pimps were only twenty years old, yet they were out there hustling young girls to make them money. I felt sorry for the girls because they had to hand over all their money they made and then the pimp would give back thirty percent of their earnings. If the girls were lucky enough, they could get a cheap motel room for the night and a cheap meal at some sleazy diner downtown. The whole set-up reeked of bullshit to me, especially when the girls were giving themselves away to strange men. The Johns came from all walks of life. They were only looking for a little side action before they crawled back to their girlfriends and wives. Johns were having sex with homeless girls for forty bucks.

I came across two police officers working the streets and looking for runaways. They stopped me in the park and asked to see my ID. I didn't have any, but I gave them my actual name. They told me to get in the back of the police car until they ran my name through the system. Sure enough, I was in the system and listed as a runaway.

The cops brought me to the police station. I was glad, though, I couldn't bear the thought of sleeping outside and not having a warm bed to sleep in for one more night. Sleeping on park benches in the cold weather while covered with broken-down cardboard boxes was not my idea of a good time. Though I certainly couldn't have articulated it at the time, I knew I was worth more than what life was offering me.

# SIXTEEN

# NOVEMBER 1969

My mother was pregnant. She hadn't bothered tell my sisters and me, of course, but we heard her and the dead man talking about it. She was expecting in the spring, and that meant that dead man was going to be part of our lives.

When my mother let him move in, it was the worst kind of news because it changed my life—the dead man's presence threw a thick garment of blackness over everything. Even the furniture seemed to have lost its colour. I watched from a distance as he sat on the couch. He looked small and cowardly, and I got real bad vibes from him. The smirk on his face was a deliberate warning that I'd better be careful. It caused a flashback about the time when my mother touched me in the bathroom. Watching his smug assuredness somehow made me see that he had planned to worm his way into the family for reasons other than just his relationship with my mother.

He moved in with clothes in an old tattered 1940s suitcase, shaving cream, Old Spice cologne, and his toothbrush. No furniture. But then he didn't need any of his own when he was living at his mother's and now at our place. He wouldn't even have moved in at all, in fact, except that my mother finally got a job working for the Ministry of Transportation.

From the moment he moved in, he knew he was in control, and so did I. His behaviour quickly changed from surreptitious to arrogant, and I knew full well what he had on his mind. He was in a position of complete control. He could now feed my mother drugs and money to keep her distracted from his real purpose, and it worked. It was so pathetic the way she would sit on the couch in her short little skirt and giggle like a schoolgirl. She worked at pretending to be naïve, just another ploy to avoid responsibility.

When she started her government job, my mother felt she was going to be a big shot, an important member of society, and would move in all the right circles. She was excited because she felt she had finally accomplished something. I think she thought she was a better person for holding a job. It didn't impress me, though, because I knew she was only looking out for her own interests. I watched her sitting on the couch lifting each leg as she admired their smooth sexy look, much too self-absorbed for my liking. I was already wondering when the dead man would leave. I was looking forward to it.

A very feeble voice inside me said, *please go away*, but it never escaped my rubbery lips. I had noticed the dead man's ulterior motives, and I needed something safe to hang onto. I started thinking about the colour green, a tree, the grass, anything related to natural things. I could not help but wonder why my mother would like a man who resembled a dead tree. He seemed lifeless to me, a dead man, a person who made everyone feel uncomfortable without knowing why. By then, my head was already too full of terrible experiences, and I didn't need any more.

My mother couldn't see it, though—she was caught up in her little world. I wondered where she could be. However, I already knew her heart was black and so focused on her pain that she couldn't see the truth of what the dead man was. I wished I could have freed her from her make-believe world and warned her of the dangers. I would have forgiven her for everything and anything if only she hadn't let him move in. I felt sad for her because, even then, I knew she didn't know what happiness was. Life for her was just one big crisis after another, just one tremendous disappointment.

I felt compelled to get away, and so I snuck out of the apartment and slipped outside, away from my mother, away from the dead man. My hair was all matted and dirty, and my shoes had partial soles. A button was missing from my second-hand blouse, and I must have looked like a pathetic creature as I went about in the neighborhood. I collected some rocks and sticks from the parking lot and took them to the backfield, where I built a pint-sized fort that became my retreat from home, an escape from terrible memories and things to come. It was a place where I went to frequently, my way of dealing with life's problems.

Something had changed inside me. I had detached from my mother by learning not to ask questions, by staying away from her whenever I could. When she would yell at me, or worse, I would pretend it never happened and replace bad feelings with lies. I worked hard at becoming invisible but felt lost, confused, and forgotten. However, it gave me a strange tranquility that eased my mind as I learned to focus away from the present reality.

That was also when I experienced mood swings—high one moment, low the next. I had to hide my anger, suppress my emotions, and I felt more and more that I could not speak about who or what I was because my mother would come undone. It wasn't fair, but that's the way it had to be because she wouldn't come out of her make-believe world. That was the worst thing about what was going on. Nobody could make her face reality, especially me. It was her protection, her way of avoiding her painful past, the *only* way she knew how to survive. And God knows she'd rub that one in—how I had it easy compared to her childhood. She'd tell me to thank my lucky stars that I didn't grow up the way she did. I remember wishing she would not mention my stars because there was no way I was dropping them as one of my survival tools, so I automatically closed down and it seemed like I no longer could hear her.

The worst thing about being outside was that, eventually, I had to go home, and every time I did my heart raced. It always scared me to death to go home, and my mother knew it. I felt I had to always hide my genuine feelings.

Six o'clock that evening, though, my mother surprised me with a bright blue tricycle. I imagined it had a red fire engine, and I would someday be a famous racing driver like on TV. Yet, I dreaded accepting the gift because it was from her, and I knew it was just her way of absolving herself of guilt. I knew it would be wrong to take it because it would be like saying, it was okay to hurt me. Besides, I had already planned to leave my mother psychologically. I could not allow her to be part of my world any longer. The process had already begun, and there could be no turning back.

Now that the dead man was in the picture, I would never again have any connection with her again, not that there was much of a connection before. I felt terrible guilt at the thought, but I had to survive somehow. The guilt, however, pressed against my thigh like a tangible thing, alerting me to the feelings of revenge. But the price was too high. I felt very naughty with my mother looking down on me like she did because her eyes dared me not to want something for myself. I decided it was better not to show her how disappointed I was about the bike.

I took the bike for a spin just to please her and pretended to have fun until she went back into the apartment. After she left, I took the bike down the elevator to a steep hill where the cars turned in from the main road. Sitting on the bike at the top of the hill, I pushed with my left foot as though I was revving up a motor. On my way down, I purposely tipped the bike from side to side with the weight of my body. I crashed, skinning my elbow and knee. Blood trickled onto the pavement, and a tremendous hatred inside me bubbled unexpectedly to the surface, bringing with it thoughts of self-destruction which seemed to grasp me by the torso in a vice-like grip. How I hated the bike at that moment, and I fiercely hated my mother for pretending that things were all right. Thoughts of suicide clashed with visions of twisted bodies and cut-outs of private parts in explicit detail. Through the cracks in the pavement, an imaginary tree appeared and laughed at me, laughed outrageously at the sight of my blood—but then it was not a tree at all.

It was my mother's face.

A car horn sounded, startling me. I looked at the driver and let him know by my facial expression that I hated the intrusion. I yearned to be alone in my make-believe world, but big people were everywhere, always ruining everything! Resentment rising, I finally picked up my bike and dragged it to an open field and buried it under some old rubbish I found nearby. Then I pulled angrily at my green grass, a symbol of hope for me until I had enough to cover the bike completely. I wanted no part of anything connected to people, especially my family, and the bike was an annoying reminder of a family I would rather have forgotten. The only thing I needed was my mind because it was my playground, and no one could enter it unless I let him or her.

Another change was taking place, a distant voice deep inside was chattering in broken sentences and riddled in some kind of secret code. I didn't really noticed the change taking place at first because it was slow, so very slow, but I was aware something was happening. I could hear the voice, but it appeared to be way down deep at the very core of my existence, hidden under layers of suppressed emotions, negative anger, and sadness. I knew it was waiting to surface, but it needed more time, a reason to present itself and the opportunity to become real in my mind.

## SEVENTEEN

# SEPTEMBER 1979

About an hour after being brought to the police station, a social worker came and got me and drove me to a group home in Mississauga. It was called Four Maples because maple trees symbolized strength and endurance—or some damn thing like that. It was owned by two married doctors who had emigrated from Africa and were looking to give back to the community by helping troubled teens. The doctors owned it, but the government funded it.

The only time I saw the doctors was when they were dropping off groceries for us. Our diets included lots of skimpy pork chops, fatty beef roasts, and macaroni dishes. And there always seemed to be an enormous amount of sweets and day-old bread sitting on the kitchen counter. I think they had a deal with one of the local grocery stores to get their expired foods.

The government was paying for my stay, and they gave me a small clothing allowance, but I never saw one dime of it. However, there was a used-clothing closet on the top floor of the house where I could grab a few things to wear. Sometimes when I fanned through the hung clothing, I would find some decent fitting blouses and jeans. Underwear and bras were always brand new, along with soap, toothbrushes, toothpaste and deodorant. There were little perfume test bottles too, but I took none because I was allergic to perfume. I really looked forward to getting into that closet on Fridays. It became the highlight of my week.

The group home had three floors. The top floor had a bathroom and three bedrooms. I had to share a room with a black girl named Aliyah. She had the tiniest waist I had ever seen. She was so cute with her nappy black hair and big brown eyes. I liked the way she folded her clothes into neat little piles before putting them into her dresser drawer. She watched her clothes like a hawk, as if her jeans were the last pair she would ever get. She had a raspy voice and spoke well, unlike me who was always stumbling over my words or talking in broken sentences.

I could be midway in a sentence and then forget what I was saying because I got stuck on some word that I couldn't form in my mouth. It didn't matter how much I tried, I could never get my words out right. Most times, I'd just say something that wasn't even relevant to the conversation. I did most of the talking while she just stood there waiting for me to go away. Then I'd get anxious and lose track of time. By the time I snapped back into the present, Aliyah would be gone. I'd just stand there like a dummy trying to remember if I had even been talking to her in the first place or whether what just happened was real. But Aliyah was real, for I'd see her at the dinner table playing with her food with a fork.

On the main floor there were two long couches in faded plaid with flat cushions and a large ottoman and a metal stand with a TV sitting on it. Even though the house was built in the fifties, it was in excellent condition and had a well-kept lawn. Some landscaping guy would come by every so often and cut the grass and trim the shrubs. I guess the inside of the house was okay. Even though it didn't have the best of things, every inch of the house was in order, right down to the fiction books on shelves. They kept them neatly in alphabetical order.

There was one other girl staying at the group home. Casey had her own room, even though there were two beds in it. I was envious of her because she didn't have to share with anyone. Casey was an odd-looking girl. She reminded me of an ostrich. Her neck was extra-long, she had no chin, and her nose was pointy and too big for her face. She had short blonde fly-away hair, which was super thin like baby bird feathers. She even walked funny, as if she weren't comfortable in her own skin. She acted like she had recently gotten a new body and was trying to adjust to it. Her head was too big for her body. Oh God, I couldn't stand her, but I didn't know why. Imagine Beetlejuice, the devious poltergeist played by Michael Keaton, and you'll have good sense for her. The one thing that stands out most in my mind about her was she had terrible body odour. Every room she went into, she'd leave behind a cloud of stink that caused my stomach to get sick. The odour was so powerful that it lingered for hours behind her. For that reason alone, I stayed clear of her because I had an overactive nervous system which goes awry at the slightest foul smells and potent scents made my throat close up.

I was at Four Maples for about a year, and so I really got a chance to know the people who worked there, which was nice because there was a sense of stability. I think that alone was probably good for me.

There was a staff of five, including the director, a guy by the name of Fred. Fred was in his early forties and handsome. He had short black hair and combed his bangs to one side to hide his one eye. His eyes were dark blue, and he sported a speckled grey and black beard. He told me he was a martial arts expert, but he didn't appear to be a tough guy. He walked calmly, never hurried, and his voice was soft when he spoke. He was a man of few words, but when he spoke it was for a good reason. He never babbled on like most of the staff. He had an air about him that demanded respect. He seemed so well put together that I wondered if he had any flaws.

I'm sure he did. I bet he had secrets just like everyone else.

One time, when I was in the basement rummaging through boxes, I found some naughty magazines. I sat there and eagerly turned the pages until I came across a woman in her early twenties sprawled out on a bed. The centrefold. Page after page, there were brief stories here and there. But mostly nude girls filled the pages. It was the first time I had ever seen such magazines, and I was curious. I flipped through the pages, admiring the beautiful women. Their bodies were perfect, and their makeup seemed too perfect. I couldn't see one blemish on their faces or any marks on their skin.

When I went back upstairs, I told Fred that there were boxes of nudie magazines downstairs, and he told me to show him where they were. He followed me down the stairs and I pointed out the boxes. He picked out a few of the magazines and scanned through them before saying he would get rid of them. Then he took the boxes and loaded them into his station wagon—never to be seen again. I wondered about those magazines a few times. I wondered if he had kept them for himself or tossed them in a dumpster.

In the spring of 1980, another girl came to stay at the group home. She looked just like one of those women in the magazines. She reminded me of a famous pinup girl from way back in the fifties when life was simpler. I called her little Marilyn Monroe, but her actual name was Stephanie. She had beautiful long blonde hair done up in a bob. Her waist was tiny, and her big sparkling blue eyes shone. I swear I saw a twinkle in her eye every time she looked at me. She had the whitest skin I had ever seen in my life, and a beauty mark on her cheek. When she talked, her voice was so quiet.

Stephanie oozed sex appeal, and it flowed right down to her perfect little toes. She curves in all the right places too. It seemed like everything she did was magical, even if she was just pushing her hair off her face, she looked like a movie star to me. I think she knew how beautiful she was because she always seemed to flaunt it. When I stood beside her, I felt like an ugly duckling, awkward, lost for words, not worth a second glance. I used to go in the washroom with her while she put on her makeup. After, she put some on me. I even took her eyeliner and dabbed a mark above my lips. Now I had a beauty mark just like her.

By the time Stephanie arrived, I had gotten used to everyone and was feeling comfortable in my surroundings. The two full-time staff members were Robin, Donna, and there were two part-time workers, named Michelle and Allison, but they only came in when someone called in sick, and that wasn't often. And there was also a professional cleaner named Mike who came in once a month to do the heavy cleaning.

Robin was a free spirit with a drinking problem. She always seemed to be on the go. She drove a white Volkswagen, and I always knew when she arrived for work because I could hear the car's muffled cough as she drove up the driveway. She had tight curly hair and usually wore a faded T-shirt, blue jeans, and a brown belt to match her brown leather ankle boots.

One time, in June of 1980, she took us girls up north to her parents' cottage about an hour out of Mississauga. On our way there, Robin stopped in at the liquor store and bought an enormous bottle of whiskey, and then she got food from the grocery store.

The cottage was white with brown trim and a tad bit rundown. To get there, we had to drive down a long dirt road. Once we got settled in, Robin cracked open the whiskey and poured us all a drink. I didn't like booze, but to fit in I guzzled my drink down. Then another. Before I knew it, I was out back in the open field where the trains come through. I wore rubber boots and was staggering around. My head was spinning, and I felt like vomiting.

Robin came up with a brilliant idea. She told us to strip down to nothing and wait for the train to come by so we could wave at the passengers in the nude. I didn't fight her on it because I was too drunk to resist. As soon as I heard the train coming, I ran down to the fence and started jumping up and down, waving frantically at the people in the train. After that, I blacked out. I just remember waking up in my clothes with a booming headache.

Later, Casey snitched on Robin. She told Fred what had happened at the cottage, and shortly before I left, Robin got fired.

My favourite staff member was Donna, a tall thin woman, who was working at the group home until she got her master's in social work. She dyed her hair a dark purple and wore high-waist corduroy pants with a belt. Her nails were long and painted to match her hair. On the weekend, we'd play records together. While she sat on the couch with one leg folded over, she watched me dance up a storm on the living room floor. I'd lip-sync to the *Rocky Horror Picture Show* album. When I thrust my hips in and out, Donna would giggle and blush. For my finishing act, I'd throw in a bum shake. Afterward I'd fall on the couch, exhausted and laughing my head off. Music was the one thing that gave me peace.

Donna was a shining light in my dark world, except for the time when she came bulldozing into my bedroom. I was sitting on my bed with my back against the wall when she came right in without an invitation. The next thing I knew she was sitting on the bed beside me, too close for my comfort, especially when I didn't want her there. My stomach even got sick from her intruding on my personal space. Quickly my mind filled up with snapshots of bare legs, a dozen slippery tongues and a hatchet.

Donna was talking, but I couldn't make out her words, everything was going in slow motion. As soon as I realized she was trying to pry into my dark world with her shiny smile, I lost it. As I raised my fists at her, Donna covered her head with her hands to protect herself from me. It felt like time had stood still, but instead of bashing her skull in, I hugged her. Both of us just sat there crying. It was my entire fault. The one social worker who liked me, I had hurt, and I could never take it back ever. The only thing I could do was mumble I am sorry.

The following week, Donna didn't come into work. Fred told me she was sick and wouldn't be in for a while. Of course, I didn't believe him. I knew Donna wasn't there because of me. While I waited for her to come back, I busied myself doing household chores. I swept the floors spotless and cleaned all the appliances. After I was done, I checked off my tasks on the bulletin board in the kitchen.

A couple weeks later, Donna dropped in to say goodbye to me. She was leaving to go to another job. She said it had nothing to do with me, but I knew she was lying. I didn't care either way, really. As I watched her car pull out of the driveway, I felt nothing. At least that's what I told myself.

# EIGHTEEN

# JANUARY 1970

After a few months of the dead man living with us, things were really becoming confusing for me—the silent voice in my head, the dead man, my mother's denial of what kind of person he was, and the make-believe world I was taking refuge in. I'd just turned six, and yet I felt tired, like a hundred-year-old woman too stubborn to let go of life because she still had unfinished business. The loneliness of it all was forcing my conscious mind to seek a place of safety. I realized a marvelous sense of curiosity and focused on nature—on the beauty of the trees, on flowers, on the brilliance of the sky. Thousands of questions came to the surface, even questions little girls shouldn't ask. My mother demanded silence, and that silence killed something inside me. It was so hard to be silent when there was so much to learn and so much to know. My need to explore my environment pressed hard against my lips, trying desperately to get out, but with nowhere to go, with no answers, with no one to ask the questions of, the loneliness just grew and grew and grew.

I wished desperately to escape from reality permanently. My body had a tingling feeling all the time, and I was already beginning to feel a detachment in my limbs as though I was slowly disappearing. This was good. I wanted to disappear. Nobody seemed to know I was there anyway, so I might just as well have been dead. Perhaps it was terrible to wish I could disappear, but it served its purpose. There was no sense trying to persuade my mother I was there because she was always saying, *I wish you were dead.* There it goes again, always back to my mother—life revolved around her.

Momma this! Momma that! Oh God, why couldn't *she* be the one who disappeared?

When it came to her pregnancy, she appeared to be happy, but she would still complain about her growing waistline, nausea, and headaches. She looked scared to death of having another baby. I always thought she didn't like children, so it came as a surprise to me she was even having another one. Early on, morning sickness had been a regular thing, and she responded by becoming more aggressive, more agitated, and her moods swung totally out of control, although it wasn't exactly a surprise to watch her switch from happy to angry in a flash.

Personally, the whole thing scared me because it was the dead man's baby. That meant he would not be going away soon. And I felt sad for the new baby in my mother's belly because I knew it was going to suffer the same fate as me. I thought her to be a selfish woman for bringing another child into the world when it was so obvious that she wasn't caring properly for the ones she already had. And I'd always hoped, way down deep inside me, that she someday, somehow, would show that she loved me. But now that another baby was coming, the chance of that ever happening had become even more remote. The pregnancy had destroyed the one and only chance I had of ever being loved because my mother would have to focus her attention on the needs of a newborn baby.

The feeling of exhaustion was overwhelming, so I imagined laying right down there in the field and looking up at the sky. It was peaceful lying there. It was peaceful inside too. Nothing happening in there, just emptiness—but it was a *good* emptiness that made me feel fulfilled. I felt connected to the universe. It was so much bigger than me, larger than life. Some people call it religion, others call it getting in touch with our spirituality, but all I knew back then was that it seemed to fill me up and take away some of the loneliness. I called it my secret garden where I could be perfect, whole, and complete. When I was there, my body didn't tingle, my mind was clear, and life was worth living even if just for those few precious moments in my secret garden. Even my untied laces, my messy hair, my lopsided smile, and my crooked teeth didn't matter to me then because I was free and alive. At that moment, I was special. Life had meaning, and the best thing about it was that it was mine, all of mine. My mother could take none of it away from me! She didn't have the power.

I had decided I didn't want to acknowledge my body anymore because my body belonged to her and was hers to do with as she pleased. She just didn't seem to get it, that what she was doing to me was so terrible I couldn't even confront it. As I lay there on the grass in my mind, I wished I could find someone to talk to about what was going on behind closed doors, or at least for someone to remove me from the situation. I wished someone would come along and see that I was waiting for something good to happen. It just seemed so unfair that I had so much to tell, so much to say, but my voice was being squashed like a bug on a wall. I felt sad for my loss, sad for my frustrating journey through life, and sad that my voice was disappearing into thin air.

I went to my secret garden as much as I could so she couldn't find me. I could play her like a fiddle and take part in her little head games. I was going to win because she could not destroy my secret garden. That was the one thing I knew about my relationship with her, and I believe she knew it too. It was the game that prevented her from ever acknowledging her own pain, and she did everything possible to make me lose. I figured out the rules of the game and that, in order for my mother to win, she would have to destroy me. I was a mere reflection of her—that's all it was.

She felt she had to destroy me to deny her own past. I had the secret weapon, the truth, and that was something she couldn't face. When I got to thinking that way about her, it made me feel stronger, and it strengthened my resolve. I wanted to win, and when I felt lost, I would return to my secret garden. Through all the pain, confusion, and suffering, I was carving out my path in life. I just needed to remember never to lose sight of my secret garden, the one place where I could really be free to be me. I felt good about that because I was only six years old, and I was gaining experience in dealing with my mother, an experience that, someday, maybe, would help us both. But now the dead man was there, and he was a problem: a problem that might not get fixed.

The dead man was very pleased with his position of control. I was watching him eyeball me one day when he got up, strode across the living room, and sat down where I was sitting on the floor near the television set. He was much too close for comfort, and I felt like he was trying to weasel into my world. I wasn't that dumb. I wasn't that detached from reality to not notice him trying to get in. Then he touched my hair with his bony fingers and tried to run his fingers through it. He caught a snag! Served him right.

He stood then and disappeared for a minute and returned with a brush. I sensed he was angry about something, probably the mess of my hair. What a jerk! My body went stiff, my head felt light, and I could feel butterflies in my stomach. But I had two conflicts going on in me, the need for him to go away and the *desperate* need for affection—it had been so long since I had felt much of anything. My mother wasn't one for hugging or any other expression of kindness, so I felt a desperate longing inside of me that slowly surfaced as he brushed my hair. I looked up at my mother, but she didn't seem to notice what was going on. Her eyes were glazed over as usual as if she saw nothing. Then she didn't have to do anything about it.

I felt strangely alive.

I didn't notice it at first—the dead man placing his hand on my back, just below my neck. When I realized it, I wanted to scream, to push his hand away, but I couldn't speak or move. My mother didn't seem to care if her boyfriend was touching me, and it made me feel sad.

I think the day when he came to live with us was the saddest day of my life. I remember feeling a significant loss, as though I had the weight of the world on my shoulders, and I responded by sinking into depression. I wasn't angry. I just felt so powerless, and there was this emptiness in the pit of my stomach. The touch of the dead man's hand on me seemed to take something away. I cried inside that day. I became a wilted flower with no hope of ever becoming something beautiful.

From that very first day, the dead man had wormed his way into my world and brought with him ghosts of everything that's black. I tried to squirm out of his reach without making a scene. I needed my mother to take control, to make the dead man go away or, at least, to stop touching me, but she couldn't and that was so hard for me to see. I felt sorry for her, for her pain, her life, her empty existence, but most of all—even though I was still so very young—I felt sorry for her inability to experience joy.

I kept a close eye on the dead man and listened to him carefully and learned that his mind was quick. It was cunning, sharp like a knife, dangerous and unbelievably controlled. I was his target, his victim, and his prey. From a distance I studied him, watched his every move, the way he talked circles around my mother, convincing her he loved her. I knew he had no genuine feelings for her, and I also knew she was no match for him. The balance of power rested on his side. My mother simply proved too easy to manipulate, to mould, and to shape into a perfect little puppet. I think I might have loved her back then, certainly the need to protect her was there. I still felt the need to shelter her from the truth about the man she had so recklessly picked as her companion. I really didn't think about how it was affecting me because I belonged to my mother and her sickness, so I was thinking about her. Nobody told me I had rights. Nobody told me I could say, no.

The dead man soon began bringing pets to our home: rabbits, gerbils, mice, and two Siamese cats named Jasmine and Topaz who scratched the shit out of me. It was his way of pretending to be kind, a deception that was very persuasive in making everyone around him believe he was so wonderful. But I knew the true motive behind all those cute bundles of fur. And I still find it hard to believe that my mother never knew how bad he was or suspected his ulterior motives. Ill intentions. She must have sensed his attention drift toward her little girls. She could hardly have missed it. Yes, she *must* have known because eventually she began reacting to him with anger. She attacked him verbally with insults. The novelty of her new relationship quickly wore off, and it even showed in her smeared makeup—I suspect from bouts of tears. Her eyes lost their sparkle because her hopes of a good life and a stable relationship were disappearing. Her perfect little world was coming undone, and her psychotic outbursts became a routine.

In these outbursts, she would even attack the pets.

One day, she had placed the rabbit in his cage on the balcony and when she raged in a violent outburst of anger, he was her first target. She kicked the cage so violently that it must have caused the rabbit to have a heart attack or something because it just lay there motionless inside the cage. She just turned and stomped off into her bedroom. As soon as I heard the door close behind her, I went to the cage. The rabbit looked dead to me, and as I looked at it, I wondered what it would feel like to die and how my mother felt about it now. I opened the cage, reached in, and touched the dead rabbit. Then I ran my fingers over its lifeless fur. I felt powerless to help him. I couldn't bring him back to life. I wanted to cry, but my mother might have heard me and turned her anger toward me, so I just swallowed my hurt in a big lump and backed away from the cage. I didn't know how to behave about such things, so I just went and sat on the couch and tried to pretend it hadn't happened, but it was all too real, too disturbing.

After what seemed like an eternity she came out of her bedroom. She appeared very calm as she stared blankly ahead.

Eventually I spoke up. "Something's wrong with the rabbit."

"It's dead," she said.

Then she mechanically removed the rabbit from the cage, wrapped it in newspaper, and dropped it down the garbage chute down at the end of the hallway. She felt no need to discuss it, or to apologize, or to explain. She just carried on as though it was an everyday occurrence. I should have been used to her rages, but my mind just couldn't seem to wrap around the concept that she was nuts. I didn't want to believe it, couldn't believe that she would always be that way, and so I pretended—like she did—that it never happened. To do that, though, I had to suppress the memory and my feelings about the entire incident. I had to pretend it was just another change to make in the life of a child.

From then on, I kept a keen eye on the pets. The dead man bought me two gerbils with all the accessories to keep them alive and healthy, even happy. But to me, it just meant two more creatures at risk, so one night, when I was sure everyone was asleep, I got up out of bed and opened the gerbils' cage. I picked them both up and placed them gently on the floor so they could escape from harm's way. I couldn't bear the thought of my mother being able to kill them in her next psychotic rage. Somehow, I felt responsible for their safety and, therefore, had to do everything in my power to protect them. But my mind was a child's mind, and I hadn't realized I was putting them in mortal danger by letting them run around the apartment. It wasn't long before Topaz and Jasmine caught the gerbils and they ended up dead, anyway. I tried to make light of the situation, but it plagued me with guilt and the constant reminder that I was responsible for the deaths of the gerbils.

One day I found a gerbil's tail underneath the living room radiator. The guilt came flooding back. I feared that I was a killer, that I was responsible. Somebody had to take responsibility, and I knew it would not be my mother because she'd never taken responsibility for anything in her life. Even if I'd had the nerve to question her behaviour, she would have just played dumb like she knew nothing. She had a great knack for turning an accusation aside and placing the blame at someone else's feet. It was a head game she played frequently, but if it didn't work—and sometimes it didn't—she would just break down in tears like a blubbering baby and become the poor victim.

My mother was in her third trimester by now and showing regardless of how she dressed. Her inability to look anything but pregnant disturbed her, and she was even more irritable and prone to fits of anger than usual.

One night the dead man came into my room as I was trying to go to sleep. He didn't turn on a light but sat on the side of the bed.

"Your momma's a cold fish, Tracey. Do you know she kicked me out of our bed? She won't sleep with me."

Maybe he was trying to make me feel sorry for him, but I was six and scared when I was alone with him like that. I didn't trust him. Or maybe he was trying to convince himself of something.

I remember him talking and talking but being unable to follow what he was saying.

. . .

The following morning, he called me into their bedroom when my mother wasn't there. He slapped his hand on the bed and told me to get up. I got up on the bed and his hands reached out and pulled me in closer. Suddenly he started tickling me as though we were playmates. His fingers dug under my armpits, trying to make me laugh. I didn't want to laugh. I didn't even want to be in the same room with him. While he was tickling me I thought he was trying to pretend it was something else, something like affection. But he wasn't fooling me. He was a fraud.

I held on tight, trying not to laugh, but I laughed anyway. Of course, laughter isn't always joy—sometimes it's anxiety, but I didn't know that. I felt so ashamed when I finally laughed because I thought he would think I was consenting, warming up to him. I just wanted to run from the room. Suddenly he stopped tickling me. I guess it had served his purpose. Now he could tell himself we had a different relationship than we did. Me and the dead man.

Suddenly my mother was standing in the doorway, arms crossed over her chest. The look on her face was angry and venomous.

I jumped quickly down off the bed and stopped breathing as I passed by her, fearful she would hit me with her hand or utter some degrading remark, but she said nothing.

Once I got past her, I took a deep breath and ran.

The door to the room slammed, and a big fight broke out between them. My mother's voice shrill and full of pain. The dead man's voice low and indistinct. I thought maybe they were arguing about me—and perhaps they were at first, but I couldn't make it out. Then it grew louder.

"I want a ring!" she yelled.

She was sick and tired of running around pregnant and unmarried. She was very concerned about what her co-workers, her mother, and her friends would think of her.

If they'd only knew the half of it.

# NINETEEN

# AUGUST **1980**

Shortly after Donna left, I was transferred to another Four Maples group home, this one very close to Port Credit and within walking distance of Mrs. Johnson's. The moving around was getting to me. It brought about a sadness in me that didn't seem to want to let me go.

When I got to the new group home, I introduced myself to everyone. There were three girls and five staff. The girls came in different shapes and sizes. I didn't really get a look at them at first because my anxiety was through the roof. The director, Athena, was a heavy-set woman with streaks of grey running through her long brown hair, and once I met everyone, she ushered me towards her office for a brief chat. I didn't want to go with her, but she insisted.

When we sat down, she told me I was going to have to attend a nearby school—this might have been part of the reason for my transfer. First they had to check my school record and have the school determine what grade I was going to be placed in. I'm not sure what my record could possibly have told them, but I was placed in Grade 10. I thought that was odd considering I was incapable of learning a damned thing. The only thing I really knew how to do was chores and more chores.

The first day of school, the teacher made a fool out of me by making me stand in front of class to say my name. I could barely get my name out, but I got through it. Afterward, I grabbed a chair in the back of the class so I could keep my eye on everyone—and so I could prevent a sneak attack on me. I tried to focus on what the teacher was saying, but her face kept changing into a wolf. I kept having thoughts of dying. I was thinking about how I would do it. I thought about jumping in front of a car and imagined myself sprawled out on a driveway with one leg bent back with a police chalk line around me. When I got bored with that, I turned my attention to doodling on a piece of paper. At first, I started with smiley faces and then things turned dark and I drew pictures of the devil's face. I thought it was a waste of time for me to go to school. I didn't know what was wrong with my brain, but it had a glitch. The writing on the blackboard looked liked scribbles. Numbers became sharp-edged sticks, making no sense to me.

I found out I was in a school for kids with learning disabilities. The only thing good about it was that the teachers had low expectations of me; in fact they expected nothing from me whatsoever. I could fail every class, and it made no difference to anyone including myself. It was just one big babysitting facility where they put kids with no future. Besides, I was a failure, so nothing was going to change.

I had to go to a life skills program with the other kids, the ones who had problems socializing. It was okay at the beginning, but then one of the girls' boyfriend started talking to me, and I guess the girl felt threatened, so she began hurling rude comments my way. I thought she was an idiot—I had no interest in having a relationship with anyone. I tried not to look at her boyfriend, but I could still feel his fiery gaze on me. At one point, the girl even told her boyfriend to stop looking at me. I didn't really know why the boy would look at me, anyway. He must have liked ugly girls.

I had to go on a school bus to go to an excursion out in nowhere land. I can't remember where we went, but that girl in the life skills program was making fun of me on the bus. She was accusing me of hitting on her boyfriend and trying to steal him, but it was the other way around, he was hitting on me. She began throwing rolled up pieces of paper at me. I tried to ignore her, but then she got two of her friends to join in. The next thing I knew, she had me by the hair and was dragging me down to the floor.

I didn't react.

I just got back up and sat in my seat. But after that, I started obsessing about how I would get her back. In imagined her sprawled out on the ground with two stakes stuck in her eyes. I had bludgeoned her to death.

Then I started pretending I could implant thoughts into the other kids' heads. I sent them a message: *I am the chosen one*. I imagined a bright light encircling me. It seemed to suppress my fear of being in open spaces. I was so fearful that the other kids would sneak up on me that I'd hide in the stall in the girls' washroom every chance I got. When the school bell rang, I knew it was my cue to go to my next class. But it was hard for me to be in a crowd. I didn't like anyone looking at me. So I watched them talk amongst each other in the hallways. It seemed like everyone was having fun except me. When I thought they were busy, I slipped past them and quickened my step to get to class on time.

I hated school. I found it too hard to concentrate on anything, but I had to go. To pass time, I pretended to implant messages in the other kids' heads. I'd zap them with secret information that I only knew. Things like I was the chosen one, sent down from heaven to do some good in the world. Before long, I didn't see them anymore—their faces were just a blur, a mere nuisance in my world. I couldn't wait to get out of there and back to the group home.

When I got back home and ran up to the porch to open the door, I watched my hand float in the air. My hands were so tiny. I got inside and put my shoes neatly in the closet and then headed straight to my bedroom without saying a word.

Athena started working with me and taught me sophisticated words like *couth* and *gallantry*. When her boss came around, she'd get me to say them out loud. I was so embarrassed. Athena would look on proudly, as if she had taught me something important. Her boss would just give a slight smile and move about his business. I think he was one of the head honchos down at the Children Aid Society in charge of overseeing all the group homes to ensure they were running right. I knew they *weren't* being run right. The facility was only geared to getting chores done and going to school, and that's all.

While I was sitting on the couch one day, one of the staff named Meredith kept trying to get me to talk. She was tall with long curly blonde hair and was going on about how she made brownies laced with marijuana and how her mother came over and ate one by mistake and got stoned out of her head. I don't know why she was telling me that—it crossed my mind that she was asking if I smoked weed in a roundabout way. I didn't.

Another staff by the name of Ellen kept telling me there were ghosts in the house who told her how, years ago, boys got beaten to death in the basement. Eventually she got fired for making stuff up. The people who were trying to help me were just as crazy as me. The only one who had some common sense was Athena. I liked the way she walked around with her nose stuck in the air—so *couth*—like she was someone of great importance. She always seemed to be in a cheerful mood and in charge of her emotions, unlike me, a bundle of nerves.

One time she called me in the office just to chat about nothing, really. Then she started going over my family history. Apparently, she had a file on me that dated back to the time when I was in the orphanage. I asked her if I could read it. She told me she wasn't supposed to show it to me, but she would make an allowance for me. As I read through it, the words, *paranoid schizophrenia* jumped out at me. Even though I didn't know what it meant, I was curious. I didn't ask Athena questions, however; I just handed it back to her and ended the chat by leaving the room. Later, I started thinking about how Athena knew everything about me. I wondered if they had been watching me all along and knew my deepest and darkest secrets.

# TWENTY

# APRIL 1970

My brother Billy was born in April. Deep down, I still longed for my mother to wake up and acknowledge me, to recognize that I was there wanting love and waiting with open arms for a chance of getting a hug. I clung to that thought desperately because I didn't want to believe that I was an unwanted child. It would have broken my spirit permanently. Sometimes I imagined I had a magical rope and that, if I could throw it high enough and get it around her neck, I could climb up it to get inside her heart. That is where I wanted so badly to be and, if that didn't work, maybe I could just put it around her neck and choke her to death.

Most of the time, though, I believed it was my fault she couldn't love me, that maybe I was unlovable, mentally crippled, an unworthy human being, damaged goods, deserving abandonment. It just seemed natural to blame myself for being an unworthy person. I hung in there, though, out of sight, staying away from her as much as possible but waiting patiently for her to see me.

There were so many times when it was quiet in the apartment, times my mother was alone in her bedroom, that I wanted to go to her and tell her I needed a hug or a kiss, anything to connect to another human being. I knew it would never be her coming to me. If a change was going to take place it would have to be me going to her, but I was only six years old, and my mother had forgotten to show me how to love, so I did not have the courage to make the first move. I was afraid I would never experience the love between a mother and a daughter that should have been. I don't think she knew how to love, to share, to bond, or show any kind of affection at all, at least not toward me. That was the sad truth about both my mother and me—we were both mentally impaired by her past, and while I didn't understand it in so many words back then, I recognized it all the same. She just never had the proper tools to be a mother or to raise a healthy, happy child.

Spring turned to summer, and it seemed like every time I felt somewhat relaxed, almost normal, reflecting on my own needs, my mother would come down on me like a ton of bricks. One time she flew out of her bedroom in a tremendous rage, and I did not understand why she was so upset. I wondered if it was the quietness, but there was no time to think. No time to run and hide. She came towards me at full speed and slapped me across the top of my head. Then she kicked me in the stomach and punched me until I had to put my hands over my head to protect myself. Then she had both hands around my neck and started choking me.

I could see the rage in her eyes, all the bad things I could imagine—fire, blackness, the dead man's mouth, my mother's hands, evil. I hyperventilated. My chest was tight, and my lungs were bursting. A funny sound came out of my mouth, not a scream, just a deep gasping sound. Quickly she put her hand over my mouth and pushed on it so hard that my mouth bled. She was making sure no sound could escape and alert someone to what she was doing. She had me pinned down with one leg weighing heavily on my chest. She looked directly into my eyes, seeing my fear, seeing my pain, knowing she had hurt me.

Then, suddenly, I was free. When she felt I had calmed down enough and the funny noise from my mouth would not give her away, she just got up and walked away. All I could do was to lie there on the floor like a broken doll. I escaped into my imaginary world, placing the incident up on an imaginary shelf inside my brain where it would be safe. My mind seemed filled with children's building blocks. Eventually, over time, those blocks would fall, then crack, and break into pieces, one by one.

Then I imagined a door slamming shut to keep her from entering my world. No more tears, no more feelings, and no more truth. I didn't need her anymore because what she was doing to me caused me to slip into a clay model of a child. I pronounced myself dead to her. I then heard laughter.

My laughter.

Laughter would be my way to escape. I would laugh at everything—pain, people, smiley faces, evil, the world. For now, my mother could try to destroy me, for she had me. I was hers to keep, her victim. But I had put on a dangerous mask of denial to handle the lies, the terrors, and the haunting memories. She was always closing the curtains back and forth, back and forth. But this time, I was going to close the curtains on my world, for good.

I just lay there, in the middle of the floor, for the longest time, listening for her footsteps coming back into the room. I guess she had gone to her bedroom or something because the entire house seemed lifeless and void of activity.

Where was the dead man? Out, I suppose. What about my baby brother? In my mother's room perhaps. My sisters... I really don't know—so many of my memories from back then in that apartment have me locked in a kind of emotional solitary confinement.

My head felt dizzy from shuffling all those imaginary boxes around in my brain, piling them up high inside my head. Every bad experience I could remember, I compartmentalized in my brain, putting each into a separate box and placing them all neatly on an imaginary shelf. This latest incident was a big one, and so I needed a big box with lots of room on the shelf to store it. I had to move some little boxes around so I could get it up there, out of the way. Once everything was neatly in its place, I could forget about it, so I finally got up and went to look out the balcony door. I stood there admiring the sunshine, the blue sky, the white clouds, and the treetops. I so loved the outdoors. It was my sanctuary. I stood there wishing I could fly like a bird—if I could have, I'd have been long gone. I would have flown away leaving just one feather at my mother's door, a reminder of the child who got away.

Suddenly, she was there and still enraged and screamed at me to get out of the apartment. I stood frozen to the spot, at first unable to move, and staring at her burning gaze. I searched frantically with my brain for a proper way to respond. Finally, I mechanically went and got my shoes, put them on, and walked out the door, down the stairwell, out to the front of the building, into the fresh air, and out of my mother's reach.

I wandered around the building until I got to where I thought my mother's balcony door would be. Every once in a while, I looked up towards the third floor where we lived just in case she might peer down seeing if I was close by. I sat down in a large patch of grass, shifting my position every so often to appear as though I was doing something interesting. People were coming in and out of the front door. Cars were driving up and dropping passengers off. I didn't want to appear lost, so I pretended to be looking for dandelions and four-leaf clovers, *anything* to pass the time while my mother stewed upstairs in the apartment. I thought it was so stupid that she threw me out of the apartment when she was obviously the crazy one, making stuff up in her head. I wanted to kick her in the stomach. My anger increased as I sat there, and in my mind, I imagined horrible things—my mother's death, punching, kicking, and even scratching my own eyeballs out so I couldn't see her anymore.

Hours later, I heard her calling me from the balcony. She wanted me to come back upstairs. But I was still angry, so I pretended not to hear her. She could holler until she turned blue in the face for all I cared. I imagined her with a blue face, rubbery lips, no eyes, bald, miniature, and then I imagined her being like a balloon and I popped her. Then she was just a small piece of rubber lying on the ground and I could walk all over her. But I knew something about her—she wouldn't show her anger when she was in public. She had a different mask for the public; it was pretty, nice, friendly, funny, charming, easy-going, giving. Well, she could hide behind her pretty mask with them, but she wasn't fooling me. Because I knew that underneath that beautiful little mask, there was a devil in disguise.

It got dark, and so I finally decided I'd better go back up. The dark stimulated my imagination, and I started thinking of sickos lying in wait for a nice little girl to eat. Yet, I was afraid to go back into the apartment too. There was no safe place for me—I had to go back. As soon as I got back into the apartment, my mother just laughed at my stubbornness as if nothing else had happened. I forgot about everything. It was just another chaotic day living with my mother.

Whenever there were big chaotic blow-ups, I would use the opportunity to get out of there. I remember one day when Billy was still a baby—neither my mother nor the dead man were getting any sleep—there was a big fight about something, and I snuck out of the apartment and walked down the hall. I could still hear the yelling, but I didn't care because I knew they were both crazy. I opened the back door of the building and discovered it was raining hard, so I pulled my sweater up over my head and did the two-step across the water puddles like I was Gene Kelly singing and dancing in the rain. I didn't care who saw me acting nuts because I was expressing my true self.

I was me—as free as I could be.

As soon as I got to my field out back, I took my shoes and socks off, rolled up my pant legs and started dancing in the rain. I raised my arms up, looked up toward the sky, and let the rain bounce off my nose, my mouth, and my chin. What a great feeling! The rain was coming down, and tears poured out of my eyes and slid down my face, mixing with the rain. This was my connection to the world, nature, and innocence. I wanted to live in that moment forever. I opened my mouth and allowed the rain to enter it, catching the drops on my tongue. It cleansed me, my body, my mind, and my spirit.

Then I sat down on the ground where the grass was high enough that no one could see me. I was grateful that no one ever bothered to cut the grass there because it allowed me my personal space where I could play and detach from the real world. It was great there, not like the real world with its conflict and poverty. At that moment, in that place, I found out where hope lived. It lived inside my soul. It was a place where my mother didn't live, where the dead man didn't live. It was just me against the world, alone to find the love within my heart. The best place of all is in the human heart where anything is possible. I loved myself that day in the rain. I loved my being, my feet, my hands, and I loved that lopsided grin on my face. To others, I would have resembled a statue, emotionless, hard, and heavy of heart, but when no one was around, I removed my mask, came alive, and danced in sync with life, tapping my feet on the ground in time with a song written just for me.

Other times, however, I would leave our apartment and walk up and down the hallways aimlessly, pretending to be searching for someone. Back and forth, I went from one floor to the next, listening closely at some doors. Sometimes I heard conversations and sometimes a cat meowing. It took away the loneliness I felt inside. Sometimes I walked to the top of the landing on the fiftieth floor and sat quietly for hours on the cold cement because I needed to be alone while my mind raced wildly with disturbing thoughts of death. I knew the boxes and compartments in my mind were sealed tight, but it was as though things were moving around, shifting, trying to tell me something. I did not want to focus on what was going on inside my mind, but it was getting very difficult to distract myself from it. I felt detached from both the past and the present. I even came to enjoy the loneliness of the stairwell. Yet, somehow, I felt powerful. It gave me freedom. I felt a spiritual oneness with myself.

Detachment had become a simple thing, and I was spending so much time outside that the other children who lived in the building started asking me to play with them. They wanted me to play hide and seek, spin the bottle, and doctor. In the building's parking garage, the kids would take the grocery carts left behind and use them as make-out points.

I started copying them, and before I knew it, I started kissing up a storm with a boy I didn't even know as we both sat crammed inside a cart. I didn't like it. It was awful and gross, but I was so lonely for human contact that I settled for any kind that came along. I often wondered where their parents were. We hung around in a tight little group. We were the misfits. None of us had any money. Joining sports or a club for kids was out of the question because we were too damned poor to afford much of anything. We'd be lucky if we could get three meals a day. I also wondered if the other kids had parents like mine. I wondered if their parents were bad too. I never asked them about their parents, though, and they didn't ask after mine—it was just something us kids didn't talk about. It seemed everyone wore a mask, everyone had two lives, a pretend one and a painful one, just like me.

# Twenty-one

# January 1981

One day, just before my seventeenth birthday, Athena called me into the office and told me that my time was up and I had to leave the group home soon because the government would not pay for my stay anymore, even though I was a ward of the courts till my eighteenth birthday. I didn't question her about it because I didn't know what to say, so I walked out the door, but before I could get far, she stopped me in my tracks and promised to help me find a job and a place to live. What good was that when I didn't know how to take care of myself, never mind do anything else?

A week later, Athena handed me a resume and off we went in her car to go job hunting. We went down to the industrial area in Mississauga's Lakeview neighbourhood where all the factories were lined up in a row. As I got out of the car, she told me to brush down my hair with my hand and then she wished me luck. Against my will, I grudgingly made my way to the front entrance of the factory and then went inside to the front desk where sat a lady with brown hair.

"How can I help you?"

I mumbled to her I wanted to apply for the assembly line position that was available. She took my resume and told me someone would get back to me. Then I walked back to the car, kicking up the gravel. I didn't like what was going on. It petrified me to think I had to make it on my own.

Two weeks later, I got called in for an interview at the factory. It was on Rangeview Road, and the manager hired me on the spot. I could start the following Monday. In the meantime, Athena found me a room to rent in an old lady's house near Ogden Avenue. It was walking distance from my job. It wasn't much of a room, though; it only had a single bed and a nightstand with a small lamp on it. The curtains that hung on the window were a dingy brown.

After Athena inspected the place, she said it would do and wrote out a cheque for the sum of two-hundred and fifty dollars and handed it to the lady. I tried to keep positive, but the only benefit I could see was that I didn't have to go to school or do anymore chores.

At work, I helped make picket fences, the ones designed to hug flower beds or line up along a walkway. I had to stand on my feet all day, putting the fence parts into a gigantic machine that automatically welded the pieces together. I didn't mind doing the work, even though it was repetitive. To pass time, I worked on my speed. And after a while, I got great at my job, enough so that my boss took notice. His name was Richard, and he couldn't believe how fast I was. He'd come over to where I was standing and watch me work, and then he'd shake his head in amazement, and cover me in compliments.

"You're so fast, I bet you can run this machine by yourself," he'd said. "Keep up the splendid work."

He was so impressed with my performance that he offered me a job running the machine and getting the other workers to follow my direction. I had no interest in barking out orders, so I turned him down.

After work, I'd go to a burger joint on Lakeshore called P&J Hamburgers. While I waited for my order, I'd play an arcade game. Then when my order was ready, I'd take it to the back of the restaurant and sit down facing the front door so I could see who was coming in and going out. It made being out in public a little less stressful.

One time, as I was eating my French fries with gravy, I got a nasty taste in my mouth and it tasted like poop. I thought someone had put something in my food, so I pushed the plate aside, got up and left the restaurant, but before doing so I went to the washroom and rinsed out my mouth.

Another time, when I was sitting in the back of the restaurant, I saw Richard through the big window as he got out of a black Cadillac. He was wearing a long heavy grey coat, and he had a scarf wrapped around his neck. When he noticed me, he came and sat down next to me. Then when the server came by, he ordered a coffee from her. I felt uncomfortable because I didn't even invite him to sit down with me. I didn't mind him talking to me at work, but out in public? It wasn't like he was a friend of mine. I watched him take a hundred-dollar bill and slap it on the table.

"How would you like to make that much in the next hour? There's a motel we could—"

"No."

"Are you sure? It'd be easy money. Nothing you wouldn't enjoy."

"No, I don't want to."

"Are you sure?"

I was sure nobody was going to be touching me, especially a grown man who had no business asking the question in the first place.

Work became difficult after that. I wasn't sure when my boss would approach me again to ask if I would sleep with him. To avoid running into him, when he came around, I'd take off to the washroom or hide behind one of my coworkers pretending not see him. Eventually he called me into his office and apologized for his behaviour, but I wasn't buying it. I quit.

I had no job and no way of paying rent, so at the end of June, I left my belongings behind and hitchhiked to downtown Toronto, the only place I knew where to go. I didn't call Athena to tell her I'd failed. Besides, after setting me up with a room and a job, I never heard a peep from her again. She didn't even give me a proper goodbye, zilch.

Once I got downtown, I went to Clarence Square Park where all the homeless kids hung out, but before getting there I sat in front of a store and people watched for a while. People were running around everywhere, men in business suits and young people going in and out of shops. Across the street, there was a vendor sell-ing newspapers and snacks. I watched him for a bit and then I made a beeline towards the park. I saw some homeless faces in the group, so I sat on a bench nearby and waited for someone to approach me.

Soon enough, a young girl invited me over to sit beside her. I think they were hippies or something because their hair was all twisted up in knots. As far as I could tell, they weren't wearing any deodorant because of the smell. Some of them didn't even have shoes on. I could see dirt in between their toes. I was so sensitive to smell that I almost puked in my mouth a few times. Their stench of their skin got stuck in my nostrils, and I'd cover my nose in a weak attempt to getting rid of the odour. Even though the smell bothered me, I stayed close to them because I knew if I stayed on my own something bad could happen. I also knew that there were pimps casing the park, on the lookout for vulner-able kids to exploit. I had to be on high alert at all times and use my supersonic radar to zero in on any kind of danger. There was no doubt in my mind that, if I put my guard down, someone would get me and do horrible things to me when I was alone.

Before long, I met another group of kids. They were more like me, and blending in wasn't a problem. When they laughed, I laughed. When they swore, I swore. It was that easy. Another thing I liked about them was that they only talked about their dreams, never about why they were on the streets. Hanging with them eased my loneliness, but it never took away what was going on my mind. I was still thinking about dying around the clock. I was still having visions of being splattered on the concrete, blood coming out of my ears and nose, and the voices in my head were calling me names, but I didn't give into them. Over time, I had learned to ignore them.

Sometimes when the kids were talking, I drowned out their voices by fantasizing about being a celebrity with a chunky, gold chain hanging around my neck and standing on a platform talking into a microphone about the coming of Jesus. When things got quiet, I'd slip away to the library around the corner and search through books, hoping to find my actual identity. Mostly I would read books on biblical studies. I'd stay at the library reading various books for hours and losing track of time. Once I stayed there until closing time, and when I got back to the park, I could only find kids lying near a bush, so I quietly crawled in beside them and tried to get some sleep.

First thing in the morning when I got up, I headed to the mall to use the washroom. I splashed water over my face and used a bit of soap from the dispenser to wash my armpits. Then I dipped my finger into the water to brush my teeth. Then I looked in the mirror to check my hair. It was messy, so I used my fingers to comb it out. After I finished, I went back to the park.

Eventually a kid told me about a place across the road that was taking in kids under the age of twenty-one and providing them with a short-term place to live. I made my way over there and rang the doorbell. Someone answered the intercom and told me to come back around two o'clock. They would interview me then.

When I returned a few hours later, I pressed the door buzzer and then wiped the sweat off my brows. I hated meeting new people. It made me nervous. While I waited for someone to answer the door, I practiced a karate move, the one I had seen Bruce Lee do in a film.

Soon, a lady with grey hair opened the door and let me in. She told me to hold on while she fetched a social worker to come get me. When the worker appeared, her appearance pleasantly surprised me. She was wearing a funky knitted hat, faded blue-jeans, and white sneakers with no scuff marks. She had a bounce to her step. She took me to an office where the walls were glass. The place had nice furniture and walls painted in bright colours that I felt at ease.

I sat on the chair across from the social worker and stared out the glass at the other kids sitting on couches and round tables in the kitchen lounge. Everything looked normal, and I was happy to be there.

I can't remember the name of the social worker. By that time, I was struggling to remember names and faces, and I kept slipping in and out of reality throughout the day. She asked a bunch of questions.

"Where are you from?" –and– "How old are you?" –and– "Do you have a social insurance number?"

I just made up that I was from California and was passing through and just needed a place to stay for a while. But soon the gig was up because I found out later that Fred was working there, and he probably brought my file with him. When the social worker asked me about my lies, I denied ever knowing Fred. I then dropped the issue. But I knew they knew I was lying.

One rule at the shelter was that I had to leave during the day and couldn't come back until dinner time. The place only provided night-time sleeping and brief contact with the staff, and that was fine by me since I had nothing to talk about.

At the park I met Darryl, a guy in his thirties from Nova Scotia. He was a painter by day and a thief evenings and weekends. He talked fast, but he had a strange accent. He was a trickster. He wanted me to steal merchandise from the stores. He'd be the lookout, and he promised if any floorwalkers tried to catch me, he would intervene. Back then they didn't have anti-theft tags on clothes; they just had security pretending to be ordinary people shopping. Darryl offered a fifteen percent cut of the money. It sounded like a million bucks to me.

On Friday nights, I would meet Darryl in front of the downtown shopping mall where he'd tell me to go into Eaton's and take bags from behind the clerk's counter and then go to the men's section and stuff suits in bags. Beforehand, he told me the colour and sizes of the suits before I left his sight. One time I almost got caught, but I dropped the goods near the store elevator and then went down the escalator. On my way down, I ran into two security guards who were hot on my trail. I smirked at them, shot them the finger, and then disappeared into the crowd outside.

Eventually, Darryl let me go with him when he dropped off the stolen goods. It gave me a chance to meet some buyers. One of them owned a restaurant on the corner of Yonge and Dundas. I think the store was some kind of front for bigger crimes. I met by a man with thick bones and short black hair. He had olive skin, so I assumed he was Italian because of his accent and the way he spoke with his hands. When Darryl got the money, he handed me my cut and then told me he had to go. I watched him go down the street and felt somehow cheated.

I got to thinking my cut wasn't enough, especially when I was risking getting arrested and Darryl would have gotten off scot free since he wasn't doing the stealing. It didn't seem fair he was getting the bulk of the money and me next to nothing, so I stopped talking to him and went to see the man at the restaurant on my own.

This time, I made a deal with the man that I would fill his orders for fifty dollars per suit. I don't know how much Darryl was getting, but the man seemed pleased. He gave me the sizes and colours of the suits and off I'd go. I soon got to know all the employees at the restaurant and took plenty of orders.

One day, the guy at the front counter pulled me aside and asked if I wanted to score a lot of cash. Apparently, he was stealing cars and selling them. I didn't ask questions because my fear was kicking in. Stealing cars was out of my league. Besides, all I could imagine was being locked up in jail and that was the last thing I wanted. So I turned him down. After that, I stopped going to the restaurant. I figured they were part of the mafia or something. I didn't want a bullet in my head or dumped in some lake with cement boots on my feet.

Instead, I headed back to the park where there was safety in numbers and forgot all about the restaurant guys.

At five o'clock I went back to the shelter for dinner. As I was sitting at a table in the lounge, a girl named Nicole came over and sat next to me. She weighed around two-hundred and fifty pounds and was complaining about her feet being sore. She took off her shoes and kicked them under the table and then rubbed her feet to-gether. When I looked down at her feet, they turned into walrus flippers. Then I focused on her face. Her teeth were white and perfectly straight. She had big blue eyes and a dimple in her chin. When she smiled at me, I knew we would become grand friends right away. I just had that feeling.

At dinner, Nicole got a plate and put a mountain of food on it. Then she sprinkled a triple helping of parmesan cheese on top. I watched her shove the spaghetti in her mouth. After she ate the first plate, she got a second helping to my surprise. But I didn't care. The key thing was she liked me and didn't mind all my devil talk.

Later, Nicole told me she was heading back to St. Kitts where she grew up. She was only in town for a short while and wanted to get back to her family. I hadn't known her long, but she insisted I go with her.

"We'll get a room," she said. "You'll like it there, it's quiet, no traffic."

And so, in August, Nicole and I hitchhiked to St. Kitts (St. Catharines). We stayed in a shelter for woman for a little and then we got a room to rent in a house where we could walk downtown. It wasn't much of a downtown, though; it only had a major street with shops and a big hotel.

The landlord charged us five hundred dollars a month for a shared room, and that included our food. But there wasn't much food. The room had sheer curtains and sparse furnishings with two single beds and a closet. After we got settled in, the landlord took us to the kitchen and showed us a large jar of peanut butter and where the bread was so we could eat when we got hungry. He told us the next time he went grocery shopping he'd get some cereal and milk for us. That was basically the menu, but I didn't care—I just needed a bed to sleep in. It didn't bother Nicole because she had family to go to for help. All she had to do was call her mother, and she'd come running with groceries in hand.

It was a strange and unexpected turn of events for me. Nicole and I got along surprisingly well, and suddenly I didn't feel quite so closed off. It also helped that I had escaped the GTA and put around a hundred kilometres, and the western tip of Lake Ontario, between myself and my mother.

# TWENTY-TWO

# AUGUST 1970

I soon stopped playing with the other kids in the apartment building because I found it boring when they started playing kissing games. My need for human contact wasn't that important, and besides, it reminded me of the dead man's mouth. It just wasn't that much fun smooching up a storm with some dumb ass kid pretending to be a doctor.

What I needed was to feed my curiosity about the low-income housing across the parking lot and on the other side of the fence. My mother warned me that *bad people* lived there, but I was living with my mother and the dead man, so the idea of bad people didn't strike me as that frightening.

There must have been at least five paved pathways into the complex where I was certain I would find some interesting characters. I climbed up onto the fence then jumped down into on the other side, feeling like the intruder I was, yet not really caring what others thought because my curiosity had the better part of me. I took the path closest to the fence near my field of long grass, just in case I got into trouble for being on private property. I started thinking I should have practiced running fast before beginning this adventure, but I was too excited about it to wait any longer. I figured I could probably switch to my marathon runner mask to get me out of trouble if I had to.

Finally, I was in, and as I walked down the path, I noticed an old woman hanging wet laundry on a clothesline. Her dress looked old and faded. There were no flowers or print of any kind, nothing but grey to match the greying hair she wore tucked in a bun at the base of her neck. As I passed by, I tried to see into her eyes, pretending I was a mind reader or a fortune-teller. I'd use different masks for that too. But she was too far away for me to tell what her soul was saying. Oh, the wonders of magical thinking played into my need to feel special.

At the far end of the complex, there was an enormous park with three swing sets, two sandboxes, and climbing equipment. Talk about an adventure! The kids from the complex hung out there regularly, talking or playing, and I could see the teenagers gathered around in a circle smoking some rotten smelling stuff that the wind blew my way. I knew it wasn't cigarettes. As soon as they looked at me, I turned and ran quickly back down the path, climbed over the fence, and ran back to my property.

Then I went back and crawled on the grass alongside the fence to do a little private investigating. I had an imaginary machine gun just in case one of them spotted me and I had to blow their brains out. The thought made me chuckle. On my hands and knees, I crawled in a tactical position, as though I was a little green plastic army man in combat boots, inching my way toward the enemy lines. My mind was razor sharp, my eyes focused, and I tried not to blink, but when I did, I pretended that they had shot me. I rolled over and pretended I was dead. Lying there, I felt the breeze in the air, watched the sky and the sun, and wondered why life couldn't be that easy all the time.

After a while, I got up and went inside again. I strolled casually down one of the inside paths, looking from side to side at the backyards, the big picture windows, the dogs barking, and the chain-link fences. It seemed so deserted. I wondered where the kids were. Now and then I jumped as high as I could and tried to sneak a peek in a window, but all I saw was my reflection changing from pretty to ugly, ugly to pretty, and then back to ugly again. I had two selves. I think that was when my mind was splitting into a thousand fragments.

I also wanted to meet some new friends, see some fresh faces. Something. *Anything.* I didn't like the feeling that had overtaken me, the realization and loneliness of having no real friends. I also felt a deep connection to the appearance of the grounds around the buildings: dirty, lifeless, meaningless, and gloomy. I kicked a rock with my foot and looked down. I was feeling great hopelessness when out of nowhere I heard another kid.

"Do you want to play with us?"

I looked up. She was a young girl, maybe five years old. There were two other children in the yard with her. One of them looked to be about my age. The other one was maybe nine years old. They all seemed lonely playing in their backyard with some old dolls. The youngest was holding a doll that looked like it had been through a war, one eye was missing, an arm dangled dangerously from a single stitch that held it onto the body. And they looked badly soiled. Looking at those beat-up dolls brought a smile to my face, though, because I thought it might just as well have been me they were holding. Just the sight of those three girls, standing there looking so pitiful, waiting for me to play with them, kind of took my breath away. I liked them immediately. There was no doubt in my mind that we were all going to be friends.

I had seen no other kids until then. I thought the four of us were alone. The complex seemed otherwise deserted. But before long two kids came whizzing by on their bikes, their voices a cruel singsong.

"Where's your stinky father?" –and– "Everybody hates the Prestons."

Apparently, that was their last name. The girls told me their names were Krista, the youngest, then Kimberley, and Katherine, the eldest. They were nice girls, and my heart sank when I heard those insults hurled at them. Mrs. Preston opened the back door right about then and ushered the girls inside, away from those rotten neighbourhood kids who had already learned to make the Prestons' the scapegoats.

"Can my new friend come in too?" asked little Krista.

Mrs. Preston agreed, and my heart almost jumped out of my shirt with excitement. I had to touch my chest to make sure my heart was still there. My hands became sweaty.

She looked down at me. "What's your name?"

"Tracey," I muttered.

It was so easy. I'd expected a thousand questions and that she'd be all over me with the third degree.

The next thing I noticed was the stench inside the house. It smelled like dirty armpits and green mould. In the kitchen, there was an old wooden table covered with dirty dishes. It looked like Mrs. Preston didn't take a liking to washing dishes or cleaning countertops, sweeping floors, vacuuming, or putting laundry away. She was the total opposite of my mother, who couldn't bear to leave even a glass in the sink. The mess bothered me a bit because it wasn't something that I was used to, but I overlooked that fact by pretending it didn't exist. As soon as I calmed down, I observed Mrs. Preston's appearance. She seemed too old to have such young kids. She was more the grandma type, a very unkempt grandma type. She told all of us to go upstairs and play in the bedrooms and not to bother Mr. Preston because he was resting in his bed.

I found out later that Mr. Preston had a mental health condition called schizophrenia and that he had to take his medications so he could act normal, but I had never seen him act normal. He worked part-time as a crosswalk guard just down the street, and the kids in the neighbourhood taunted him every day. They called him a mental case to his face and teased him about getting locked up. The first time I saw him was when the girls took me into his bedroom. His bedsheets had urine stains on them, and the room just reeked. His hair was uncombed, and his clothes were wrinkled and dirty. Actually, his hair kind of resembled mine.

The girls started nudging him to wake up and called him piss pot. I thought they were told to leave him alone, but I said nothing. I just watched it. Suddenly, Mr. Preston woke up and started punching the air and swearing in a language I didn't understand. But as I looked on, watching the girls being so insensitive to their daddy's needs, I felt terrible for their father. That was the first time I'd seen someone in such a state of confusion, and yet—compared to my mother—I think I would have preferred him as a parent.

The one thing that stands out in my mind about Mr. Preston is that he always seemed to wet his pants, and Mrs. Preston would change him like he was just one of her babies. I didn't like that part at all. I wanted to reach out to him and ask him some questions and give him a pat on the shoulder because I understood him in some strange way. I identified with him. I felt the need to protect him from his own kids. I think that was the first time in my life that I felt the need to know someone on a personal level. I wanted to be close to him, to give him a hug, or maybe I just felt safe with him because he couldn't talk to me, I don't know. Mrs. Preston told me it was when her husband came back from fighting in the Second World War that he lost his mind. I thought about that for a while and concluded that life was one big war. Mr. Preston had a profound effect on my life, and once in a while I think of how that old man made out. He has now passed on, but I wonder still.

The night before I was to start Grade 1 still felt like summer. Humid and still. I went to bed with my stomach in knots. I lay in bed a long time, hot with anxiety, in and out of sleep. When I heard the doorknob to my room turn, then click, I came awake from a feverish dream.

Then there was dead man.

His face close to mine, shiny and sweating. He was nervous and excited, like he was about to tell me a secret. He said he wanted was a kiss goodnight. I became hyper aware of my surroundings—the one small bed, the beat-up dresser with the scratched top, the closet whose folding door hung crooked, the poorly patched walls—and realized how shabby it was, how poor we were.

Then the dead man was kissing me on the lips, pressing hard like he wanted to eat my face. The bed sagged and creaked. Then I must have lost time or left my body or something because the next thing I was aware of was the closing of my bedroom door and of being alone.

## TWENTY-THREE

# AUGUST 1983

I'd been living with Nicole for about two years in our room in St. Kitts. The good thing about getting a permanent room to rent was that I no longer had to depend on shelters, and since I had a place to live, I got welfare with dental and medical included. One of the first things I did was go to the dentist to get my teeth fixed. I had a cavity that was causing me a considerable pain, so I ended up getting it removed even though the dentist argued with me it didn't have to get pulled. I got my teeth cleaned for the first time. I ran my tongue across my teeth, and they felt squeaky clean.

Nicole had depression, but I couldn't tell. When she got down in the dumps, she'd call her mother, and she'd bring food, usually a big box of glazed donuts. She'd also give her money, and then we'd go on long walks to the grocery store where Nicole would get sore feet and we'd have to sit on a curb for at least fifteen minutes until she rested up.

One night, early on in our time together, Nicole brought home some red hash. It was my first time smoking it, and I didn't know how to hold it, so I watched Nicole do it first. When it was my turn, I dragged so hard on it I almost blew out a lung. A few minutes later, I was higher than a kite. I got super high, so high that when I looked at Nicole, she looked like an oversized model. Everything around me looked brighter and clearer. Nicole's eye makeup seemed to have a shimmering effect. She reminded me of a goldfish, the way her eyes popped out.

In August of 1983, Nicole invited me to the house of an old friend of hers. Her name was Sheila, and Nicole had known her for years. I'd met Sheila once or twice in passing, but I'd never been to her place. She lived with her mother and brother on the bottom floor of one of those Second World War homes. Little did I know as we approached their place—a run-down house behind the CHSC-FM building on Queenston Street—that my life was about to change.

I was nineteen years old.

That first visit I didn't meet Sheila's mother, Judith, who was in bed, but I did meet her older brother Paul. And for the first time in my life I felt an electric charge for another person and knew that something was about to happen.

Paul was twenty-one, and I liked the way his thick wavy brown hair draped over his shoulders and the way his crystal blue eyes seemed to exude an aura of softness. He was five-eleven feet and too thin. He looked like a model. When he looked at me, I'd shy away, but I could feel his eyes were roaming up and down my body. I didn't know what to do with myself, so I just stood there with my hands to my sides. Eventually he told me to come and sit at the kitchen table with him. I sunk in the chair and then played with my hair while pouting my lips and slightly closed my eyes, giving my sexy look. As I sat there, the silence was killing me. I didn't know what to say, so I told him a dumb joke. He laughed and his face came alive with the most beautiful smile I had ever seen. His teeth were perfectly straight, but they had nicotine stains on them.

About an hour later, Nicole came out from the living room and told me it was time to go. So I got up from my seat, pushed the chair under the table, and told Paul I'd see him later and walked out the door.

When Nicole and I got halfway down the street, I jumped up and down with a big grin on my face that reached my ears. I told her that Paul was hot. I had a warm tingly feeling in my stomach. A thousand butterflies in my stomach were bursting to get out. I never felt so alive in my life. Nicole's face lit up with a smile, and then we laughed like crazy as I jumped around while spitting out my words that made no sense. I was practically drooling.

Soon, I started going over to Paul's without Nicole. One time, when I was sitting up on my bed and dreaming about Paul, I heard a knock at the door. It was Paul. He had come over to ask me out on a date. He was taking me to a junior hockey game down at the recreation centre near his house. He told me to come by the house and we'd drink two beers and then off we'd go to the game. I remember saying okay and shutting the front door, but I couldn't remember if I had all the details, so I ran upstairs to my room, grabbed a pen and wrote the date and time down. Then I stuck the note in my dresser drawer. I must have checked the drawer a hundred times to make sure the note didn't disappear. I must have read the note a thousand times.

On Friday, I went to Paul's house just like he told me to do. When I got there, he answered door. As I went past him to sit at the kitchen table, I got a strong whiff of his cologne. He smelled so good. He was wearing a white shirt and faded blue jeans that looked two sizes too small. I watched him a grab two beers from the fridge. Then he handed me mine and sat down across from me. I didn't know how to behave or what to say. So I just asked him what he did all day. He told me he was out about doing not much of anything. Then we talked about the weather and the hockey game we were about to see. I told him I liked hockey.

"It'll be a great game," he said.

At the game, Paul threw his arm around me and was practically sitting on my lap. I could feel sweat streaming down from my armpits, but I wasn't too worried about it because I wore an extra sweater to absorb the wetness so nobody could see the sweat marks. But I was uncomfortable with Paul's arm around, so I excused myself and went to the washroom. On my way there, it felt like I had a million eyes on me. I hated crowds.

After the game, Paul walked me home with his hand in mine. I just wanted to run. I hardly knew him, and he was already making moves on me. I hurried just to get the night over with. At the door, he leaned in for a kiss and I didn't move away. I stayed in the moment. It was the best kiss ever. It felt like we had melded together and were totally in sync. I could have stayed there forever. I finally pulled away.

"Why don't you come by tomorrow night after dinner," he said, his voice low.

I said I would. Then I went into my house, straight up to my bedroom, lay on the bed feeling like I was on cloud nine. I was in love.

The next day, I went to Paul's and met his mother who looked like a tomboy, short dark hair, no makeup, a shapeless figure. Paul's family was dirt poor. Judith had lost everything in a fire and had to go on welfare to survive. Most days she'd be in bed, laid out with a cold facecloth on her forehead. When she was up and about, she'd complain about all the twists and turns in her life, and all about people who had let her down. Yet she had a way of making her hardships sound funny, and after each story she'd roll her eyes as if to say *that's life*. I could tell she had a hard life by the dark circles around her eyes and how they had no light in them, not even a little spark of hope that things could get better. She had given up on her dreams and let everyone know it. She was the first person I had met who didn't have a shower. Instead, she'd clean herself with a warm facecloth and then leave it on the bathtub edge to dry out. I thought it was weird, but I said nothing about it.

Before I knew it, I was over at Paul's house every other day. I got to know his family really well. Judith had divorced Paul's father, David, many years ago when Paul was little. David had remarried. According to Judith,

David had married the woman he had a fling with. They might have been divorced but David didn't leave his kids like my dad did. He played an active role in his kids' lives, taking them on weekends. His new wife Susan was nice enough. But I could tell Judith hated her. Frequently she called her a home wrecker and a bitch. I don't know why she was holding a grudge because it had happened many years ago.

After Judith and David had divorced, Judith had remarried Bob, a man with five or six kids. It was their house that burned down to the ground. Even though they too had divorced, he was still coming around to do things together, but it always ended up in fights and sometimes he wouldn't come around for weeks. I think the only reason Judith kept him around was because he'd buy food for the house and take her over to the hotel up the street where they'd get drunk together and come back to the house to argue and then Judith would throw him out.

By October, I'd given up my room and moved into Paul's house. Paul also had an older sister by the name of Carrie, but I didn't get to see her much because she lived across town with her partner and son. Sometimes I'd go over there with Paul, but the visits were short.

Paul's sister Sheila didn't like me. She didn't need to tell me either, I already knew. But I liked her. She looked like a model. The primary reason I liked her was because she was kind enough to give up her bedroom for Paul and me. She took over Paul's spot on the cot in the kitchen. She didn't even seem to mind either. When I fetched a glass of water in the middle of the night, I had to be quiet. I would tiptoe across the floor and let the water run slow. Then I'd close the bedroom door slowly too.

One day, out of the blue, she told me the reason guys like her so much is that she could wrap her legs around head like a contortionist. I watched her as she got down on floor to show me. It impressed me. We got to talking and she was candid about her feelings.

"I didn't know how to take you at first, Tracey. And to be honest, when you look at me, sometimes it's like you have evil eyes or something. But my brother loves you."

I guess it was her way of telling me she didn't like me. I didn't know how to respond, so from that day forward I never looked her in eyes again. I would still hang with her though. Sometimes she would take me over to the house of a friend of hers. Alfred was an old man who lived in a run-down house. He had no family, and Sheila would go over and clean his house for free. Then she'd pull up a chair and Alfred would bring out his guitar and play while Sheila sang in perfect pitch to songs I had never heard before. But I enjoyed listening to them.

Mostly, I'd stay away from Sheila, but it was hard to do since we were living under the same roof and the place was only around eight-hundred square feet. It only had two bedrooms and a small living room that fit one couch, a chair, and a TV stand. The furniture was old, like they had bought it from a second store. The landlord's son Steve lived upstairs. I'd see him leave for work in the morning. He dressed in a suit and tie. I think he was some kind of finance guy. Steve had a roommate that Sheila was seeing. I can't remember his name, but he would always buy her expensive jewelry. She would come down from upstairs showing off the stuff. I figured he was a finance guy like the landlord's son. But it turned out he was a bank robber. The news had a nickname for him, but I can't recall it. While I was living with Paul and his family, Sheila's boyfriend was caught, tried, and got fifteen years in prison. That upset Sheila and she cried about it a lot.

## TWENTY-FOUR

# SEPTEMBER 1970

The morning I was starting Grade 1 was difficult because I was still feeling queasy and jittery about the night before with the dead man. Also school was just going to be difficult for me. Too many people I didn't know. Too many eyes on me. Too many strange adults I had to interact with. I would be walking on my own because, although Martha went to the same school and was only a grade ahead of me, I found it impossible to walk beside my big sister. We didn't have that kind of bond. Not like most sisters. I would always run ahead in my own little bubble.

My mother gave me easy instructions to follow. I was to wait for the light to turn green at the corner in front of the building, then cross the street and head straight down the main road, and when I passed the shopping mall, I would be able to see Elmlea Junior School.

As I walked down the main road, I watched the morning traffic pass by and wondered about the people driving by in their cars. I wondered if all adults were bad people. I had to be careful because a driver might intentionally swerve off the road and hit me. My mother had warned me about that that very morning.

The lunch she made me was in my hand, a peanut butter sandwich and an apple.

"Get some water from the drinking fountain if you get thirsty," she said.

My hand felt detached, and I had to keep looking down at it to make sure I didn't drop my lunch. Or was it because my lunch was so damned light?

As I've said, my nerves were terrible that morning for a number of reasons. And I was angry because school just seemed like it was a good excuse for my mother to get rid of me for the day. She looked happy that morning, putting on a fresh coat of eye makeup and checking her nylons for runs and brushing lint off her outfit. She seemed unaware of how scared I was to have to walk to school on my own that very first day. I thought she should have been walking with me, but I guess it was her way of pushing me away. I thought about the dead man, wondering what he was doing as I walked alone, but nothing came to mind because there was no space in my brain for him.

I finally made it to the school grounds, and when I saw all the other kids, I froze. Suddenly my clothes felt too tight, my hair too neat, my shoes too shiny. My mother had me dressed up like a clone, exactly the way the other children looked. I looked down at my dress: brown, ordinary, pressed. I suppose I looked like I fit in, but I felt very different inside.

The baseball diamond caught my attention. There was a bunch of children gathered around it—one boy holding a ball, another boy holding a bat, and others standing on the baseball plates or waiting in line. It was just the way I had seen it on television. I scanned the school grounds looking for something else that looked familiar, but it was quite unlike my isolated world. I could hear laughter, screaming, and most of all what I saw was a life I had never known. I wanted to get a little closer to that ball. I wanted to hang from the school climbers. I wanted to run wildly across the open field. I honestly think I felt something that day, and without being fully aware of it, I think I fell in love with sports. It was my ticket to personal freedom, a way to escape from the control my mother had over me. I now could move, run, and jump when I wanted to. And most of all, I could make lots of noise that my mother would never find out about, never hear.

The school bell rang, and all the kids headed for the doorways to go inside. I just followed along, trying not to draw attention to myself. I took the piece of paper out of my lunch bag that my mother had stuffed in there for me and read my new classroom number: 110. The halls were crowded, and I sensed the excitement in the air. I didn't feel any excitement myself because I was just worried about making it to my new classroom. The strangeness of the experience bothered me to the point that I just wanted to run. To remain focused, I counted the tiles on the floor as I walked and followed the black lines that might lead me to my new classroom. Now and then I would look up so I wouldn't miss my door number. Finally, I found number 110. I sat down on a hard blue plastic seat attached to a desk at the back of the classroom and adjusted my hair over my eyes so I could hide behind it.

At the front of the room, some kids were showing off their new clothes, and others were talking about their summer holidays. Others were just standing around trying to be funny by telling stupid jokes. I felt comfortable and safe in the back of the room because I thought nobody would approach me there and try to engage me in conversation. I watched the other children, admiring the handsome boys and the pretty girls who had their hair all done up nicely.

There was one boy I thought seemed nervous—he was bouncing around like he couldn't find a place to fit in. He was interesting to watch, the way his facial expressions would change from seriousness, then to a clown, and then to fear. I was just waiting for his face to explode! His face was expressing how I was feeling inside except that I didn't have the courage to move, let alone smile, not even to move my legs out from under the desk. I had to be quiet and still just the way my mother taught me. I sat quietly, looking for something to distract me from the fear I felt inside. The butterflies in my stomach had lost their wings; they lay silent now, breathless. The fear seemed to lay silent too.

I don't remember much else of that first day, and so it must have passed without incident.

Every day I went to school I just sat there, trying to fit in by not doing anything obvious. And when I had to move, or become obvious, I mimicked what the other kids were doing, and it must have worked because nobody seemed to notice me. I learned quickly that I could avoid drawing attention to myself by sitting still, controlled, emotionless. It was easy because it was something I was so used to doing at home. I learned at a very young age to follow directions, read body language, to appear like I was normal. It looked like the other kids in the classroom understood the rules too. I thought it was odd, though, the way everyone around me just seemed to follow the leader, the teacher. Everything seemed too controlled, too rigid, and it boggled my mind the way we all appeared so much alike in mannerisms and actions, like little copycats of each other.

By the time I was settled into Grade 1, visiting the Prestons' after school had become a regular and enjoyable routine. All of us girls would spend hours playing with dolls and role playing. Personally, I never liked dolls because they were female, and they made me think about my mother. So I would detach myself from what I was doing by mimicking the girls' behaviour and hang on to their every word. Then, I would repeat it back to them, changing only a very few words. I don't think they noticed at all.

We told silly little stories, and to fit in, I had to have a very colourful imagination to keep up with them in that department, what else was I supposed to do, tell them I had a rotten life and a horrible mother and that my daddy had abandoned me? I couldn't tell anyone about my home life, especially about the dead man. I didn't even like talking about my sisters. The more time I spent with them, the bigger my lies became to paint a picture of the best mother in the universe. I had to because I would have cried if I hadn't. The girls just listened closely to my stories and laughed.

I wondered, sometimes, what would have happened if I'd dropped to the floor, sobbing, and told them how sick I was in my head? I didn't think they would understand, so I just went on pretending to be normal. I matched every movement they made, every gesture, every intonation of their voices, every pattern of their speech. I was a stranger in their lives, a virtual impostor, and none of them knew it. Or maybe they did.

Every day I rushed home from school, changed into my play clothes, and left my mother's world to go to the Prestons' place. My mother didn't care just as long as I was home for dinner. I guess that made our family appear normal. Whenever it came time to leave and go home, I would become very anxious. My feelings would be up and down, as I walked back home with my head hanging low. I would get lost in thought and before I knew it, I was turning the doorknob into my apartment.

One day when I got home, I saw my sisters sitting on the couch watching TV while the dead man sat at the kitchen table smoking a cigarette. My mother wasn't home from work yet. I was careful not to make direct eye contact with anyone, but I thought it was so pitiful the way everyone around me appeared to be filling some pre-assigned role. Things looked normal, nothing going on, so I just went over and sat on the floor in front of the TV and pretended to watch cartoons. But my mind was wandering around in circles—flashbacks jumped around in there like yo-yos. The boxes in my mind were shifting again as though by routine. By then I could ignore both past and present realities because I carefully organized everything in sealed boxes, lined up on their respective shelves, each in its place.

One night near the end of September, the dead man came to my bedroom again. It was late, and he woke me up when he came in. I lay very still as he came and sat on the bed. He wanted to talk to me about my mother. Billy slept in their room and he cried most of the night, keeping the dead man awake so he had to sleep on the couch.

"I'm lonely," he said and reached under the blanket and took my hand.

...

The next morning, I awoke on a bare mattress. The bedclothes crumpled on the floor. I swung my legs off the bed and felt dizzy and anxious. I had to walk by the dead man on the way to the bathroom, and he just smiled. As soon as I got to the bathroom, I turned the water on and started washing my hands. I scrubbed and scrubbed and scrubbed.

At the breakfast table, my mother said something... and it made my throat close up. I had a mouthful of cereal and couldn't swallow. My head swam. I looked at her and there was something in her eyes that really scared me. Already I couldn't remember what she had said. All I knew was that I had to choke down the cereal in my mouth or I'd be in big trouble.

Later, when I was sitting on the couch waiting to leave for school, I took a good look around. My sister Sarah was sitting at the kitchen table, eating porridge. She was three. I looked at her and admired her beautiful moon-shaped face and almond-coloured eyes, her innocence. She looked like a wallflower, never saying much, just going with the flow. She was cute as a button. Something stirred inside me, an awareness of my environment. But I didn't have time to dwell on it. I just got up and left for school, tucking the memory into another box in my imagination and placing it routinely on the shelf.

In school, I couldn't focus on what the teacher was saying because I was obsessing endlessly about what to do with my hand. I hated my hand because it had become infected by the dead man. During lunch hour, after the other kids left to hang out in the playground, I hung around inside. Then I purposely went over to one of those big heavy wooden doors that seem to take forever to close and put my hand between the hinges. I had been holding the door open with my other hand and let it go just standing there, waiting for it to close.

When it closed, it squeezed and twisted the ends of my little fingers, squashing them. The pain was intense. I opened my mouth and let out a high-pitched scream, which echoed all the way down the hallway. Yet, the pain also felt good because it meant that I was alive. The door crushed my fingers and blood was oozing out. A student, having heard my scream, rushed over and saw that I needed help. Then she ran and got some paper towels and wrapped my hand up. She offered to take me to the nurse's office, and I had to say NO!

But soon the school nurse came and led me to her office. She asked me if I wanted to go home for the day. I didn't respond. I knew my mother would freak out if I drew attention to the family. I hadn't meant to draw attention to myself. I just wanted to feel something, anything, and if it took crushing my hand to do it, then that's what I had to do. I just had to find out if I were dead or alive. I had to wake up the dead hand that the dead man had poisoned. That wasn't the only time I did that trick either. I did it many times over the years. I just wanted to get rid of that dirty, poisoned, hand.

# TWENTY-FIVE

# JULY 1984

In July of 1984, I got a job picking strawberries on a farm with Paul. A truck would pick us up on Welland Avenue not far from his place. For eight hours a day, six days a week, I'd fill four-quart baskets with strawberries in the scorching sun. I didn't mind. I enjoyed counting things and improving my speed. It wasn't good for my skin, though, and if I didn't put sunscreen on and wear a hat, I'd burn to a crisp. I used the money I made to buy groceries for the house and give a little to Paul's mom. I'd also saved some for myself to buy a box of beer because by then I was drinking like a fish.

I remember one time Paul and I got so drunk that, as we stumbled down the street to go home, I saw a beautiful large plant on someone's porch and told Paul to bring it home with us. We laughed about it all the way home. Instead of coming in the front door, we cut through the radio station parking lot to a wall that backed on to their yard. The wall was high, and we couldn't figure out how we were going to get the plant down, so I jumped down from the wall onto the grass and told him to drop it to me. But he didn't. He jumped off the wall with the plant in his hands and landed on his knees. I heard a cracking sound. It was his knees. He let out a scream. Then he told me he had broken his legs. I broke out laughing. I thought the whole thing was comical, I could see the headlines in the news: two dummies steal a plant, one in serious condition with broken knees. After I pulled myself together, I went over to Paul to help him up. But he couldn't move. He was in too much pain. He told me to take the plant and go inside, and he'd be there in a while. So that's what I did.

I placed the plant beside the stove. It must have weighed fifty pounds. I was glad to get it in there. I went out back and helped Paul get back on his feet and into the house. I had to hold him up because he could barely walk. As soon as we got in the door, he went straight to bed. I covered him in the blanket and went to get a drink of water. Judith came in from the hotel loaded. I watched her stumble to the plant to have a look at it. She asked me where I got it, and I told her we stole it off a porch. She went to the kitchen drawer and pulled out a pair of scissors and told me the plant needed trimming. I told her not to ruin the plant, and off to bed I went. In the morning when I awoke, I went out to the kitchen to check on the plant, and it was down to three leaves.

Around that time, I started thinking about my family. I was missing them. Besides, Paul and his family kept questioning me on their whereabouts. So far I had only told them very little because that's all I could remember. To make my stories more colourful, I made stuff up. But I told the truth about where my mother worked and that I had a stepfather and three siblings. I kept my answers short and sweet, which was enough to keep them from prying. If that didn't work, I'd take the attention off me by asking about their lives. They had no problem going on about their pasts and their plans. I'd get so bored with it that I would drift off into my world in search of godly secrets. As long as I nodded in agreement every few minutes and pretended to be interested, nobody suspected I wasn't listening. It was something I did regularly.

Soon after, I looked my mother up in the phonebook and called her. When she picked up, one of the first thing she had told me was she had been searching for me. She had driven around all the places she thought I would be. I didn't believe her. While I was under the care of Children's Services, she didn't visit me once, not even a lousy phone call, which would have taken five minutes out of her precious day. Instead of arguing with her, I let her ramble on. Before getting off the phone, we made plans for the following weekend. I gave her the address, and that was the end of the phone call.

Four days later, there was a knock at the door. It was my mother. She came in trotting like a show-horse standing on its hind legs, looking down on everyone, including me. She looked the way I had remembered her. She was wearing blue jeans and a black and silver sparkly blouse. I went to hug her but changed my mind. Instead, I put my hand on her shoulder, and then I felt my hand go numb.

It had been six years since I'd last seen my mother, storming out of the assessment centre with Martha and Sarah in tow, slamming the door, and leaving me with Mrs. Johnson. Even then, my mother had already seemed like a person from another life. Now, six years later, it struck me that I could trace myself back to the girl on the bridge, the girl who walked away. Me. But that everything that had happened to that girl before the day on the bridge was dreamlike, almost like it had happened to someone else. Maybe that's why seeing my mother again shook me so badly.

Inside, my mother took a seat at the kitchen table. Paul's mom was standing at the sink with a dolly in her hand but put it down to join us. Paul was already at the table. I took a seat across the table from my mother, just waiting for my mother to open her mouth. Sure enough, without missing a beat, she started talking.

"I could never control, Tracey," she said. "She was always trouble, crazy."

I almost fell off my chair, but I kept it together. She and Judith talked for a while, but I couldn't concentrate on what they were saying. I hadn't expected to be so unsettled. After a while I spoke up telling my mother I was feeling sick and had to go lay down. She got up, pushed her chair in and went and put her shoes on. I walked her to her car. Just before she got in, she turned to me.

"Why are you with those people?"

"I like them," I said.

I watched from the sidewalk as my mother drove down the street and disappeared. Suddenly I felt suffocated, just like I did as a kid. I pulled the top of my shirt down a bit to get some air in there. I felt dizzy, like I was going to pass out. I stood there for a few minutes, pulled myself together and went back inside. I told Paul and Judith that my mother thought they were great.

"I like your mom," said Judith. "She's a nice lady."

I almost puked. And just like that, my mother was back in my life.

After that visit, she called me every couple of weeks, and it always left me feeling a little off balance. I could never talk for long and would make excuses to let her go once talking to her was starting to upset me, but I slowly learned what had happened after I left.

She and Robert had separated during my time at the first Four Maples home around when I was getting drunk at Robin's parents' cottage—that would have been about a year after Robert had come to visit me at the detention centre—and by the time Robin had been fired, my mother and Robert were divorced, and Robert had taken Billy and moved to Vancouver. The thought of Robert thousands of miles away on the other side of the country gave me a queasy giddy feeling I didn't like.

There had been some trouble with Martha and Sarah after that, and my mother had kicked them out shortly after Robert took Billy. Martha would have been sixteen going on seventeen at the time and Sarah fourteen. But now my mother was living with Sarah in an apartment at Jane and Finch. Sarah, now eighteen, had a boyfriend, and was working as an apprentice to be a cabinetmaker and making good money.

My mother had a boyfriend, and they were talking about getting a house someday, and Martha too was living with someone.

## TWENTY-SIX

# MAY 1971

One weekend, on my way over to the Prestons' house, a woman stopped me.

"Do you know God?"

Who the hell is God? I thought.

I was seven years old.

I took a step backward and observed her appearance. There was something too inviting about her, and I felt awkward, as though she could see right through me. She had beautiful light blue eyes that seemed transparent. It was like looking into the deep blue ocean and the clear blue sky, and when I looked into her eyes, they appeared that they were closed off from reality. She seemed very peaceful, like she had come from a peaceful world where beautiful fairies flew around, telling wonderful worldly secrets. Her dress was very simple, fit her loosely, and seemed designed to hide rather than accentuate her figure. Her light brown hair had golden highlights and was pulled back into a ponytail. I didn't catch her name when she mentioned it at first because I got swept away by her sweet voice, lingering perfume, and my anxiety. I listened to her ramble on about the Lord's plans as she stuffed a pamphlet into my hand.

She wanted to know if I would be interested in attending Sunday school. If so, I could meet her and the others on the main road and wait for a school bus that came by every Sunday morning at nine o'clock sharp. The pamphlet, she told me, contained consent forms for my parents to sign.

Before she left to search for other would-be followers, in and around the complex, she reached out and touched my shoulder.

"Jesus loves you!"

Jesus loved me.

Now, that last statement sparked my interest. I ran home, burst into the apartment excitedly and found my mother sitting on the couch looking like Mr. Potato Head with too much makeup, raccoon eyes, rosy cheeks, pink lipstick and eyelashes that looked way too thick. She was wearing a low-cut blouse and that mighty tight short skirt, but I had no time to give much thought to what she looked like to me at that moment, even though I found it to be odd.

I sat alongside her, back straight, legs nicely together, and practically begged her to let me go to Sunday school.

"Keep your mouth shut," she said. "Church people have strange ideas. They think they are better than everyone else, and they also think they are God's chosen ones, while we the little people are nothing more than peasants."

She also suggested that they like to take people's money. I didn't know she knew anything about God. She'd mentioned nothing to me about it before, but then again, we never talked about much of anything that was important.

I nodded, anything to get her to sign the consent form. It overwhelmed me that she would even consider letting me go to Sunday school. I sprang up from the couch, jumped around like a grasshopper, and smiled shamelessly. Her face lit up with a smile too. She found it amusing that I had gotten so excited about something so simple. I think she thought I had no emotions at all, but today she witnessed her daughter expressing joy.

When my excitement became too much, she ordered me to settle down or else I wouldn't be going anywhere. Quickly, I shut down and pretended to be a Potato Head too. After I got her to sign the consent forms, I left the living room, went into my bedroom, lay down on my bed, and soon got lost in deep thought about learning something new about life. My mind conjured up the idea that I could impress others at Sunday school and people would soon like me. That was me, always dreaming about being accepted.

That Sunday, I brushed my hair and my teeth and got a shirt and a pair of pants out of my dresser drawer. I hummed quietly to myself as I dressed and then went to sit at the kitchen table to eat a bowl of Sugar Crisp by myself. The cereal tasted good, and my tongue tingled as I ate and watched the hands on the clock slowly turn until the smaller hand reached the eight and the big hand reached the twelve. I didn't have to be there until nine o'clock, but I wanted to leave early enough so I wouldn't risk missing the bus. I put on my shoes and left the apartment, closing the door quietly behind me because everyone else was still sleeping. Besides, I didn't want to wake my mother up. She might change her mind, and I couldn't bear the thought of that.

I headed for the main road, walking on the grass. It was wet with morning dew. I enjoyed being out walking so early in the morning when there were so few cars on the road, people out walking their dogs, and birds singing in the trees. The sky was a little cloudy that morning, but I sensed that the sun would make a full appearance soon. My mind felt clear and free that morning as I walked on the grass by the side of the road and then waited patiently for my bus to arrive. It wasn't long before more children arrived to wait with me— boys dressed in white shirts and nice sweaters, shiny black shoes, and pants freshly pressed for Sunday school. The girls wore dresses, leotards, and shiny shoes. That's when I started to feel uncomfortable. My clothes, although they were my best, were nothing compared to theirs, but I didn't really care because I was going to go to Sunday school, anyway. Despite how I felt inside, I held my head high and pretended not to notice there was any difference between us.

From where I was standing, I could see the bus coming up the road, the engine making all kinds of rumbling sounds as though it was about to release one final cough and die right there. But it arrived, and we all got on. I hurried to the back of the bus, sat down, and stared out the window, thinking about what mask I should wear that day. Since I really had no identity of my own, I decided that maybe I could be a detective investigating my new environment.

Oh! What the hell, I thought finally, I'd just be me, a lost little soul in search of whatever I could find.

I enjoyed the ride. It was fun as the bus made its way down a winding road and into the church parking lot. The other children were whispering amongst themselves. I was too far back to hear what they were saying, but I imagined they were secretly mocking my clothes. I heard a voice tell me I was no damned good.

I cursed my mother. If she knew so much about church, she could at least have warned me that there would be a dress code. The very first time I was invited to join something interesting and already I had a black mark against me.

When I entered the church, the first thing that caught my attention was the smell. At first, it smelled flowery, but somewhere in the recesses of my mind, I had picked up the scent of mould. It reminded me of secrets—old secrets passed down through many generations. I looked up at the walls and admired the stained glassed windows. The colours seemed to give the room a sense of power. The surroundings impressed because, oddly enough, it also gave me a sense of power to feel such freedom. I felt connected with the colours. Colours, to me anyway, meant permission to explore the artistic side of myself.

A young-looking woman, maybe in her early twenties, put us into groups according to our ages, which meant I ended up in a group both boys and girls between seven and ten years old. We all gathered in a circle on a carpet around a chair where the mystery woman sat and handed out booklets to us all. I took mine and tried to read it, but I really couldn't read too well. The woman read it aloud to all of us, instructing us to change the page when necessary. There were more pictures than anything else in the booklets, so that relieved some of my anxiety. I hadn't expected that it would be anything like school. I thought there would be more interesting activities like playing games and maybe even refreshments. It was just like school, except that the Sunday school teacher was going to teach me the meaning and purpose of life.

After she read to us she closed her booklet and looked up.

"Who knows one of the Ten Commandments?"

A few hands went up, but not mine because I had never ever heard of the Ten Commandments. The teacher pointed to one boy who had eagerly raised his hand as though he was trying to reach the top of the roof.

"You shall not murder."

"Very good," she said.

And the boy's face beamed as he settled back with pride.

The teacher then told us the rest of the Ten Commandments rather hurriedly. The one that bothered me the most was honour your father and your mother, that your days may be prolonged in the land which the Lord your God gives you.

I didn't quite understand what it meant, so I raised my hand and asked the meaning.

"To obey and listen to your parents as they instruct you through life."

That stung.

I felt confused because it didn't sound right that I should follow my parents' orders, especially when my mother who had brought the dead man into my life. I lowered my head in shame, feeling a deep sadness. I stayed, though, wanting to learn more.

Over the next few Sundays, I learned a lot. Especially about good, evil, and how there is only one path that leads to the Lord. I learned about Satan, the dark angel who the Lord had banished from the heavens and was creating havoc on earth. I learned that Satan would tempt me to follow his ways. I was told I must stay in the light of God and it would protect me.

The one good thing about that experience was that I learned right from wrong, although I figured I had a good understanding of it already. I sensed I was already born with that knowledge. The teacher said Satan was also called the devil. I believed in the devil because he sure had influence over my mother and the dead man. I started thinking very hard about the devil. I wondered if it was possible that the devil was making my mother do the things she had been doing to me.

I also thought about the dead man and wondered if it was possible that he was actually the devil himself. That would mean that I was living with the devil and he was influencing my mother. Then I started thinking about the possibility that if I lived with the devil and evil had touched me, then I was a baby devil. I got very paranoid just thinking about all that so, I rearranged my sitting position and thoughts of the devil seemed to go away.

It wasn't long before I had to leave Sunday school. The teacher said I was too hyperactive. I could tell she was trying to be all nice about it, but I knew she knew that I was nothing but a problem child. I could never settle down. I ran around when I should have been sitting quietly. I asked too many questions, which disturbed study time when the teacher wanted us all to sit still—like good little puppets—and follow her directions. There were just too many rules for me to follow. The church wanted good kids who were more easily controlled, and I couldn't be easily controlled because I had too much on my mind. I found it very hard to sit still or take care of everyday stuff while concentrating on all those boxes in my head. If things were too quiet and still, the boxes would start moving around or disturbing thoughts would swirl around in my mind. I guess that's why I so often resembled a grasshopper. It was my way of handling the anger.

In one sense, I didn't really mind being kicked out of the church because, deep down inside, I knew I wasn't one of them. Still, I regretted having lost the opportunity to belong somewhere. The church evoked feelings of guilt inside of me for not being worthy enough to be a member. It saddened me.

I felt a sense of loss when it finally sunk in that I had to leave the church, and I wondered where I would go from there. The only place I could think of was back to my mother's dark world.

Therefore, I left the church that day telling no one I was leaving and walked home, sadly reflecting on my lack of self-worth. I guessed that mother had been right about whom I was—an ugly little slut. I didn't really know the true meaning of the word *slut*, but the way my mother said it made it sound so rotten, so I knew it had to be terrible. I felt ashamed of being rejected from the church. I thought a lot about my mother, the dead man, and on the world as I knew it. I thought about where my place in the real world should be.

One good thing about the whole church experience was learning about the power of prayer. The teacher showed me how to put my hands together and pray.

"Whenever you feel afraid or troubled," she said. "Just ask God for guidance, and he will show you the way."

I already knew that I would do a hell of a lot of praying from that time forward. I took that with me that day, knowing it would prove a very useful tool in my survival because I knew things would not get any better from that moment on.

In the short time I spent going to Sunday school, I learned a lot of things, but when they turned me away, I saw them differently. I thought, if there really was a God and his son Jesus who was so loving and who taught that everyone was equal, then why would God's followers turn away a child? How I loved to think about those things and allow my imagination to mingle with the ideas of faith to challenge this new awareness and to analyze the meaning of life. My curiosity was expanding, my knowledge growing, and a new understanding was leading me to my own personal beliefs—beliefs I knew would build my character. Besides, I had my secret garden, and that seemed pretty close to God to me.

As soon as I opened the door to the apartment, I turned off all my emotions, holding them in tightly so they wouldn't escape. I was not about to let my mother know that my heart was filled with sadness. Holding my feelings in was hard, so I just pretended I was plastic and stared blankly ahead like a little toy robot. That way my mother could not break my heart again like she'd already done so many times before. In addition, I was not about to let her know that the Church asked me to leave, that they didn't want me in Sunday school anymore.

My stomach felt sick as I tried to become invisible, so that my mother and I wouldn't need to communicate. It hurt like hell, though, because I needed to talk to her, to tell her the truth about my disappointment and how weak and insignificant I felt. And how especially disappointed I was with the people who followed God's Ten Commandments.

Every Sunday morning, I left the apartment under the pretense of going to Sunday school. I could not face my mother mocking me for being such a failure. I knew that, even though she may have said nothing right off, she would have used it down the line, when it would have been most useful to make me feel small, to humiliate me. So every Sunday I went to my secret place in the field out back and sat for hours at a time, imagining

I was in Sunday school. I did this until I became bored with my disappointment and my churchgoing days became a distant memory.

But I still hoped the day would come when another such opportunity would present itself. I still hoped that, one day, others would accept me although I was different. I so needed a place to fit in. I needed acceptance from others with all my faults, with all my defects, with all my awkward ways. When I think back, I can't help but feel that such acceptance would have made a major positive impact on my life despite what was going on behind closed doors at home.

## TWENTY-SEVEN

# JANUARY 1985

In January of 1985, I got pregnant. I had just turned twenty-one years old. I had been on birth control pills, but they hadn't worked. I thought about having an abortion, but then gave up the notion because of the pressure put on me by Paul and his family to have the baby. It seemed like every time I brought up the topic, I would get disapproving stares from them. Deep down, I knew I was in no shape to have a kid. After a while, I just kept my fears to myself and never mentioned it again.

Morning sickness came quick and steady. Within the first three months of pregnancy, I was barfing up a storm. I couldn't even keep toast down, and to boot, Paul seemed uninterested. He didn't give me any emotional support. He carried on like I didn't exist. Most days I just stayed in our bedroom, sleeping, and getting up to go to the washroom or a bite to eat.

We weren't going to be able to stay there with his mother after the baby came, there just wouldn't be room. And due to Paul's indifference, it fell to me to find a place to live, so I went to look at apartments. I finally found a large upper one bedroom in downtown St. Catharines about a twenty-minute walk from where we were living. Welfare paid for first and last months' rent, and Paul's dad and stepmom gave us a gold and red sectional from the fifties and red curtains to match.

Then when I was close to my due date, they had a baby shower for me. There were people there I didn't know, mostly family from Paul's stepmom's side. I got all the things I needed for the baby, a brand-new crib, playpen, an expensive stroller, blankets galore, and enough baby clothes to last two years. I appreciated it so much. I couldn't thank them enough.

By that time, I was in tight with Paul's stepmom, Susan. I adored her. Out of blue, she'd call me to ask how I was doing. We'd talk for hours until my ears would get sore from holding the phone to them. Mostly I would listen while she went on about the family business and her family. She worked with her father, and apparently the business was very successful. I can't remember what it was, but I knew they had money. I'd go over to her parents' house for dinners sometimes, and their house was big with expensive stuff in it, stuff I was afraid to touch. They had an in-ground pool in the backyard with a dome covering it. The water was warm, and if they'd let me, I would have swum in it all day.

David and Susan's house was not as big or nice, but they decorated with splendid furnishings. The curtains were beautiful. When we sat in the living room, I was careful not to spill my drink because they had white rugs. Come Thanksgiving, Susan cooked up a king's meal. She even taught me how to make gravy. I liked when Susan had a bit too much wine because she'd let loose, and then I could relax and have fun with her. It seemed like we never ran out of things to talk about. I felt guilty because she didn't have the same rapport with Paul as she had with me. After a while, though, it became a little too much because sometimes she'd call me two or three times a week. I think she was lonely. I didn't like her crowding on me, but I didn't know how to tell her I needed space. I didn't have the words. So eventually I cut her out of my life.

Aaron was born in October. He weighed five pounds, six ounces. Labour was hard on me. I screamed so loud that the nurse had to come into my hospital room to tell me to be quiet because I was scaring the other women on the ward. But I couldn't help it. The pain was unbearable, so unbearable that I begged the doctor to give me another shot of Demerol. I think he must have given me a super dose because afterward I felt numb from the waist down. When the doctor said push, I didn't move. I laid there like a dead fish. The poor doctor had to use a forceps to pull Aaron out by the head. When it was all over, I just lay there like a torn rag doll, stuffing everywhere, exhausted.

Once the doctor clipped the umbilical cord, the nurse brought my son over to me and laid him on my chest. I asked her if I could rest first.

"You'll be taking care of him for the next eighteen years," she snapped, "so get used to it."

I only got to hold Aaron for a few minutes before they whisked him away, but I remember it feeling like the afternoon sun shining on my face. I just wanted to bask in it for a while. It was the day my heart opened wide. It was love at first sight. I had a reason to live.

Aaron had jaundice, which made his eyes and skin turn yellow. They placed him under bright lights in a warm, enclosed bed in the nursery. I'd go down there first thing in the morning and stare through the window at him. I was dying to get at him. I wondered how he felt being apart from his mother and if he was suffering at all.

In the morning, the nurse came down to my room and took me to a private room just down the hall from the nursery. She had me take a seat in the rocking chair while she grabbed a breast pump out of the cupboard. I watched her fumble around with it. Then, she centered the breast shield over my nipple, and the milk came flowing out within minutes. I did the other breast all by myself. Then the nurse took the bottled milk to the fridge, and I went back to my room.

The first time I breastfed Aaron, the feeling I had was indescribable. I felt connected to him. I felt I was doing something right by him. Even though my head was a mess, I could ignore it as if I were bystander listening in on a two-way conversation from a distance. I couldn't quite make out the words, but I knew it was there. However, the fear was still there. A gut-wrenching knot remained in my stomach. I think nothing was going to make that go away.

There was just one hitch in the hospital—every time I went down to visit Aaron in the nursery, I'd find him tangled up in an oxygen tube in the incubator. I'd tap on the window, and the nurse would come out, and I would explain to her my concerns about the tube. Then she'd go back in and move the tube away from Aaron's face to make me feel better. The separation from my son was killing me. He belonged in my arms. To cope, I'd go back and forth from my room to the nursery window and stand there watching him like a hawk. Then paranoia would kick in, and I'd check for cameras watching me. I would imagine that the doctor and nurses were trying to steal him from me. The scene in *Rosemary's Baby* played out in my mind, the part where Dr. Sapirstein tells Mary her baby died. I didn't act on my crazy thinking. I bit my lip and kept quiet because I knew I'd risk losing my son.

Finally, I got out of the hospital. David and Susan drove me home. When I got in the door, the place was a mess. Dirty dishes were all over the countertop, used towels were lying on the bathroom floor, and I could see cup rings on the coffee table. There was a weird stench in the air too. Paul wasn't around. I felt my anger bubble up at the sight of the place, but I knew to remain calm because I had my son in my arms. I put Aaron on my bed, rolled two towels up and put them on each side of him so he wouldn't fall off. And then I cleaned the house.

Afterward, I went back to the bedroom and lay down beside Aaron. I stared at him, lovestruck, and touched his little toes and hands. He looked so innocent laying there. Then when he woke up, I breastfed him, changed his diaper and put him back down where he soon fell asleep again. I watched him for a while and then I drifted off to sleep, content.

# TWENTY-EIGHT

# SEPTEMBER 1972

A few months before my ninth birthday, we moved into the Elms, a quiet Etobicoke neighbourhood right next to Rexdale. My mother and the dead man had rented a three-bedroom house with a finished basement on Hadrian Drive right across the street from Elmlea Elementary. It was a well-maintained older home, white with brown windowpanes. Attractive green bushes lined the property, and in the backyard, there was one big tree and a few smaller bushes alongside a wobbly fence. The fence, however, was in dire need of repairs.

My mother put me in the upstairs bedroom, across the hall from where Sarah and my baby brother would share a room. My older sister, Martha, was to have the bedroom in the basement, just off an adjoining room where the dead man set up a games room. There was one more sizeable room that would become a playroom for us kids. Instead of using the dining room for eating, my mother turned it into a bedroom for her and the dead man. She hung curtains across the open space between it and the living room and furnished it appropriately for its new designation. I had an uneasy feeling about the space as soon as I saw it set up.

From their bedroom, I could see into the kitchen where everything appeared well organized. My mother had a place for everything, from the teapot to the deep fryer. I could also see into the living room. I didn't like that because I knew the dead man could see me no matter where I was, except upstairs. And I knew that, even if he couldn't see me right off, he could hone in on me with his special radar that could detect my presence anywhere, even detect my scent. He was like a blood-hound, nose to the ground, always sniffing around, and his tail wagging in friendly fashion to keep others off their guard.

As soon as we settled in, my mother talked endlessly about all the new stuff we would get—all materialistic items—but not one word about how a new start might be a time for new behaviours. She had high hopes of making a go of it, though. I guess she thought if she could change enough aspects of her life, then maybe it would change her mood. With the dead man's income and hers combined, they had a nice little pile of cash. I guess we were middle-class citizens by then.

She decorated the house with dark green, yellow, white and brown furniture. I loved the colour green in my surroundings, but since it was a colour my mother liked, I considered changing it to blue because she didn't like the colour blue. I had determined that all ties with my mother had to be severed, and my liking of the colour green would have meant that there was still a connection. I wrestled with that idea for a long time and finally decided that my favourite colour could still be green since there were all different shades of green.

All I had to do was pick one. It could be lime green, or pale green, or forest green, or frog green. It didn't have to be her green.

My mother enjoyed fresh starts. Her eyes sparkled with delight as she put the finishing touches on our new home. She seemed happy for a while, but I worried about how long that mood would last. I wanted to be happy for her, but I knew that my mother's happiness was usually artificial. I think nothing could have filled up her emotional tank except for maybe some real good loving. As I watched her eyes sparkle, I felt the need to fill up my own emotional tank. I longed to find a way to transfer my version of what love should be to her empty heart and to make her a whole human being instead of a lost little girl in a woman's body. As I watched her play at being happy, I adored her and admired her childlike innocence. I wanted so badly to get close to her at that moment, but I knew better. I knew I did not have the power to turn the fantasy into reality.

Those were the times when I was open to her—the times when she didn't appear to be a threat. Those were the times when I was most aware of her need for help. I knew she was unwell, but that was the part I had to deny the most fervently to protect myself. Even though I had consciously set about to sever any connection with her, it was really she who had done the severing. She was incapable of love. She must have rejected me even before I was aware of it. I remember reflecting on all that, one day, and how I felt. Suddenly, I just had to get out of her sight. I was angry. I jumped up and ran out the front door, slamming it hard. I wanted her to at least know I was there and how angry I was at her for rejecting me time after time.

The first Saturday at the Hadrian Drive, I headed for the school grounds. It was the afternoon, and the grounds were pretty deserted—just for a few people playing with their dogs and children playing on the climbing equipment—unlike the weekdays when the grounds were more crowded during school hours.

From there I descended into the Humber River Ravine; there was a path right behind school property that led down to the river. When I listened closely, I could hear water. I walked down the hill and, as I walked, I embarked on an adventure different from any adventure I had experienced so far. This adventure involved imaginary children I was seeing for the very first time.

Imaginary but real *to me.*

There were at least three who were visible, and they wore bizarre clothing: flowered hats, tight-fitting skirts, high-heeled shoes. Not the clothes a regular real-life child would have worn. I did not realize they weren't really there—that they were only a figment of my imagination. They talked in a scrambled language that I did not understand, and they followed all my moves if my arms went up, so did theirs. The experience was as real as the green grass I was standing on. I laughed out loud at their physical appearance and awkwardness, but it was only a reflection of how I saw myself and perhaps a distorted glimpse of how I saw my mother and the total control she had over my life.

As the children ran down the path in front of me, I experienced a sense of detachment from the real world, as though I were floating. I imagined these new friends loved me. They took away my loneliness.

As I explored my surroundings, I was drawn deeper and deeper into the ravine. I soon felt a sense of terror. My new friends had disappeared, and in their place, I saw odd-looking strangers lying in wait behind the trees, strangers I knew could do me harm. I picked up my pace, slowly at first, and then ran. I turned my head to see where my new friends had gone, but they had disappeared into thin air. I could hear laughter in my head, but it seemed far off like it was not a part of me, as though it were just an echo from my distant past. Deep down inside, I screamed, a muffled desperate scream, because I knew I was losing my mind. I knew something was wrong, and I was frantic with fear.

Eventually, I had to stop running. I didn't know where I was, and my head felt dizzy. I stopped dead in my tracks and listened to the buzzing noise in my head and realized my heart was pounding. The children disappeared, the strangers disappeared, and the loneliness was back.

I wanted to cry, but to do so would have meant acknowledging that the experience was not real. My face went blank. The feeling of being dead came back. I was numb and lifeless. I walked toward the edge of a path and climbed up a small hill that led to a treed area where I thought I spotted a man lying on the ground beneath a tree. I tiptoed over to him and saw that he was wearing a feathered hat, leather boots, and a one-piece blue outfit. He did not look like any regular person I had ever seen before. In fact, he looked like a fictitious character right out of Robin Hood. He had a very long sharp knife strapped to his belt, and it glowed strangely. It looked inviting. It was like the one my mother once held when she threatened me. I imagined that, if I looked a little closer at his face, it would have resembled hers. That was the entire purpose of these hallucinations, of course, to disguise my mother so I would never ever have to confront the truth. The man was not real, but I could not acknowledge that fact at that moment in time. I had to go on pretending he was real to enforce the belief that I was not crazy. I had to believe he was real to protect my sanity.

I climbed out of the ravine and wandered back towards the low-income housing by our old place. The walk seemed way too long, and my feet felt like they were floating above the ground, detached from the real world. As I walked, I sensed the imaginary compartments with the boxes inside my brain stuffed to the rim. I felt overloaded. I skipped and jumped along pretending that I was avoiding the cracks in the sidewalk, counting in my mind, two, four, six, and eight. But the real reason for doing that was that I believed if I could jump high enough the boxes would fall down off their shelf and make more room for the future traumatic events I knew were sure to come. I thought my mind well equipped to deal with trauma—it happened automatically. But I don't think any of the boxes fell off the shelf.

When I got to the complex, I gathered some kids in a circle around me, telling them what I had seen. They weren't really in a circle, but I pretended they were to feel some kind of control. Actually, they were a little hesitant even to hear what I had to say, but they drew a little closer. Besides, living where they lived, there wasn't much to do, so gathering to listen to the crazy words of that funny girl was just another way to fill up time in their day.

I convinced them to visit the ravine to see for themselves. They were quiet and seemed a little confused, yet excited at the possibility that I just might be telling the truth. But when we got there, there was no man, no knife, not even a suggestion that a man had been there at all. I disappointed the kids because we found nothing. I had betrayed them. I was on the brink of being discovered as a fraud, as a weirdo, and I was desperate to make them believe that there had been someone there. So I checked the grass for the indentations we all knew would have been evidence of a man's presence. I searched as though I was just as disappointed as they were about his disappearance.

Finally, we all had to admit there was no way we were going to find anything, and as we walked away from the ravine, I felt compelled to scream at the top of my lungs. I don't know why I did it, but it didn't just scare the other kids, it terrified me. Somehow, though, I thought maybe a demonstration of terror would convince them I had seen something. It had seemed very real to me. However, as traumatized as I was about that experience, I did not put it into one of my imaginary boxes.

The boxes were only for real trauma, like sexual, physical, and mental abuse. The hallucinations were my reality and part of my conscious mind. I let it be real in my mind because, in some strange way, the experience felt good, and I knew it couldn't hurt me. The real world was very dangerous, too dangerous to confront, so holding onto what wasn't real was a survival mechanism, my way of coping with life, as I knew it.

Yet, the experience in the ravine somehow led me to believe that I was in real danger, so when I got home, I took a knife from the kitchen drawer and put it under my mattress. Every night I would check to see if it was there before climbing into bed. I had to be sure neither my mother nor the dead man had found and removed it. Some nights I put the knife under my pillow where I could hold on to the handle. I held it in my hand just in case my mother or the dead man came into my room. I never intended to use it, it was there for protection, but the thought of using it crossed my mind more than once. I fantasized about slicing and dicing my mother into pieces. I figured that would put a permanent end to the abuse. It was an awful thought to have, and I felt guilty for thinking it, but I was truly concerned about my safety, my life. I even thought of using the knife on myself because I had a growing need to die and put an end to my miserable existence, but I never found the courage to do so. I knew instinctively that it was wrong to act on my fantasies, so I replayed them in my mind, over and over again, until I became exhausted enough to go to sleep. As I lay in bed, I put my hand on the knife and it allowed me peace of mind.

One night, as I lay on my bed, I heard creaking noises and realized someone was coming up the stairs. I did not understand who it was, so I pretended to be sleeping. My mother came into my room and nudged my shoulder with her hand. I opened my eyes, and she told me to be quiet and come downstairs. Slowly, I got off my bed and followed her with suspicion. She led me into her bedroom where the dead man lay awake and waiting.

He was naked.

I looked at him, but only indirectly. I felt my heart sink and my body grow weak. This was like a bad dream. My body shut down, and my hearing grew indistinct. I could hear the two of them talking, but it was as though they were far away, far enough that I couldn't really make out what they were saying.

...

The following morning my mother was diligently, even anxiously, cleaning the house. She went from one room to the next with a rag in her hand, dashing it over the furniture. I tried to make eye contact with her, but she avoided meeting my gaze.

I felt sorry for her, though, as I watched her spin through the house like a robot without a shut-off button. I still harboured the fear of repercussion if I interrupted her. I feared it would re-ignite her anger and spark more verbal and physical abuse. So once again, I felt compelled to store another traumatic experience in a box and put it on the shelf and remove it from conscious memory. Amazing how much storage there is in the mind of a little girl.

I not only hid stuff inside my brain, but I hid my physical self. I let my bangs grow to hide my face. And I didn't pull them across my face just once in a while anymore. I did it every day. It was, in fact, my way of slowly disappearing from the real world physically, mentally, and emotionally. I used every excuse to hide. And I would literally hide in my bedroom closet. Inside the closet was a small door that led to the attic. I would quietly sneak into the attic and stay there for hours, lost in my imaginary world, lost to a world that was unreal and unsafe for me. I felt safe in there, yet also found it terrifying because it seemed to become a way of life. The private world I had worked so diligently to create in my mind without being aware of it was slowly growing in size, consuming my true identity.

And also, unknowingly, I was about to travel even further down the road of madness.

## TWENTY-NINE

# FEBRUARY 1987

After Aaron was born, Paul and I were having a hard time making ends meet, so I took a job at a factory making wooden pallets. Paul worked there too, and one of Paul's friends—also named Paul—would babysit Aaron while we went off to work. When I got back home, I'd have a shower and then pump out my breast milk and put it into the baby bottles for the following day. Then I'd skip dinner, take Aaron to bed with me, and crash.

Mostly, my Paul wasn't around. Sometimes he didn't even come home. In the morning, I'd find him passed out on the couch with his clothes still on. He didn't really bother with Aaron or me. He'd grown distant and disinterested. In fact, he didn't really make any attempts to connect with Aaron as a baby. Once in a while, he gave us a little attention. Occasionally, he'd even give us a hug here and there, but nothing special. Physically our relationship had grown cold, Paul claiming that pregnancy had ruined my body. He wasn't attracted to me anymore.

When he was at home, he didn't even help with housework. He did very little of anything except go to work and disappear. After a while it didn't even bother me that much. Sometimes I'd hear stories of him sleeping around, but I would ignore them. It didn't matter, anyway—my feelings for him had changed. I think we both knew that our relationship was dead. We had nothing in common. The only thing that held us together was our inability to get close to anyone. So he went out to drink, and I stayed home to take care of our son.

Paul's friend Paul Kelly, our babysitter, approached me after work one day. I could tell he was nervous about something. It didn't take much prompting for him to blurt it out.

"Paul doesn't love you," he said. "You're with the wrong Paul."

It never dawned on me he had a crush on me. I shut down at that point, I think, and walked away without responding. This was how I handled anxiety around men, through avoidance and denial. I don't know how he interpreted that non-response, but his feelings for me were never brought up again.

Avoidance successful.

I knew, on some level, that men found me attractive, but never seemed real to me. I had my mother's fine looks, and just like her, I drew men's attention. There wasn't a place I'd go where men weren't cat calling me or trying to strike up a conversation with me. I ignored their attempts more times than I can remember.

Aaron was sick all the time. He wouldn't stop crying, and I tried everything to soothe him. At first, I thought I wasn't changing his diaper often enough, or he wasn't getting enough breast milk. But my breasts were full, for when I pressed down on them in the shower, milk squirted everywhere. So I knew that wasn't the problem. I wasn't sure what to do, so I took Aaron to the doctor, hoping to solve the problem. The doctor suggested he might be colicky. He told me to give him grape seed oil after each feeding and then give him a good burping session. I followed his instructions, but it didn't help. I'd spend entire nights walking around the apartment with Aaron in my arms, trying to settle him down. Things got so bad that I quit my job. I couldn't take care of him and work at the same time. It became too much for me. I couldn't get out of bed to get to work on time. It tired me all the time.

When Aaron turned six months old, I started him on solid foods while I was still breastfeeding. Things got worse, though. He was crying even more than usual. I took him back to the doctor, and he told me Aaron would eventually grow out of it. But he didn't.

It turned out that the root of Aaron's crying was he had food allergies. I don't know why the doctor didn't test him earlier on for it. It also turned out that Aaron had asthma. I felt so much guilt over it because I could have killed him by accident without my knowledge.

Things, however, got a little better when Aaron started on big people's food. I first gave him mashed potatoes, and I was pleased that he didn't have an allergy reaction. I still gave him baby food though, just the bananas and vegetables from a baby food jar.

My mother dropped by one Saturday and stayed overnight. I got a babysitter so that Paul, my mother, and I could go out for drinks. By the time we all got back, we were all half in the bag. I felt tired, so I jumped in bed beside Paul after making a bed for my mother on the couch. I was just about to drift off to when I heard my mother whisper from the end of the bed to move over—she was coming in. It happened so fast I didn't know how to react. All I can remember was her giggling like a little schoolgirl in between Paul and me. Then my anxiety bounced off the wall and I got up muttering how I wouldn't be able sleep there like that.

"It's okay," my mother said suddenly, "I'll go to the couch."

The following morning when my mother left, Paul turned to me, bleary eyed.

"I could sleep with your mother if I wanted to."

I had no comment.

I'd reconnected with Sarah by this point and had heard her side of the story when it came to her relationship with our mother. I found out that the apartment my mother had been living in at Jane and Finch when I first got back in touch with her was actually *Sarah's* apartment. My mother had more or less taken it from her, moving in by degrees after they had first reconciled and then claiming it for herself when Sarah decided to live with her boyfriend—and keeping most of the contents as well.

More recently, I knew that Sarah had again briefly lived with our mother and her boyfriend when they finally got the house they'd been talking about, but what I hadn't known—until Sarah told me—was that she had provided the five-thousand-dollar deposit to make the house purchase possible in the first place. Not that that hadn't stopped my mother from throwing Sarah out shortly thereafter. Sarah was hurt by this, of course, but she'd come to expect very little from our mother and maintained a relationship with her regardless. Poor Sarah had been mistreated by both our mother and Martha and had been looking after herself for a long time.

In fact, back in the summer of 1980, shortly after Robert had taken Billy to Vancouver, and around the time I was being sent to the second Four Maples home, my mother had kicked both Martha and Sarah out of the house on South Service Road. Martha would have been sixteen and Sarah only fourteen. Sarah had moved, with Martha, into the place where Martha's boyfriend lived and had ended up getting raped in the basement by some other roomer. Shortly after that, Martha too had kicked her out.

It's difficult when your own family does hurtful things because they occupy emotional ground unique to family. I felt a lot of anger on Sarah's behalf, which only complicated my relationship with my mother and Martha.

In June of 1987, while visiting my sister Sarah at her apartment, I ran into her friend Jeff. I had met him a few times before, but I was about to get to know him a lot better.

He had jet black hair and a thick body. He was an Elvis Presley wannabe right down to the sideburns. He oozed sex appeal and wore a gold bracelet with his name engraved on it. His hair was naturally curly, but he spent hours straightening it out with a round hairbrush and a blow dryer. The kicker was he could sing like Elvis, which blew my mind. I don't think there was ever a time he wasn't breaking out in song and dance. The sight of him pulled me in like a cat to milk. He was a magic man, dazzling women, dragging them down to their knees just with his words, smooth, charismatic, magnetic, glib.

Enough though I didn't know him well, I felt like he had put some kind of magic spell over me—though I could break it by adjusting my focus onto something mundane as a cup. Over time, we just fit together like a hand to a glove. It felt like I had known him all my life, but I couldn't put my finger on it. When my sister was off on one of her little adventures, she left us alone. He even convinced me to go over to his place, an apartment left for him by his mother who had recently moved out of the country. She had left all her furniture behind along with an expensive cappuccino machine.

After sipping on an espresso, Jeff showed me his bedroom. His closet was halfway open, and I could see a full-length mirror pressed up against the inside wall and facing outwards. I thought it was odd, so I asked him why he had a mirror in the closet. He told me he used it to watch himself "bang girls." Then he went on about how he wished his penis were bigger and longer for a good ten minutes.

As I sat on Jeff's couch, I listened to him go on about his childhood. Strict Jehovah's Witness parents raised him. His mother would force him to study the Bible late into the night. After his mother put him to bed, he'd swap out the Bible for a girly magazine he had stolen from his older brother's room. They were ten years apart, and I found out later that his brother hired hookers on Friday nights, which to him was normal.

Jeff also told me God had sent him down from heaven above to "make love to all women." And he was trying to make good on that. So far he had slept with five-hundred women. When I challenged him on that number, he said he kept a tally. With that, I got up from the couch, brushed my dress down and told him I had to go.

A voice told me to back away—in fact, to run like hell. As I walked down to the elevator, I got an eerie feeling that someone was scratching at my back with long fingernails. Once I got out the front door of the building, the feeling went away.

In April, Aaron had a full-blown asthma attack, and I had to call the ambulance for him. The ambulance came fast, and before I knew it, Aaron was lying in an oxygen tent in the hospital. My anxiety was through the roof. I didn't know where Paul was, and he would sometimes stay away for days on end. I tried to get a hold of him by calling Judith, but she didn't know where he was. So I called Paul's dad, and he and his wife came to the hospital right away. I was happy to see them when they walked in. I could see genuine concern on their faces.

"Oh my god, where's Paul?" Susan asked.

"I don't know," I said. "I have Judith tracking him down. I'm sure he'll show up eventually."

But he never did, not that day.

Aaron was in the hospital for over a week, and I never left his side. I got the nurse to get me a cot out of storage, and I slept there every night at the foot of his bed, waking up every so often to check on him. After two days, they took him out of the oxygen tent, and he was sitting upright. The nurse would bring him cherry and orange popsicles. I think it was the highlight of his stay. He looked content sitting there in the hospital bed licking at a Popsicle like a kid would do. As I sat there, watching him enjoy his treat, the love I felt for him washed over me. He was my greatest gift in life so far, and I'd do anything for him. Anything!

At the end of Aaron's stay at the hospital, Susan and David came and picked us up and drove us back to my place. They dropped me off at the curb because I was too ashamed of our living conditions to invite them in. So I just thanked them for all their help while grabbing Aaron from the car seat and then disappearing into my house.

Sometime in July, I got a call from Susan, and she told me David had got Paul a job at a fish plant through one of his golfing buddies. He could start immediately. He just had to go to an interview. The only catch was that we had to move to Hamilton, about a forty-minute drive away. As soon as I got off the phone, I had the desire to pack my bags. I couldn't wait to tell Paul when he got home. In the meantime, I fantasized about our new place and having nice things and giving Aaron and me a better life.

When Paul walked in the front door, I could hardly contain my excitement as I told him about the conversation I had had with his stepmom. As usual, he responded with no emotion. He told me he had to think about it first. Then he went and sat down on the couch to watch TV.

# THIRTY

# JUNE 1973

It'd been nine months since my mother had woken me in the night and brought me to the bed she shared with the dead man. Long enough that it wasn't clear what had happened. Nine months to an unsettled mind can obscure a great deal. A lot can be lost, or packed away.

I was nine years old, and my mother again come to me in the night and told me to come to her bedroom. I remember the quiet of the house as we walked down the stairs. In her room, behind the green curtain, she ordered me to get undressed. Though he didn't speak, I could feel the dead man's eyes on me. Terrified, I slipped out of my pink nightgown and watched it drop to the floor, my mind flickering back to the last time this had happened. I had no choice but to obey. I was a child. I clumsily climbed to the top of her bed.

Although the lights were out in the bedroom, I could still see the shadow of the dead man on the bed because of the stove-light in the kitchen. I slyly looked at the outline of his body sprawled out on top of the covers. Although I knew he was a coward, I imagined him as the king of the castle. I guess, because of the power imbalance, my mind was playing tricks on me, so I saw him as ten feet tall and as strong as an ape.

...

Later, on my way down the hall to my room, dragging my nightgown behind me, I stumbled against the wall with the tainted brown and green flowered wallpaper. I was running but as though in slow motion. Nothing was real. I was in pain, but it was hard to track—there was the physical pain, the split in my mind, and the tear in my heart. Somehow, I made my way up the stairs to my room. Everything was spinning around, and my vision became blurred, yet things I hadn't noticed before seemed to come into stark clarity. I studied everything with great intensity, as though what I had just endured were no more important than going to the bathroom, as though it was not an unspeakable thing. I noticed the chipped paint on the walls, the faded sheets on my bed, and the stains on my pillowcases from my drool for the first time. I could see the minutest of details. I had become a human microscope. It was fascinating, yet terrifying.

I lay in my bed, but I couldn't relax. Flashbacks of past traumas were flickering in my head so fast that I couldn't make out the pictures. My head started throbbing, and I felt compelled to flee, so I got up and went downstairs to the back door.

The door seemed to close loudly behind me, although I tried to close it so they wouldn't know. Overwhelmed with emotion, I was unsure what to do next. All I could think of was to run. I started running and jumped over several fences on my way to somewhere I didn't know. I scraped my face and legs on tree branches, and my heart pounded violently in my chest. Later, I realized I was on the ground, curled up in a ball in the corner of someone's shed. I dared not move. I felt like I was being terrorized by some outside force. I felt something evil in the shed with me. Images of the devil flashed through my mind and, just like that, the devil was now standing in the place of my mother and the dead man. The wind whispered in my ear, telling me to kill myself. But I knew it was only one of my mother's sweet voices demanding that I surrender to her demands. Behind the images, I could still see the devil breathing hard. But it wasn't the devil. It was the dead man in disguise.

I spent an eternity in that shed. Then finally I broke through the terror and went back into the house. I walked mechanically into the kitchen, took the butcher knife out of the drawer, and went into my mother's bedroom. I stood there for a few moments watching her sleep. I felt like a giant standing there with the saber in my hand. I looked around the room. It looked so ordinary with its queen bed, a modest dresser and end tables, her favourite lamp, and a shoe rack in the corner. I was suddenly enveloped in tranquility. It seeped in and became a part of me. I watched as she slept peacefully and listened to her snore.

Then I looked over at the dead man and rage welled up in me so powerful that it took over my every move. I had never felt so much hatred in my nine short years of life. I wanted him dead, and my mother too. I wanted to pierce her heart and let her breath expire. I wanted her to feel what it was like to have a broken heart. But before the rage got the better of me, I got control of myself and logic kicked in. I realized that if I killed my mother, it would probably wake the dead man up and he would take the knife away before I got to him. And way down deep inside, I knew it was wrong. In effect, my conscious mind brought me to my senses, and I walked away with no blood dripping from the knife blade.

Silently, I walked into the kitchen and put the knife back in the drawer. I felt bad about what I'd almost done. I felt guilty to think about how close I came to crossing the line from victim to perpetrator. And I felt a great sadness. But thank God, I wasn't evil.

When I woke up in the morning, I remembered nothing about the night before. It was as though it never happened. I didn't remember that I had lost my mind. I didn't even recognize my family. I felt like I was suddenly deported to some foreign land where the people spoke a different language and I didn't have a clue in how I was going to communicate. My mother said something to me, but I couldn't make it out. It was so strange. It was like being in enemy territory with my every movement being watched. I had to be careful of these strangers around me who might try to trick me into believing I was safe. I watched my mother's mouth move and tried my best to decipher the words, but nothing registered. I just nodded my head and went to my room.

I went to my hiding place in the attic where I sat quietly obsessing about my survival and how I was becoming ever more enmeshed in my imaginary world. I had stolen matches from the kitchen drawer and started lighting them one by one. I watched, mesmerized, as they burned down to my fingertips. It occurred to me to burn the house down, but all things considered, I didn't really want to die. Death was a too permanent solution. Besides, what would they have written on my tombstone, HERE LIES THE FAMILY NUT?

The attic felt like a cave. I felt cut off from civilization. It was primitive times, and I had daily rituals to perform. I rubbed my hands together, and then touched my hair and my eyes. I was trying desperately to think of ways to distract myself from the demonic visions and thoughts I was having. I counted the wooden boards, rubbed my hands sensuously across the beams, and listened carefully for noises coming from outside the attic.

There in the attic was the first time I truly confronted the voices in my head. They were loud and were telling me to kill myself. They were messages from my mother who wanted me dead. In a panic, I bolted from the attic, thinking I could escape them and maybe even lock them in behind me. I became queasy. I reached down and rubbed my stomach, then went to the window and vomited. I hoped that I had vomited up all the demons and that my fears would now settle down, but they didn't. So I sat on my bed, listening to the voices, and found solace because, at least, I wasn't alone.

From that day forward, any vestige of the real me ceased to exist. They had finally broken my spirit. My mother had won and so had the dead man because my voice was now permanently silenced. And I chose not to remember. I could no longer relate to people on a normal level because people had become stand-ins for the devil. I could not see people for who they really were because it would mean confronting the abuse, and to me, it didn't even exist. My mind had brilliantly designed an escape from reality. It replaced human faces with animal faces.

Sometimes when I looked at my mother's head, it turned into the head of a wolf. It seemed so much safer to see her as a wolf than to look into the face of the one who had caused me so much harm.

I felt so detached from reality that I would walk around the house constantly touching the furniture to make contact with something I knew was real. The pictures on the walls would move and change into terrifying images of devils and ghouls. From that day forward, I began a journey into a bizarre and wonderful and frightening world, where I searched desperately for my identity, my missing self.

Frequently, I lost track of time. Sometimes I would discover myself in the ravine searching for insects and frogs. Especially frogs. The frog prince. I thought a lot about frogs becoming human beings. I thought of myself as a frog. To me, frogs symbolized hope and inspiration. Somehow, they made me believe that I too could become greater than what I was. I went down to the creek often to look for frogs, and when I found them, I picked them up and stroked their backs, hoping some of their magic would rub off onto me.

Sometimes, kneeling on the ground, I would look up at the trees and the sky. When I was in the frog kingdom, it made me feel like it was my kingdom too, where even little girls could dream big. Nothing compared to the feeling of imagining me as a king. And in that little kingdom, there was a lot to do. I'd stroke the smooth surface of the pebbles, run my fingers through the slivers of grass, touch the rough bark on the branches of the trees, trace the veins in the leaves with my fingertips, and enjoy the water rushing through my hands.

I really loved nature. Oh, how I loved nature! It was possibly my saving grace. All those tactile sensations rippled through and became a part of me. It was a mystifying experience that seemed to tell me that there was more in store for me. The voices seemed to enjoy it too because they were always quieter when I was there, and it seemed to take the edge off my psychosis. The sound of the water, the antics of the insects and of the wind in the trees always seemed to ease my pain. Together they were like a soft hand caressing my back and a soft whisper calming my fears. Life wasn't all that bad when I was in the ravine.

I had discovered salamanders too—black ones with orange and red specks. They were so beautiful, and I liked the way they felt wet, like they were always ready to swim. Somehow, they instilled enough courage in me to go into the creek and play around. But sometimes when I was in the water, I saw the rocks on the bottom turn into the devil's claws. Or I'd see my mother looking up at me with a sly grin. But then, it wasn't really my mother's grin, it was the devil's. It was weird. It was a good thing that I learned about the devil in Sunday school because then I could see the devil instead of my mother. The devil was only masking her presence, but it was easier for me to accept him being evil than it was to believe my mother was. So my subconscious just turned her likeness into his, and that allowed me to avoid confronting the reality of my young life.

I was always careful when playing around the rocks. I'd try not to touch them with my hands, but it was hard to balance without them. Sometimes I'd slip and land hard on the rocks, and it would always terrify me by bringing on disturbing thoughts of something or somebody out to get me. I guess there was just no way to escape the madness. It was like living with an enemy every minute of every day. Still, nature had the power to ease my suffering. I would leave the water weighted down with drenched clothing and then have to hang around for hours for my clothes to dry. I couldn't go home with wet clothing. My mother didn't like to do laundry on her days off.

## THIRTY-ONE

# AUGUST 1988

Five weeks later, Paul got the job, and we moved into our new place in Hamilton, a run-down apartment building on Granville Street that was no better than the one my mother had when I was little. Every time I opened a kitchen cupboard door, cockroaches would scatter and find refuge elsewhere. It didn't matter how many times I bleached out the cupboards, I couldn't get rid of them. They multiplied at lightning speed.

Three floors below our apartment, a woman named Sandra lived in the corner unit. She had dark circles around her eyes, which reminded me of a raccoon. She was overweight and wore a baggy sweater to hide her bulging gut. She was a single parent with a six-year-old daughter named Ashley.

Sandra was collecting welfare but had a boyfriend on the side by the name of Bruce, not Ashley's father. He had a good job down at a factory where they made car parts. On the weekend, he'd come over and supply Sandra with beer and weed and bring gifts for her and Ashley.

I am not sure how Paul met Sandra, but they were hanging out with each more often than not. It never dawned on me that anything was going on between them. I just thought they were friends. Besides, I was too busy looking after Aaron to think about much else. By then Aaron was nearing his third birthday, and I was enjoying my time with him immensely. I would take him down to the store in the building's basement. As I held his hand on the way down, he'd ask me questions.

"Can I get candy, do they have the black ones I like, and can I pay the guy the money?"

Occasionally I'd go down to Sandra's with Paul, but I suspected she didn't want me there. Every time I said something, she'd roll her eyes, so I left them to their becr and weed and took Aaron home. Besides, I didn't want Aaron in that kind of environment. He deserved better, and so did I.

The next time I saw Jeff it was during a visit to Toronto see my mother—he and Sarah were over at the same time. We went dancing at a club, and afterwards Jeff and I took a long walk, talking about whatever crossed our minds. I found out later that Sarah had been calling him to let him know that I was in town.

Once I got back to the apartment, I carried on as best as I could. I was having a hard time staying focused on the present. I was being bombarded by intrusive thoughts and found it hard to get through the day. I was still thinking about suicide, but I had to ignore that thought because I had a child to care for. I didn't see any other option. In my mind, I made a list of things to do. It helped me to set small goals like bathing my son, feeding him, and playing with him. I cleaned the house with a pail of bleach, vinegar, and water. I scrubbed the walls and baseboards until my hands turned raw and the outer skin was peeling off.

Meanwhile, Paul went to work. When he got home, he'd shower, splash some cologne on his face and head straight down to Sandra's place. I didn't bother fighting with him about it because it was useless—I wouldn't be able to change his mind. But deep down, I really wished he would stay home with Aaron and me and try harder to be a better family man. The only thing he was interested in was doing drugs and getting drunk. By that time, he was snorting cocaine with his friend Donny, who he had known from way back when he was a teenager. Donny had two children, and the mother of his children was a stripper, so he wasn't hanging out with the best of people, the kind I wanted nothing to do with.

While bathing Aaron, a hand flashed through my mind, but I couldn't see who it belonged to. I tried to zoom in on it, but it escaped my awareness and other images took its place. They were moving way too fast for me to capture. I swear the images were coming at me as fast as a machine gun. Before I got lost in my little world, I grabbed Aaron, wrapped a towel around him, dried him off and then took him to the couch so he could watch a children's show. Then I went and grabbed him crackers from the cupboard and smeared them with peanut butter. Afterward, I brought him the plate. He seemed content as he sat there munching on the crackers.

I had no money, so I had to rely on Paul. And though he doled out only a small allowance, he always seemed to begrudge it, even though he was now making good money. His father had got him a union job working at a food warehouse that specialized in seafood and expensive cuts of meat. Even though Paul was set financially and always had a roll of twenties in his pocket, he'd steal lobsters and prime beef from work. Aaron didn't seem to mind eating lobster while he sat in front of the TV watching morning cartoons in his pyjamas.

One time Aaron had a sleepover over at a friend's house. Derek was only a little older and the son of Josh—one of Paul's drinking buddies from the building—and they lived on the ninth floor. Anyway, it meant that I had the night to myself, so I went with Paul down to Sandra's place for drinks. Sandra was talking to her friend on the phone and, without warning, told me that her friend Tammy wanted to talk to me. When I got on the phone, I could tell right off the bat she was looking for a fight. So I mentally slipped into a coat of armour, ready to battle. At first, I thought she was just joking with me, but then I realized she had it out for me. If I had known that, I would have not got on the phone. Instead, I would have left and gone home.

The next thing I knew, I heard a loud bang on the door. It was Tammy, and she was now right up in my face challenging me to a fight. I didn't know how to handle the situation. I was too drunk to protest or come up with a reasonable excuse to get out of it. So we ended up outside the apartment and in the hallway. I didn't even have time to block my body. Tammy was all over me, swinging left and right. She then pulled out a chunk of my hair. Out of the corner of my eye, I saw it lying on the floor. I tried to fight back, but I was too drunk. By the time the fight was over, I was black and blue. The thing that hurt the most about the fight was that Paul didn't lift a finger to help me. He just stood there and watched the whole thing go down.

The next morning, I lay in bed with a big bald spot on my head and my legs and arms had bruises all over. I could barely move without something hurting. While I lay there in bed, Paul took Aaron back up to Josh's place on the ninth floor.

In the afternoon, Sandra's boyfriend, Bruce, came over to see how I was doing. He told me if he had been there, the fight would have never happened. He couldn't believe that Paul had done nothing to protect me and watched as the mother of his child got beaten senseless. I didn't blame him for it, though. I knew I shouldn't have got drunk or gone down to Sandra's place based on how I already suspected she felt about me.

Soon after that, I found out that Paul and Sandra were more than friends. I ran into Bruce at the shopping mall, and he told me that Sandra dropped him and was seeing Paul on the sly. He didn't seem upset about it, but I sure was. I was fuming. I flew home on a broom. I put on my invisible witch hat and marched in the front door. I found Paul sitting on the couch with his feet up on the coffee table, eating a bag of chips. Before I could even get off my shoes, I started screaming at the top of my lungs.

"How could you do this to me and Aaron? What were you thinking? I'm leaving."

Paul denied he was cheating.

"Sandra and me are only friends. I don't like fat chicks. She's my drinking buddy."

After that, there was nowhere to go with the argument, so I dropped it. And he continued to go see Sandra at her place.

In November, I got into a heated argument with Paul over him never being home to help me with Aaron. He told me he was too busy with work and was too tired to do anything else. But it made me mad because he always had time for Sandra and his drinking buddy upstairs.

Eventually, the argument turned physical. In a rage, Paul grabbed the broom from the closet and started beating me with it. I ran out the front door to get away, but Paul caught up with me and continued to beat me. He hit me so hard that he broke the broom in half. A lady came out her door from across the hall to see what the commotion was all about. But as soon as she saw what was going on, she went back into her apartment and slammed the door shut.

The breaking of the broom ended the fight, so I went back inside and lay on the bed, hurt and crying. It's a good thing Aaron was upstairs playing with his friend. I wouldn't want him to see that kind of violence. By the time Aaron got back home, I put on a smile and pretended like nothing happened. I couldn't tell the truth to Aaron, so I lied and told him I had a nasty fall. But deep down inside, I knew I was a lousy mother for being with the wrong guy, even if he was Aaron's father.

From that day forward, I never questioned Paul about his whereabouts. I knew our relationship was over, but we stayed together.

Aaron was now three, and I figured I had done a good job of raising him so far. He didn't want for anything, except a father who was more active in his life. I wasn't sure how it was affecting him to have a father that wasn't around much. I had doubled up on giving as much love as my heart could give. Everywhere I went, he went. I loved taking him to the park or down to the candy store while he talked a mile a minute asking me all kinds of questions.

With Paul coming and going as he pleased, I was afraid to ask him for any money for the bare necessities, and Christmas was just around the corner. I didn't feel like sharing the holiday with him, so I called my mother and asked her if Aaron and I could stay with her for a few days. I told her I didn't have any money for Christmas presents. She told me no problem, that she'd put on a good Christmas for her grandson.

When the time came to go to my mother's, I packed a bag of clothes and headed down to the front lobby of the building and stood there with Aaron waiting for my mother to arrive. As she pulled up to the front of the building, I toyed with the idea that I was making the wrong decision, but by that time, I had had enough of Paul, the invisible man.

As soon as I got in my mother's door, I looked over at her Christmas tree. They were lots of gifts stacked under the tree. I turned to Aaron and told him, look lots of gifts for you. I watched him as he smiled at me. But it turned out all those gifts weren't for Aaron, and on Christmas morning I watched Aaron's excitement turn grey. I knew I shouldn't have believed my mother, that she would give my son a terrific Christmas or help me. There were four gifts for Aaron, two wooden puzzles, a children's book, and a toy truck.

I felt terrible, especially when I had told my son that Santa was bringing him splendid gifts for a special little boy. It was heart-wrenching to watch my son's excitement turn to disappointment. I could see it in his face, I had let him down. It was just one more little thing to add to my son's disappointments in life. I don't know why my mother couldn't see how much I loved my son—her grandchild—or how important it was to me she didn't let us down. But she did. I was mad, but I didn't let it show. I took my son to the side and whispered in his ear how sorry I was and promised him our Christmas would be so much better next year. Then I hugged him as tight as I could. Meanwhile, my mother hollered out that my son was a spoiled little brat, which made things worse. It was the first and last time I allowed her to hurt son. I couldn't wait to get out of her house.

In February of 1989, I found out I was pregnant again—my second pregnancy on the pill. Having an abortion didn't enter my mind. I felt far more confident in having another baby. The only thing I worried about was how a new baby would affect my relationship with Aaron. I had just spent three years with my son, and we were close, for I had spent every waking hour attending to his needs. There hadn't been a day gone by where I wasn't interacting and laughing at all his silly antics. He was my world. A new baby would mean adjustments for me and Aaron, but I knew, deep down, I would love the next child the same.

## THIRTY-TWO

# SEPTEMBER 1973

It was a Sunday, and I'd spent the whole day by myself in the ravine—I was nine years old. When I got back home, my mother was hurriedly preparing dinner and setting the table. I could hear the clanking of the plates and cutlery. We were having roast beef with mashed potatoes and gravy, and supper was almost ready. I was starving because I hadn't eaten all day.

I went down to the basement to sit on the floor and waited to get called upstairs. I fidgeted. I counted on my fingers. Then I moved my arms up and down to check to see if they were attached to my body. I noticed that my hair was sticky and there was mud under my fingernails from playing in the ravine. I wanted to go to the bathroom and clean up before dinner, but somehow, fear struck me. Instead, I just sat there waiting to be called to the table. As soon as I heard my mother's voice, I got up and slogged up the stairs to the kitchen. I imagined hands reaching out and trying to get me from between the steps. I just couldn't shake the feeling that someone was watching my every move, invading my every thought.

I ate dinner meticulously, closing my mouth properly, chewing methodically, and kept my eyes down as I pushed my food around on my plate between bites. I didn't want to look like a pig because my mother's hot gaze would have burned a hole in my skull, and I didn't want to trigger an episode of rage.

Suddenly, I laughed.

I had imagined a big fat pig on a platter in the middle of the table, and it was speaking in riddles. No one else was laughing. The dead man was looking at me, and both Martha and Sarah were staring down at their plates. I looked over at my mother and could see the anger on her face.

"Shut up," she said.

I got quiet, and I felt embarrassed for having brought attention to myself. My face turned red, my shoulders slumped, and my stomach ached. I wanted to get up and run from the table, but I knew better. I knew enough to pretend I was behaving myself.

When everyone else finished, I put all their leftovers on my plate and gulped it down. It wasn't really because I was hungry, though. It was really because I had such an empty void inside it didn't matter how much I ate, nothing filled it up. Afterward, I did the dishes because I had to clean the counters, and then went into the bathroom, where I stuck my fingers down my throat and brought my dinner up. It gave me a strange sense of control.

I watched TV for a while with the family, sitting on a La-Z-Boy chair and glancing back now and then at the dead man. I sensed his gaze while pretending to be watching

TV, and sometimes I caught him staring at me. I tried very hard to concentrate on enjoying the show, but when commercials came on, I was sure the man selling cars had a secret message for me, something about how the world was ending and I was the only one who could save it.

Eventually, I gathered enough courage to get up, leave the room, and go into the bathroom to brush my teeth. When I looked in the mirror, though, I saw the devil there. I panicked. I went into my bedroom and put my pyjamas on. I lay on the bed and stared at the ceiling. Then I got up to check the door to see if it was closed. I knew it was but felt compelled by some inexplicable force to recheck it. I had to check the window too, again and again. Until, hours later, I finally fell asleep.

In the morning I threw on some clothes, brushed my hair, and sat down at the kitchen table to eat breakfast before leaving for school. My mother had already left for work, but the dead man came into the kitchen and sat down beside me. He gave me the creeps. He rambled on in a language I did not understand. I had changed my words and reorganize my sentences to create distance between those and myself around me. It was a very effective way to avoid closeness. I made a game out of it by doing such things as replacing actual words with my own, like using salami for a salamander. I was the only one who understood it. It was beautifully crafted and designed to keep others out of my make-believe world. I felt very smart, like a genius. I imagined myself unique, magical, and destined to greatness beyond what a normal person could hope to achieve. I lost myself in the fantasy: A brilliant way to avoid the truth of abuse.

Just as I had become absorbed in the fantasy, I heard the dead man's voice.

"Come with me!"

It was loud and startled me. Breaking me out of my reverie and spinning me off balance. His hand on my shoulder.

…

The next thing I knew I was getting up off my knees. Then I was crossing the street to the school. Then I was sitting at my desk in front of the teacher. I looked at her with intensity and took great pains to observe her long checkered skirt, her crisp white blouse, her bright eyes, and lovely chestnut hair. For the first time, I was aware of what a fine creature she was. Then I was aware of a nasty bitter taste in my mouth. And I was sure that, somehow, she could sense it on me.

I raised my hand, and she allowed me to go to the washroom. I turned on the tap and quickly rinsed my mouth. I shut off the tap, grabbed some paper towels, dried my hands hurriedly and went into a stall. I didn't have to go to the bathroom. I just needed somewhere private to regain my composure, but the more I tried, the more panicky I became, thinking about how close I had come to being discovered for what I was. I imagined the police showing up, handcuffing me, and putting me into a small room at the police station before getting interrogated. Eventually, I went back to the classroom where I found it impossible to concentrate on anything for the rest of the day. I just fidgeted with my pencil between my fingers and daydreamed about rescuing the world.

From that day on, the dead man had complete control over me whenever my mother was at work, and he took full advantage whenever he felt like it. One night he took me into the bedroom and ordered me up on the bed with him where he told me to touch him. He could see I didn't want to, but he didn't care and because I wasn't in control of the situation physically. I imagined myself resisting him, used my mind to escape. I felt trapped, as though I was locked in a block of ice, frozen to the core, unable to move.

"Do it," he said, "or I'll get your mother to kill you!"

He even dared to close in on me when my mother was home. They planned it together when my sisters and little brother were in bed, and my mother was puttering around in the kitchen with those stupid fuzzy pink slippers on her feet. I could easily see her since the kitchen was only a few giant steps away from the bed. I could also see the damp rag she held in her hand. Sometimes when I saw it, that rag, something flashed through my mind, and it gave me an eerie feeling. I felt like something was trying to surface, but I had become good at burying memories. It was kind of like when you have a word on the tip of your tongue, but you can't quite speak it. I saw the dead man as a wild animal, a wolf stalking its prey, waiting patiently for just the right moment to pounce.

When I looked at him, one moment I'd see his face, and the next the head of a wolf. It helped, somewhat, to distract me from what was really going on, so I felt nothing inside. That was the good thing about it. I didn't have to feel a damned thing. Ever! My emotions had become flattened like the Prairies, without a ripple of emotion anywhere to rest the tired eye.

The dead man was always on the prowl. After a while, I pretended that I was a detective tiptoeing around looking for imaginary clues to imaginary crimes. I wore an imaginary straw hat with a Hawaiian shirt, green pants, and a thick gold leather belt that was all loaded up with what I perceived as tools of the trade such as water guns, boomerangs, slingshots, and ninja throwing stars. They weighed a ton, and my pants practically dropped to the floor from the weight. I'd spend hours searching painstakingly for clues, carefully avoiding the mines and grenades buried somewhere in the house. But I found nothing of interest or use, just dust balls and an assortment of broken crayons.

One night, I looked down at my hand, and it suddenly turned into an enormous claw. It scared me. It seemed whimsical the way things would appear one minute and then gone the next, and yet when these hallucinations appeared they were so damned real—and whenever the dead man grabbed my hand, they flowered and withered so fast in my mind that I wasn't able to focus on anything in particular. I didn't want to, anyway.

One time, I found a dollar bill on the school grounds. I picked it up and ran home excitedly, but by the time I got home, the bill had mysteriously disappeared from my hand. My dirty little hand was playing tricks on me again. I thought that maybe I possessed magical powers of some kind and could turn things into whatever I fancied. Then I remembered the dead man pressing the dollar into my hand that morning, and my stomach clenched, and I felt a wave of shame and confusion come over me.

By that time, I had utterly lost touch with reality. And it was desperately hard to distinguish between what was going on in my head and was happening around me on a daily basis.

For instance, one time I was home alone (where my sisters and brother were, I don't know) and I was sitting on the couch in the living room, observing the front door, when someone knocked. I crawled on my hands and knees across the old green carpet, edged my way across the vinyl floor in the foyer, and reached up and opened the mail slot to see who was there. I peered out cautiously and saw a woman dressed in black. She had jet-black hair, and when she smiled, she showed yellow fangs and two gold caps on her front teeth. It startled me. I even thought I saw a hatchet in her hand. It was a long time before I got up and ran to the phone. I called the number my mother had left on the kitchen counter and told her to hurry home because there was a sinister looking woman in black outside trying to break into our house. She just laughed, said she would be home shortly, and slammed the phone down.

Shortly afterward, she arrived with the dead man. He walked hurriedly around the house, poker-faced, and said nothing. He appeared sharply dressed in brown slacks and a V-necked yellow sweater and was very careful not to get mud on his shoes. As I watched, he turned into a circus clown.

My mother was furious with me for telling such a whopper of a lie, but to me, it wasn't a lie. To me it was very real. She was furious with me for acting so crazy. Eventually, they determined that it was my fault because there was no lady in black outside the house, and so they went back to whatever they were doing. I waved goodbye, then watched my arm descend slowly to my side. I stood on the front porch and watched the car until it was out of sight, then went into the house and locked the door.

I ran through the kitchen and slid in my socks—that was fun—and checked that the back door was locked. Then I ran and slid back and checked the front door again even though I knew I'd locked it when they left. Then I checked them again about ten minutes later. Then I went into my mother's room, the only room that couldn't be closed because it didn't have a door and checked the wardrobe. I ran my fingers through my mother's clothes, but not the dead man's because I didn't want him in my thoughts. Touching my mother's clothes somehow made me feel like she loved me. I hated her for rejecting me, yet I still longed for some kind of bond between us. The feel and smell of her clothes when she wasn't in them gave me some relief in not feeling so alone.

I went into the wardrobe lots of times when she wasn't home and put on her nylons and bra and her prettiest dresses. I'd look down the side of my leg, just like I'd seen her do, and imagined I was just as irresistible. I enjoyed looking at myself in her full-length mirror, then—with the music down low—I would go out into the living room and dance with the curtains closed. Sometimes, I'd interrupt my reverie to make sure the door was locked and sometimes even to put a chair up against it for extra security.

Dancing was one of the few times I could feel something. I pretended I was someone else, a famous ballerina or movie star. The constant whirling around settled my nerves. I had long since discovered a special spot inside of myself where I could be anyone I wished, and it was like flying high against the wind. Nothing could hurt me there, nothing could touch me. It was my special place, a place in my head where neither my mother nor the dead man could exist. It was much the same feeling of freedom that I had when I went down to the ravine, only there was music.

I also had the same feeling when I prayed in the early morning hours, when there was just the tiniest light coming from the moon and the stars. In all that silence—well, except for the voices in my head—I felt united with something much larger than me. I knew there was hope out there in a variety of different places, so I still believed there was still hope for me. I even imagined that I was God's assistant, the Chosen One, on a mission to rescue the world. Everything I had experienced was merely a test to challenge my capacity for faith. It just had to be the reason for all my suffering!

## Thirty-three

# August 1989

It was in the second week of August when my water broke. I was walking from the living room to the kitchen when I felt the splash in my underwear. I called my doctor and was told to go to the hospital immediately, so I did. After an examination, the nurse told me that the doctor was going to induce labour because nothing was really happening. Within hours, I was almost ready for delivery.

In the meantime, Paul called my mother to tell her I was in labour. The next thing I knew, my mother, Martha, and Paul were in the delivery room with me. I didn't want them there—I wanted them to wait in the waiting room—but I was too afraid to protest or make any waves. Martha was helping me regulate my breathing. My mother and Paul were standing at the side of my bed, watching. I don't know why, but the doctor had to use forceps to get the baby out. I think it was because I had no strength to do it myself.

When the doctor called out that the baby was coming, my family raced to the end of the bed. At that moment, shame took a hold of me and I couldn't shake the feeling. I was mad too because I had not given them permission to watch. I didn't want them to see my private parts. It felt like they were invading my privacy, as if I were on an enormous TV screen for everyone to get a close-up look. I'd rather being doing somersaults for them. To get rid of the uncomfortable situation, I turned my attention to Paul, who looked like he was going to pass out. His face was all white. I don't even know why he was there in the first place since he had so little to do with his first child. I suspected it was for show, the pretense of being a father.

My second child was born at ten fifty in the evening just like her brother. She weighed six pounds, seven ounces, and I named her April. I'd asked Paul what he wanted to call his daughter, and he said it didn't matter.

April was perfect. She was one hundred percent healthy. She looked like her brother and had the same dimple in her chin as her father. I swear, when I first saw her, she ignited something magical in me. It was pure love at first sight. She made me smile. She was my little shining star. Her hair was orange-red, and she had big brown eyes that held the same innocence all babies do.

A couple of days later, the doctor came in to see me, and I told him to tie my tubes. For a good thirty minutes he argued with me, telling me I was only in my twenties and might want to have more children later. I assured him I didn't and that, if he didn't do it, I wouldn't leave the hospital. Finally, he bent to my wishes, and I had my tubes tied. No more kids for me.

It was a breeze looking after April. She was sleeping throughout the night at two months old and only waking up to get breastfed and to have her diaper changed. Sometimes I didn't think I had enough breast milk because she never seemed satisfied, so I started her on pablum at three months old, and it seems to quench her appetite. She drank less breast milk, but I knew she was at least full from the pablum.

Our second baby tore Paul and me completely apart. The days of us talking about anything were long gone. He had lost all interest in me. He didn't touch me anymore. He said my breasts were flat like pancakes and didn't stand up anymore. Of course, they didn't, I'd had two kids.

One morning, shortly after April turned one, I woke up thinking about leaving Paul. I couldn't get the thought out of my mind, so I obsessed about it throughout the day. The next day, I called Susan and told her I had to get out. She told me she didn't blame me because she had seen her stepson in action, not taking any responsibility for his family. She whole-heartedly agreed and said that Paul's father was washing his hands of his son for his behaviour.

I grabbed a babysitter and headed down to the office for low-income housing and filled out an application to get a place. The office clerk helped me fill out the part where I needed urgent help. In October, I got a call from housing that they had a three-bedroom townhouse for me near Hamilton General Hospital. Paul's parents helped with the move. I had little, but David and Susan helped me set up my new home. It was shortly after that that Paul moved in with Sandra. It wasn't a surprise to me. At least, he wouldn't be bothering me.

I went on welfare. Paul wouldn't give me a dime, so social services told me I had to take him to court to get child support, so I got myself a lawyer through legal-aid and got the process going—at which point I didn't have to do anything except sign some forms. Paul had to pay two hundred dollars a month in support. I didn't see any of the money directly, for it went straight to family maintenance, a branch of the government that took care of men who refused to pay child support. Then the money went directly to social services. I got full custody of the children, but the judge granted Paul visiting rights. He was to take them every second weekend.

The townhouse near the hospital was only a temporary place to live, however; and in November, I moved to a new three-bedroom apartment on Barton Street just down the street from the Hamilton Public Library. The original purpose of the building was to provide housing for paraplegics. They designed the apartments with wide hallways and low kitchen countertops. It was a beautiful apartment with new shiny appliances and spacious bedrooms. It was a tremendous change from living in shit holes. I couldn't have been happier.

As Christmas 1990 approached, I took the twelve-hundred dollars I got back from my tax return and spent every penny on my kids. Back then, I could claim my taxes before Christmas. The government even allowed low-income families to claim a month's worth of rent. My rent was less than three hundred, so to me it was like getting free money. It was free money because I didn't work. My monthly welfare check was for a thousand dollars, and the government also gave me a child tax benefit. To save money, I'd bake and cook everything from scratch. I had learned to stretch a dollar. I tried to cut every expense down to a minimum because my hydro bill was outrageous. Sometimes it would come in at a hundred and fifty dollars.

For Christmas, I took every dime I had and splurged it on my kids. I bought April stuffed animals, clothes and toys, anything I could think of that little girls liked. I bought Aaron over twenty Ninja Turtle action figures—the kind he'd spend hours playing with in make-believe play. I'd also got him the vehicles, buses, weaponry, most stuff that came in the set. I carefully wrapped them and piled them high in the back of the hall closet.

A few days later, I heard a noise coming from the closet, the sound of the crinkling of paper. When I got up to go check what the noise was, I discovered Aaron in the closet. I tried to open the door, but Aaron had lodged the gifts in front of the door so I couldn't get in. I was yelling for him to open the door and come out. When I finally got in, all the gifts were open. And I was mad, but I didn't stay mad long after I looked at my son's face, his fear that he was in big trouble.

I sent him to his room so I could calm down, and when I did, I went and spoke to him about the incident. He said he was sorry, and he told me he wouldn't do it again, and that was the end of that. I hugged him and he went off and played with the toys he already had. I couldn't blame him since I had ripped apart all my gifts as a kid.

At sixteen months old, April would whizz around in her floor walker. I had to strap her in tight so she wouldn't climb out. With her feet she'd push the floor and go everywhere she could go. She made me laugh. Her hair was bright, orangey red and sticking straight up like static had attacked it.

Every time my mother visited, she'd bring me a stupid porcelain doll, which I put on top of my bedroom dresser. I had never mentioned liking them, so I did not understand why she had brought them for me. I showed my appreciation by smiling and wrapping my arms around her while telling her I loved her. Then she'd grill me about being a lucky bitch for getting the doll.

I don't know how many times I had to hear her talk about how, when she was young, she got nothing from her mother. It infuriated me that my mother could just not give me anything without rubbing it in. Instead of voicing it, I just gave in and told her thanks, I really liked it. That was her cue to bring me another doll every time she came around. Eventually I had seven of them lined up in a row on the dresser. It never failed, every time she visited me there was some price to pay, usually a bit of my self-worth and dignity. I thought the only reason she came to visit me was to dig into me, pointing out all my flaws, one-upping me every chance she got. It wasn't like she was coming to see her grandchildren because paid no attention to them. She never offered to take them for the night or on an outing—not that I would have let her. I didn't know why, at the time, but I knew it was best that I not leave my children alone with her, which made it hard for me to even go to the washroom. I was just waiting for her to say one mean thing to them so I could throw her out. It was such a relief when she had to go home.

I loved being a mother. I loved the times when Aaron would wake me up in the middle of night, come to my room and complain about not being able to sleep. I would tuck him under the blankets then kiss his forehead, and off he would go back to sleep. First thing in the morning, he'd go grab a few of his Ninja Turtle action figures, spread them out on the bed, and one by one he would tell me all about them.

"Mom, they fight bad guys. They got hit by a can of ooze and mutated. Do you know all their names, have you heard of Splinter the rat?"

Of course I had, but I'd have him tell me more. As I listened to Aaron, April would wake up, and I would go down to the bedroom and picked her up out of her crib and change her diaper and grab her blanket and bring her in bed with Aaron and me. I pulled down my pajama top and breastfeed her while Aaron talked more about the Ninja Turtles. Then I'd take April to the living room, lay her on her blanket with a few toys, and get Aaron's cereal from the cupboard. I would watch him at the kitchen table dangling one of Ninja Turtles over the side.

"Don't jump," he'd yelled. "Watch out."

Once I had a shower, I'd get the kids dressed and pack a few snacks in the stroller before heading out. But before doing so, I'd checked the windows to see if I had locked them. I also unplugged the toaster and other electrical gadgets I thought could start a fire. Sometimes I'd get down to the elevator and then need turn back because I couldn't remember if I had shut everything off or even if I had locked the balcony door.

There were always free things to do in the city. If I wasn't at the park with my kids, I'd be attending an outdoor music concert or at the library in the children's section. There was always something going on around town for families. Then when we got back home, Aaron would go to his toys or sit down at the table colouring on paper.

My children were my salvation. They were the moon, the stars, and the entire galaxy to me. If it weren't for them, I'd probably be dead. I considered it a privilege and an honour to have these two beautiful children in life—till death do us part. As I went in and out of my psychosis, I hid it from my children. They couldn't see it because it was invisible. I would excessively clean while letting my sickness run wild, one step from a coffin.

There was a lady named Gloria who had an office up on the fifth floor in my apartment building. Some not-for-profit organization ran it, and Gloria was to oversee everything. There were nurses and doctors coming and going throughout the day. I was taking out my garbage one day and ran into her in hallway.

"How's it going in the apartment, Tracey?" she asked.

"Good," I said. "Things are fine. I mean, it's hard, the kids and all, but it's good. Great actually."

As I reached the door, she called back to me.

"Why don't you come up to the office on the fifth floor. I have some donated items, and if you're interested you can have first dibs."

"Thanks," I said. "I will."

A few days later, I put April in her baby sling and took Aaron by the hand and we all went up to her office. As soon as I walked in, she was all smiles. She grabbed her keys off her desk and told me to follow her. She took me down to the basement and unlocked a door. Inside there were things to furnish an entire apartment. She was storing them for the tenants in need. She told me to pick out what I wanted, so I picked out a couch, end tables, cutlery and some sheets and blankets. Then she told me to take the single bed for when my daughter got older. She would have the stuff delivered to my place tomorrow. As we went back upstairs, I thanked her repeatedly. She was my angel in disguise.

The best thing about it was Gloria genuinely cared for me. When she had time, she'd come down to place with leftover sandwiches and desserts from an office meeting? And every time she ran into me in the hallways, she'd stop and talk to me. It was nice to have someone on my side, someone concerned about the well-being of my children and me. It wasn't long after that, that she would stop by my place for a visit. Sometimes she'd stay over an hour just asking me how I was making out. I had nothing to complain about because she was watching over me.

Anyway, the following afternoon, the stuff arrived. I threw the sheets and blankets in the wash. I had a washer and dryer at the end of the hall in a closet. My favourite things were clean sheets and comfortable pyjamas. If I had my way, I'd live in my nightwear. I loved the times when Aaron and April were on my bed with me. My little family of three!

## THIRTY-FOUR

# OCTOBER 1973

It was a Monday morning, which meant I had to go to school again, so I put on my ugly brown and blue checkered dress that was two sizes too big and which hung down to my bony knees. Then I went down to the kitchen where my mother was sitting at the kitchen table drinking a fresh cup of coffee. I smelled her perfume in the air. As usual, it was too strong. She bent down to fix a hole in her nylon. The hole was near her big toe, so she just turned the nylon around so the hole would be on the bottom instead. If it was somewhere else, she used nail polish to patch it up. That day she wore her basic black dress with accessories artfully applied for a fresh look. She liked black because it made her look slimmer and believed that, if it hadn't been for having children, she'd still be the bomb. She was nearing her forties and starting to show her age, but when she was all dolled up, she looked younger. Mostly. She had little bulges around her waistline, so she camouflaged them by wearing looser clothing, but she didn't like it because they just made her feel "like an old hag."

I grabbed my lunch from the refrigerator and slammed the door on my way out, as I usually did when I went to school. I went down two steps, sat down, and tied my shoes. Halfway across the road, I realized I had forgotten to do my hair and brush my teeth. I went back into the bathroom trying very hard not to touch the walls because I knew my mother checked them every day for smudges. A single smudge would send her to her room where she would sulk like a spoiled brat. Those were peaceful times for us. For me, it meant freedom. At least when she was in her room, there were no restrictions, no rules. But then again it meant the same for the dead man who was always lurking around.

The school was somewhat like living in a sardine can, much too close for comfort. I would have protested, but I feared my mother would slap me. She accompanied me to school—in my head—and was constantly monitoring me, dressed in her tight little black dress and holding a butcher knife at her side.

And then there were the voices:

*I wish you were dead... I don't want you... Nobody wants you... You might as well kill yourself...*

The voices would laugh too, and the laughter sounded a lot like my mother's, the one that sent cold chills up and down my spine.

I'd get to school about seven thirty in the morning and play ball and jump rope with the other kids. I had lots of fun until someone became interested enough in me to ask my name or what class I was in. I hated talking to anyone about myself because I was different, and I didn't want anybody to know me. It set off the voices, and they immediately became very abusive. Even my voice bothered me; it sometimes startled me. I would get all flustered then and walk away saying nothing at all. They probably just thought I was shy. They probably did not understand I'd lost my mind.

But I know my mother and the dead man did.

When bell rang for recess, instead of racing down the corridor and outside with the rest of the kids, I stayed back, waited for a few minutes, and then hid in the girls' bathroom. When the coast was clear, I came out and sat on the wooden bench that was closest to my classroom. I looked up at all the bare brass hooks now free of all those coats and jackets. I loved the shape of them. They reminded me of little golden seahorses lined up and waiting for the kids to come back. Soon bored with that, I got up and walked up and down the halls. I turned my shirt collar up and tilted my head down like a spy. Occasionally, a kid would come in for a drink of water, but I didn't speak to them nor they to me.

There was a teacher in the hall just outside the entrance to the library, and he casually walked towards me. He licked his index finger, turned a page in the very heavy book he was carrying, and continued to read. I half-closed my eyes. So he went all fuzzy looking, and I thought he looked like a penguin with a giant beak of a nose, pinhole eyes, and arms unusually long for his height. He was going bald, and it was obvious he had combed his hair carefully to hide the fact, but it didn't work. I somehow felt tiny and young compared to him. And, strangely, I felt the way *he* looked.

He stopped in front of me without looking up from his book.

"Why aren't you outside?"

"Sick," I said quietly.

I put my hand on my stomach, groaned a little and held my breath until my face turned red. It worked like a charm most of the time, but this time I saw him turn into a beast of a woman with oversized breasts that I could see easily through her transparent dress. Yet, she had no face. No distinguishable features. It reminded me of the headless horseman from a black and white movie a long time ago. The string of bright white beads around her neck somehow made me feel demoralized.

*"You lazy bitch, get out!"* she screamed.

But I just stood there imagining her panties with too much starch like the dead man's shirts after my mother finished with them. Like the beads, her white gloves seemed to glow, and she used them to run a pointy finger across the clean benches, turning them black and as thick as asphalt. I turned away from her and felt my body seeping into the bench, and just when I thought she was gone, she spoke again.

*"You dirty little girl. Nobody wants you. Die you, bitch!"*

I clenched my fists until my knuckles turned white. Then I started swearing and jumping up and down like a maniac. I banged my head on the wall to stop the evil pictures that were flashing at me in my mind.

"Please, God, help me!" I chanted, repeating it again and again. "Please, God, help me! Please, God, help me!"

He didn't help, nor did I see an angel, but it made me feel calmer. Then I saw my mother sprawled out on the floor in the corridor, spread-eagled, and with her head crushed in like a pineapple. I wanted to cry, to scream, to get up and run away. But I just sat still.

Then the bell rang. Recess was over. And I suddenly realized that both the real teacher and the imaginary one were gone as though they'd never been.

The next day I did the same thing on the same bench, only this time, when the coast was clear, I rummaged through all the kids' lunch bags. They had names on them, some written in pencil and others written boldly in black magic markers. I took the homemade chocolate chip cookies, jellyrolls, candies, and cans of pop, but never the sandwiches or anything that would have been good for me. I hid the food under my clothes and put the small candies in my pockets. Then I went into the farthest stall in the girls' washroom, crouched on the toilet bowl so that someone coming in couldn't even see my feet, and proceeded to eat all the goodies. When I finished, I wiped the evidence from my mouth and jumped down. On my way out, I stuck my hand in the doorjamb and then closed the door on it. Just like all the other times, people came running to my rescue when I screamed in pain. But, that day, I wanted to bleed to death. I even imagined that I could suck out all the evil with a straw and spit it out onto the floor.

The following week, during his morning announcements, the principal told everyone that lunches had disappeared from the benches. I sat up suddenly in my chair and my face turned fire-engine red. My knees shook, and I knew my classmates were whispering among themselves as they speculated on who the culprit might be.

There were several suspects, but I knew the truth. I was the real culprit. In shame, I put my head on my desk and covered my ears with my hands. I hoped that by some miracle they wouldn't even notice me. I was afraid they could read my mind and would know the truth by looking at me. Then the voices in my head started getting louder and louder until they drowned out everything else. They told me I was rotten to the core and mocked me for being born.

Feeling the urge to run—but not being able to do so—I *imagined* running for the door and finding it locked. I panicked. I had to do something. So I focused my attention on the ridge below the blackboard where the white chalk was kept and watched it magically turn into a wand. I used my telekinetic powers to bring it to me and then used it to tap myself on the head and make me disappear. That was all there was to it. I was no longer a suspect!

Soon I started bullying other kids by hitting, spitting, and calling them names. Some of them would squeal on me to the teacher on recess duty, but I'd deny everything. The teacher made me stand with my face to the wall, anyway, but it was close to the entrance where the grade four kids came in and out, and when the teacher wasn't looking, I'd seek the kid who snitched on me and give them the stink eye. It was all I could do in retaliation, but I found solace in fantasies of revenge on the kids I blamed for my miserable existence.

One day after school, I saw a disabled girl walking alone. I started calling her a slut and pushed her into the bushes—her weakness reminded me of myself, and it felt good to punish her for it. But then she started shaking all over, and her eyes rolled back in her head. I was so scared I ran home as fast as I could, slammed the door behind me, leaned against it, and waited for my heart to slow down. Then I sat on the couch where I tried to melt into the furniture.

Soon the girl's mother was at our house. At first, she started hollering at me about what I'd done to her daughter, and then she lectured me on the dangers of pushing people around. Finally, she made me apologize. I put on my best sad face and complied. But I did not feel empathy. How could I feel empathy when I had no interest in people? I only liked objects.

I learned my lesson, though. I never wanted to do that again. I was too afraid of getting caught. Too afraid someone might learn about my secrets—and my secrets had to be protected at all costs. So from that day forward, whenever I picked a fight with someone, I used only powder puff punches that landed ever so gently on their cheeks. And when I got them in a neck hold, I never squeezed tight.

Even still, I developed a reputation for kicking ass. A boy named Patrick invited me to a boxing match down in the ravine where they often went to play after school. Patrick had blonde hair and blue eyes and was a nerd. But since he was the first boy interested in me, I had a crush on him. I started fantasizing about dressing up in one of my mother's dresses and going out on my first date. I couldn't wait to slip into a pair of my mother's nylons when I got home.

So every day for weeks, at about four, I met Patrick in the ravine with all the other kids. My fans. It was kind of like trying out for the Olympics. For half an hour, Patrick worked on helping me carve out my personal path towards being a prizefighter. It was ludicrous considering that I was only in Grade 5 and weighed less than seventy pounds.

But he had faith in me.

"You're a natural," he'd say. "A great left hook. I'm your coach."

He showed me how to shuffle my feet, jab, and poke, and smoke out my opponent, just in fun. Eventually, some of the most popular girls from school appeared on the side of the hill to watch. They wore the newest fashions, the latest hairstyles, and spoke a cool language. I'd heard nothing like it. I loved it. They were the cool kids, and they came to see me fight.

They wanted to change me! They wanted to fight me! They wanted to be friends!

I can't remember their names or their faces—so I guess they weren't *that* popular—but it meant the world to me that they invited me to their homes after school. At last, I had real friends. The rush of it all quickly disappeared, though, when I saw their bedrooms. Their bedrooms looked liked little castles made for princesses, and it made me feel like a peasant. But they insisted on my letting them put makeup on me, and that was okay for a while because it made me look beautiful on the outside just like them, but on the inside, I still felt ugly. Glamour just wasn't me. I was a plain Jane. I was a tomboy. I was more interested in playing sports or challenging people to an arm wrestle. I really wasn't one to put on makeup, play with dolls, or talk about boys.

It was an opportunity, though, to be in with the cool kids, even though I knew it would not last long because I was afraid they would eventually find out I was a fraud. As soon as they got a look at my bedroom, they would know right away. It was better that I reject them first. It would lessen the sting for me. Besides, they were boring. So I went back to my kind, the kids from the housing project where I belonged and had nothing to do anymore with the cool kids in school. That's how I gained the reputation of a snob.

In the project, I hung out with a girl who had a terrible reputation for stealing and having sex with both boys and girls. Her name was Kim, and she had red hair and freckles like me, except her freckles were orange, and mine were brown. She was a skinny little runt like me, yet tough like a man fresh out of jail. We'd walk around the complex, mostly out of boredom, and put eggs on Prestons' doorknob, knock, and then run away. When crazy old man Preston answered the door the eggs would break at his feet.

"You little bitches!"

In the shadows, we laughed like hyenas. Eventually growing tired of our silly little game, we found some kids who were making forts out of blankets in their backyards. I remember a boy named Ralph.

The kids called him a pervert because he would show his penis to anyone who paid him any attention, except for adults. Sometimes he'd masturbate in front of me and ask me to touch him, but I just turned away in embarrassment. He never got into trouble for it because his parents didn't care where he was or what he was doing. They were too busy with their boozing buddies. He had orange hair that looked like it was on fire because he was growing an afro and never combed it. I remember him always missing school because of head lice.

Then, I met Michael. Although I had seen him rarely around the project, Kim officially introduced us one weekend. He had strawberry blonde hair and blue eyes. I liked blue eyes and light-colored hair because they seemed angelic. I developed an overwhelming crush on him that lasted for years. I hid behind the bushes across from his house, twisted my fingers in circles, put them up to my eyes as though they were binoculars, and watch him. I fantasized about having a romantic relationship with him. Sometimes I fantasized about him lying on his bed thinking about me, just like I would lie on my bed thinking about him. Other times, I would concentrate hard to put thoughts into his head and believed that I could get mental messages from him, if he ever sent them. But when I saw him come out of his house, I did not make contact.

At school, I followed him around like a little lost dog. He caught me following him twice and told me to fuck off. The rejection only got me to repeat the whole thing over again, hoping and praying that it would eventually turn out all right. The funny thing about it was that the only thing I really knew about him was his name and where he lived.

One time, a few of us kids went down to the ravine where there was a vast hole in the ground. We called it Dead Man's Hole. Supposedly, someone had buried a 500-pound man there, and no one had bothered to fill up the hole. We went down there to make out. Well, I didn't because I felt terrified of having contact with anyone, especially boys. It made me think of the dead man's tongue. I'd usually end up climbing a tree, all the way to the top. And dream about kissing Michael (*without* any tongue).

I'd take a stick with me just in case a crow tried to attack me while I was up there. Sometimes, on Friday nights, I'd watch horror movies, the kind where the Devil lives inside a kid and the kid has big black dogs watching over him in case someone tries to harm him. The kid would someday take over the world. I imagined dogs hiding behind trees while foaming at the mouth. That's why I was afraid of big black dogs.

I felt like I was the kid in the movie because evil was alive inside of me too. And the dead man was the Devil in disguise, and he had been inside of me. I knew the crows were watching me. I could hear them squawking and talking in gibberish to each other about how they were going to take over my mind.

When I felt I was getting too carried away with that kind of thinking, I'd snap the rubber band I had on my wrist. It helped to snap me back to reality. Well, a little at least.

"Tracey, you coming down?"

A vague voice from the ground.

I came slowly down the tree, digging my nails in, and once I made it to the bottom, I pretended like I was normal again. But I bet some of them wondered why I didn't want to kiss boys.

Between hanging out with my friends and going to school, I started playing sports, made the school soccer team, and became their top player. When I ran, it felt like I had tapped into some special power, a power that I alone had discovered. My heart was full, and it beat in rhythm with all that was natural. I had discovered something inside me. It made me believe there just might be hope for me.

The only thing that bothered me about sports was running around in shorts and a T-shirt. I felt uncomfortable with my bare legs exposed. Also, I didn't like anyone behind me because of... the dead man, and so I'd run fast whenever I got the ball, thinking the faster I ran, the farther I would be from sight, and the less likely anyone could see my legs. It turned out that I was very athletic, and I loved it. It was something I could control. The voices in my head, though didn't like it.

*You're a stupid slut. Whore. Kill yourself, you bitch!*

They didn't like it when I became distracted by things I liked, like playing sports. The idea of teammates. It was as though my mother and the dead man were warning me not to tell anybody about the secrets.

Although I was doing well on the soccer field, my behaviour in the classroom got worse. I repeatedly disrupted the class by throwing school supplies around and speaking out when the teacher was in the middle of a lesson. The teacher was always putting her finger to her mouth to shush me, or she would tell me to go stand out in the hallway. Standing in the hallway wasn't a punishment, though, because I could go through everyone's bags for food and check coat pockets for change.

I knew my music teacher didn't like me because she would look at me a certain way that meant I had to stand in the corner right away. I'd stand there, arms at my sides, and try hard to stay still. When I figured she wasn't looking, I sometimes turned around to admire her long silky legs, streaked blonde hair, striking features, and trim figure. I developed a crush on her. I needed a replacement for my mother and missed having a bond with the same sex and mixed up my burgeoning sexual feelings with the emotional deficits in my life. The teacher even dressed like my mother—nylons with prints of little diamonds, short burgundy skirt, and a low-cut blouse. It wasn't a lesbian attraction. I just so needed attention, whether positive or negative, from a mother figure, and the need was almost overpowering.

Then there was my science teacher, Mr. Gilbert, who seemed like a hundred years old to me because of his grey hair. He wore blue polyester pants, heavy sweaters, and hush puppies that were as old as he was. But I liked him a lot. He was kind to me. He gave me better marks than I deserved and always made excuses for my strange behaviour, like when I threw erasers across the room or flopped across my desk like a dead fish out of the water. He would try to calm me down by massaging my back. It wasn't sexual. Just a nice gentle touch to let me know somebody cared. I basked in that small show of affection. I wanted to cry, to let it all out, but I didn't know how.

Sometimes, however, I was too much even for Mr. Gilbert, and he would tell me to go sit quietly in the hallway and that if I caused any more trouble, he would have to send me to the principal's office, which is where I usually ended up anyway.

One time I went to the principal's office and sat where I was told. Then I put my foot upon his desk like I was a big shot. He ignored my cheekiness and started asking far too many questions.

"What does your mother do?" –and– "Does your daddy live at home?" –and– "Is anyone hurting you at home?" –and– "Are any the kids here at school picking on you?"

I didn't understand what he was talking about, and I didn't like the way he looked at me so intensely. Didn't he know I was the detective? I was the one who should've been asking the questions.

Since I couldn't remember anything about my family— only that I had one—his questions were useless, and I thought he was the crazy one. I noticed how clean his face was and how perfect it appeared to be. It reminded me of the moon. He seemed innocent enough, but I knew that perfect people were probably out to get me. He even offered me half of his sandwich, but I turned it down. He was getting too close to me.

But in my usual chatty mood, I rambled on about my family as if they were saints.

"My mother works for the government, and she can't talk about it because it is dirty, and she bakes cookies with sparkles on top on the weekends. Daddy cuts the lawn, builds pretty houses, does animal tricks, and digs gigantic holes. My baby sister has new dresses. My older sister babysits."

I think he knew I was lying, but he played along. I would have preferred detention instead of him dancing around me like I was made of glass. After what seemed forever, he said he had to make his rounds and that I could sit quietly at his desk and do the work that Mr. Gilbert had sent down for me. As soon as he left, I opened his desk drawer and stole his elastic bands. I put them in my pocket and then tried to do my math. I didn't understand it, so I just penciled in some wild numbers and hoped I'd get away with it.

Strangely, no one challenged my work even once. On all my report cards there was maybe one C, and the rest were F's, but no one ever said anything. I knew I'd be in big trouble if my mother saw all those F's, so I changed the letters to A's and B's by forging the teacher's handwriting. I didn't have to worry about getting caught because my mother never went to the school, nor did she answer the teachers' calls. When they caught her off guard by calling unexpectedly, she'd just say she was too busy to talk.

Amazing how easy it is to get away with stuff when parents don't care.

# THIRTY-FIVE

# JULY 1991

Now that my place on Barton Street was furnished—thanks to Gloria—I felt as though I could exhale and start building a life. The following Friday, I packed a duffel bag of clothes up for Aaron and April. They were going to their dad's house for the weekend, and he was picking them up at six o'clock in the evening. When the buzzer rang, I felt excited. The week had worn me out, so I was looking forward to having a little downtime. I was grateful that Paul came every other weekend to get his kids.

Once the kids were gone with their father, I called Jeff. I'd told him I would. He had an eight-year-old daughter with his ex-wife, and he had the weekend off too. I didn't get any details of why his wife had divorced him. The only thing he said about her was that she was "a killjoy and a materialistic bitch." Despite his negative feelings for his ex, he bragged relentlessly about his daughter.

"She's beautiful," he'd say. "My Bella, my angel."

I expected to find the perfect little girl when I would get the chance to meet her.

Saturday morning, Jeff came by my place to pick me up to go to his friend Malcolm's house for dinner. I wasn't sure what to wear, so Jeff encouraged me to call Malcolm's wife, Angie, to ask her what I should wear. She told me she was wearing a dress, so that's what I would do. I only had a few dresses. I wore my pink and white leopard print one. It hung just below my knees. I threw on some eyeliner, mascara, and pink lipstick to match my dress, and then I was ready to go.

When I got there, Angie was wearing a long sparkly gown. Compared to her dress, mine looked like something you'd wear in a nightclub. I felt out of place from the get-go. I tried to mingle, but I had nothing in common with the other people. Most of them worked in middle management, and here I was a single mom on welfare. I stayed to the side and watched Jeff throwing stardust in everyone eyes while he danced sexy in a sleazy way. I was glad when it was over and couldn't wait to get home.

As soon as we walked in my front door, Jeff was all over me like an octopus with twenty tentacles. I kept pushing his hands away like I was a kung-fu master. I finally agreed that I would kiss him. When we locked lips, it felt like my mouth my on fire. The chemistry was unreal. The kiss was soft and sensuous, with just the right amount of pressure on my mouth. Then I pushed him back and then grabbed a couple of blankets out of the closet and put them on the couch for him. I said goodnight and walked to my bedroom and closed the door. I jumped in bed, rolled over on my back, and hung onto that one big kiss in my mind until I fell asleep.

In the morning, I awoke to drool on my pillow and the smell of bacon and eggs in the air. Before I had even got up, Jeff had driven to the grocery store to get breakfast. As I sat there eating, I watched Jeff clean up the kitchen. It was nice having a man in my home and doing things for me, even though he came off a little desperate and eager to please. As soon as he finished the dishes, he asked if he could take a quick shower before he left.

"Sure, of course."

When I heard the shower turn off fifteen minutes later. I didn't know what to do with myself, so I dusted the furniture. As I put the dusting cloth away, Jeff came prancing out of the washroom with only a towel wrapped around his waist. He had a full chest of black hair and his legs covered in hair too, which looked like black blades of grass to me. His body was thick like a tree stump, and his voice changed into a low growl as he asked me if he could borrow my blow dryer. I got it out of the vanity drawer, and when I looked up at him he was pouting his lips like a model. I burst out laughing because I knew he was trying to seduce me—and he knew it too. Everything he did was for show only. I told him he should go to Hollywood because he was a brilliant actor. Then he broke out in his Elvis moves.

After Jeff left, I started doing chores. When I got to the bathroom, there was enough hair to make a toupee, black hair everywhere. With that, I broke out laughing like a raving lunatic. I had to go get the broom and dustpan to clean up the mess.

For the rest of the day, I tried to read and watch TV, but my mind kept drifting off to Jeff. I couldn't stop thinking about him. I imagined playing the piano for him. I imagined us dancing at our wedding, everything and anything that would feed my infatuation with him. I was a goner. We were going to be together. I pushed any negatives about him back in my mind, and with that I went and turned on the music really loud and danced around the living room after I closed all the blinds. I was on top of the world and wanted everyone to know I was in love.

Jeff worked for the food industry as a sales agent. He dressed in his work clothes most times—black slacks and white-collared shirts with colourful ties—and kept his hair in place with a big goop of gel. From a distance he looked like a hotshot, but close up, anyone could see the stains on his slacks and the wrinkles in his shirts. When he wasn't in his work clothes, he wore blue jeans, a sweater, and black suede boots. I don't think he had much in the way of clothes unless he was just wearing his favourites.

If I wasn't talking on the phone to Jeff, he'd be at my place. I felt like everything was going way too fast. I was feeling smothered. For a while there, I would make excuses to not see him. I had grown used to living alone with just my kids. And I liked it a lot. I think Jeff got the hint because he stopped calling as much. I found the less he called, the more I wanted to call him. I craved the company of adults, but my priority was my kids. I wasn't ready to dive into a relationship. I wanted to go slow, and I think Jeff respected that. At least I hoped he did.

# THIRTY-SIX

# JUNE 1975

In the summer of 1975, we got a dog, which is to say the dead man decided to get a dog. She was a female German shepherd, and he named her Roxy. I enjoyed taking Roxy for walks, and sometimes she would drag me across the playing field on the school grounds and jump up on me and lick my face. I only wished she could lick off the layers of ugliness so I could be normal.

But soon the dead man ranted and raved about the dog shit piling up in the backyard. He accused everyone else of being lazy and ungrateful, and I figured he should have cleaned it up himself. After all, it was his idea to get the dog. My mother just became a bundle of nerves with all that yelling and went out into the backyard with a garbage bag and cleaned it up herself.

I knew she was really pissed about it, though, and she took it out on the dog. She kicked Roxy so hard that she yelped and cowered in fear and pain.

"I hate that damn dog. I wish she were dead."

I felt sorry for Roxy and tried to protect her by taking her outside as much as I could. It was so sad to watch her hiding underneath the table in the living room, trembling in fear. Roxy ended up paying the price.

One day my mother showed up suddenly, and the dog trembled and pissed all over her precious rug. That only incurred her rage, so she subjected Roxy to a few more blows to her ribs. I stood there powerless. I remember fantasizing about being a rescue ranger, and it eased my anxiety somewhat, but it did nothing at all for the dog.

By then we also had two cats, one grey and one black and white—again, it was the dead man who brought them home. I took an instant liking to the black and white kitten and ignored the grey one. My mother named my black and white kitten Perrier. He had seven toes on his front paws and six on his back ones. He was born that way. At night I enjoyed sitting in the recliner in the living room holding Perrier real close. I used to wear a red and white checkered housecoat, and Perrier would suck on the material as though he was feeding on his momma and purr like the kitten he was. I would sit there fantasizing about running away with him, and he was content to think I was his momma. We were the perfect pair. A few months later, I couldn't find him anywhere. I asked my mother if she knew where he was, and she said he got hit by a car. I imagined him being scraped him up off the pavement with a spatula and put in a bag.

I searched for him, though, all over the neighborhood, in vain. He had vanished, and I missed him terribly. It gave me an aching feeling in my stomach. I'd lost my best friend, and my mother didn't give a damn how I felt about it. She was so cold and so detached from everything.

In the back of my mind, I believed my mother had something to do with Perrier's disappearance. I thought she might have buried him in the backyard, so I went to see for myself. I pretended I was playing, but I was looking for my dead cat. While I was digging up the garden, I heard someone speak to me from up in the tree.

It was a whisper, and unlike the voices I usually heard in my head, it scared me to death.

I wondered if Perrier was trying to connect to the dead little girl inside of me. Shaken, I got up, wiped the dirt off my blue jeans, and ran into the house. I ran down to the basement and curled up in a ball in the farthest corner and rocked back and forth. The most frightful part of it was that I always had weird experiences like that, and yet I couldn't trust anyone well enough to tell. I had no friends, and the schoolteachers didn't know how to reach me. And mother, well, she was the one I could trust least of all.

In fact, she was rarely home anymore and had arranged for me to stay at her sister's place on most weekends so she wouldn't have to deal with me. Sometimes it would be Sarah who went, but it was usually me. Martha always stayed with my mother.

Aunt Theresa would stop by after work on Friday evening and pick me—or Sarah—up. It was about a fifteen-minute drive to her apartment near Islington and Bloor. Aunt Teresa gave me the creeps somewhat because she looked more like an uncle than an aunt, with a square jawline and stiff composure. She had streaked her hair blonde and had big blue eyes and a face that only seemed to smile on special occasions. She wore her pants too tight—I imagined that they cut off the circulation to her brain so she couldn't even think straight.

And she asked me the dumbest questions. "How are you doing in school?" –and– "How are your grades?"

I didn't completely understand why I had to go live with her on weekends—unless it was because my mother wanted the dead man all to herself and saw me as competition or even a threat. She told Aunt Theresa that she couldn't handle me and that she had a hard time controlling me.

Aunt Teresa didn't live alone. She had a partner by the name of Lindsay, and although Lindsay walked and talked like a man, there was something very gentle about her. She was patient and soft in some ways. I could even see it when she strode across the floor. Before Aunt Theresa met Lindsay, she was married to my Uncle Ron, and they had adopted a three-month-old girl named Kimmy, who was a couple years younger than me. Odd as the situation was, I would like to have stayed at Aunt Theresa's, but I always had to go home to my cold-hearted mother come Sunday night.

The first time Kimmy showed me into her bedroom, my eyes bulged. It looked like it belonged to a princess. It even had frilly pink sheets. But underneath all that apparent perfection, I sensed something sinister about her, like the way she went about in her room making sure everything was in place. She warned that if I touched anything, I was to be sure to put it back exactly how I found it, or I'd be dead. Eventually, I picked up a small jewelry box that played pretty music when I opened it. I listened to it for a few minutes and then spent another few minutes trying to remember how to put it back 'just so' on the nightstand. I felt very anxious because I knew how much trouble I'd be in if I didn't get it right.

All was not well at Aunt Theresa's. There was a lot of yelling and screaming, and Aunt Theresa was forever picking on Lindsay. They both played on a woman's baseball team, and when they came home after a game, Aunt Theresa would call Lindsay all kinds of names and accused her of having the hots for another player. Aunt Theresa threw things like ashtrays, books, or even a vase. She threw them as hard as she could, and they would smash on the living room floor. Although I had witnessed violence, it didn't bother me that much because it didn't involve me.

No matter how loud they got when they fought, I just tuned them out until it was over. In between times, there were quiet moments when Aunt Theresa would sit in front of the stereo on the floor and listen to Barbara Streisand. It was heaven to my ears.

The voices continued to harass me, but when I heard Barbara's beautiful voice coming from the speakers, it touched me in a place the voices couldn't go. It made my spirit rise and made me aware of that special place inside me that remained unharmed and renewed my hope in life. Soon I had memorized the words to her songs and sang along with Aunt Theresa. She never laughed at me during those times because she too enjoyed the sharing of a special moment. It showed me she was human, that she wasn't afraid to feel, at least once in a while, and I felt I had made some small connection through the sound of music.

One weekend Aunt Theresa, Lindsay, Kimmy, and I packed a cooler with food and drove up to Lindsay's parents' cottage at Wasaga Beach. The drive was about three hours long, and I enjoyed looking out the window from the back seat at acres of naked land with the wind toying with the trees, leaves blowing around on the ground and at passersby.

Once we reached the small two-bedroom cottage, we put the groceries away then took four lawn chairs out of storage and lined them up in a circle. I was excited because there was a chair for me too. Aunt Theresa said I could go for a walk as long as I didn't stray too far from the cottage, and she warned me not to go into the lake. I immediately took her up on the offer. The scenery was breathtaking. I felt as though something had me tucked inside an envelope of beauty. I kneeled and touched the long green grass, while realizing how precious life was. I picked up rocks and admired their many colours. Then I went down to the lake, rolled up my pants, took off my socks and shoes, and waded into the water of Nottawasaga Bay. I remembered that she told me not to, but it beckoned to me. Besides, I hated being told what to do. Aunt Theresa never found out, though. She never even came to check what I was doing.

The water was chilly, but it was not too cold for me to go in. I didn't wade in too far because I was ill at ease about deep waters. I was afraid it harboured things that could hurt me.

When I came out, I noticed broken shells lying on the sand. Even broken, they were beautiful. I picked some up and put them in my pocket. Before long, my pockets were bulging. I pretended they were nuggets of gold and that they would pay my way across the water to a beautiful imaginary island. I would go there on a pirate ship and live happily ever after. As much as I was enjoying my time by the water, all the while, I kept looking around for intruders to my paradise. I had the unnerving fear that my mother was going to show up any minute and start yelling at me for being so stupid. And the devil was hiding behind the cottage, watching me.

Finally, I went back to the cottage, carefully so as not to stir the devil into action, and Aunt Theresa surprised me with a coconut. She said I could crack it open the following morning. All night I thought about the taste of coconut. Just the thought seemed to bring my taste buds alive; it was so seldom that I truly enjoyed eating. I stayed up most of the night waiting for the sun and then about six when everyone else was still asleep I went in sock feet to the kitchen, took the coconut off the counter, and spent the next half-hour looking for a hammer to crack it open. I finally found one by the fireplace and began hammering away. I almost had it open when Aunt Theresa came out of her bedroom, sleepy-eyed and obviously angry with me.

"Do you realize what time it is?" she snapped. "For Christ's sake, get back to bed."

She said nothing about the coconut until later, when she was fully awake and had had her morning coffee. I expected her to yell at me, but she didn't. Or maybe hit me. I guess, maybe, I expected her to treat me like my mother did—although I felt nervous around Aunt Theresa, I knew I was safe and that she would not harm me.

When Sunday rolled around, I felt a tinge of sadness because I didn't want to leave. But Aunt Theresa and Lindsay couldn't keep me forever, and so back I went. As they drove me back to the city, I sat in the back of the car and watched the beautiful country scenery pass by and wondered if I'd ever see it again. I imagined all the trees waving goodbye, and I waved back. I wished that I could live in the bush all by myself and pick berries and hunt fish in the lake. The cottage was one of my more pleasant childhood experiences and, again, showed that it was natural things like water, trees, ravines, insects, rocks, and even broken shells that gave me peace of mind.

# THIRTY-SEVEN

# AUGUST 1991

In August, Jeff called me and said his work was offering him a transfer to Hamilton. He wanted to know if I wanted to live with him—or rather if he could live with me. I didn't know what to say, so I just told him I'd think about it and let him know. Before I got off the phone, Jeff mentioned he would help with my kids and help pay bills. He also said that he had to know by the end of the month and that that should give me plenty of time to think about it.

I told him I'd think about it.

The next weekend, I had the kids and Jeff stayed over. I watched him play with April, and it impressed me. He had a daughter of his own, so he knew what he was doing. Then he turned to Aaron and asked him to show him his toys. Aaron was more than willing. He raced to his room and brought out a bunch of his action figures and spread them on the floor. Now I had a man in front of me who would take on two children and their mother. We got ready and took off to the park. Jeff pushed April in the swing while Aaron and I went and played in the jungle gym. Aaron was smiling, and that was all that mattered to me.

Before making my decision as to whether to move in with Jeff, I went up to see Gloria in her office to ask her opinion.

"Go for it," she said. "He can help you."

"I don't know," I said. "Say it doesn't work out."

"Make it work."

Flippant advice, but it was all I needed to hear—I decided I'd do it, just like that. There was something deep inside of me telling me to not do it, but I trusted Gloria's opinion and ignored the red flags that were plaguing my mind.

When the moving truck pulled up, Jeff was all smiles. The movers took his stuff up to my place, which was *our* place now. He had little, just odds and ends and his mother's old furniture. His most prized possession was his bed. It didn't take long to set it up. I put my old bed in Aaron's room, and he was happy because now he had a gigantic bed to jump on. It finally felt good to have a complete bedroom set. After Jeff settled in, it was time for dinner. I had taken some chicken out of the freezer earlier on, so we made chicken alfredo and it was delicious. Aaron looked content. I was content. And little April was smiling as usual. She had just turned two.

I was changing April's diaper, and Jeff was watching over me. Out of nowhere, he said something about April's vagina looking the same as mine.

At that moment, I felt the boxes in my mind shift. I didn't know what it was, so I turned to Jeff and told him not to talk about my daughter like that. It felt like the magical bubble I was living in had burst wide open.

Jeff said he wouldn't talk like that again.

And everything went back to normal, yet I knew something was wrong. Instead of questioning it more, a voice in my head told me I was dead. It took me hours to shake that feeling. As soon as I got April tucked in bed, I felt better.

On the weekend, Jeff's friend Malcolm came over. The first thing he said was he imagined me living in a dark, dirty apartment. I fired back, telling him that not all crazy people barricade themselves in dark places. We are everywhere. Later, I thought about what Malcolm said about me and concluded that he was putting me down in a roundabout way. That's when I knew he had a low opinion of me. I never invited him to my house again. He didn't exist in my world anymore. But Jeff still saw him, and I didn't mind at all.

Jeff quickly made himself comfortable and started eating my food. He had to pay half the rent because Gloria had stipulated that in our new lease, but Jeff and I hadn't had the conversation about who would pay what beyond that. When we talked about it, he said he was already paying half the rent and that made up for his part—his part of the rent came to all of two hundred dollars. It turned out he made little money and worked on a commission basis. Sometimes he didn't even have gas money for his car. He certainly didn't make anywhere near as much money as he had once led me to believe. You could tell by the state of his clothes that he was poor.

As it was, he owed his ex-wife thousands of dollars in child support arrears. I paid all the utilities, half the rent, and half the groceries. The truth was Jeff was paying so much less than he had to pay at his mother's place. It looked like he was benefitting from moving in with me, and I was losing big time. Before he moved in, I just had my kids to feed, and now I'd be cooking and cleaning for a grown man who wasn't bringing much to the table. To make matters worse, he was pestering me to wear lingerie and pose for him. He even wanted to take nude photos of me. Fat chance of that ever happening.

Soon, the apartment felt crowded. There was nowhere for me to go to get some privacy, so I went and talked to Gloria about getting a transfer. We filled out the housing forms, and the only thing left to do was to get Jeff's signature. I got Jeff to sign it the same night, and the following day I took it back to Gloria, and she faxed it off to somewhere.

## THIRTY-EIGHT

# AUGUST 1975

A few weeks after the trip to Wasaga beach, my mother left me in charge of Sarah for a good part of the day. Usually, it would have been Martha's job to watch us— she was twelve—but she'd started to complain about always having to babysit and was off at a friend's place. I was eleven and Sarah would have been nine. It was a weekend, and instead of doing as I was told, I invited a few of the kids from the project over to play. I don't re- member their names or faces, but I remember having no emotional attachment to them. I just wanted them to come over because I was lonely. It was the first time I had kids at my house, and I felt like a big shot. I wanted to prove to them how cool I was, so I took the Colt ci- gars out of the dead man's dresser drawer and passed them around. We all sat on the couch in the living room and puffed away.

Suddenly there was a blood-curdling scream from the kitchen. At first, I wasn't sure if it was real. I thought it might be a voice in my head trying to wreck all my fun. But then I realized it was Sarah, so I jumped up and ran into the kitchen to see what was wrong. She had tipped over the deep fryer while trying to make French fries and now was lying on the floor. I ordered everyone out of the house, grabbed Sarah and ripped off her clothes, and rushed her into the bathroom and put her into the tub. The skin on her stomach was already peeling upward like fire in a forest. It was like I was watching someone else run the cold water and splash it on the wound, but it was me. Then I wrapped a towel around her and took her into the living room where I rolled her on the floor, but that obviously didn't help, so I decided I'd better phone my mother. That is when I became hysterical.

With shaky fingers, I dialled the number that she had left on the kitchen table. It was all I could do to concentrate on what I knew I had to do for Sarah. I watched my hand bring the telephone up to my ear. I knew I was in big trouble, and when I heard my mother's voice and had to tell her what happened, my heart sank, and I felt like I was on fire too. She said that she was on her way, and then the telephone went dead. I just stood there listening to the dial tone for the longest time. Then I heard Sarah groan, and it brought me around again, so I went and sat beside her and listened to her sob. I rubbed her shoulder to console her but felt very helpless. I felt horrible inside. I wanted to die. I imagined us both lying down together and pretending to be dead.

My mother had called for an ambulance, and it arrived first. I let the two paramedics in and stood silently by with my head lowered. They put Sarah on a stretcher, covered her with a blanket, and then asked me a few questions. My mother pulled into the driveway in her long green car just as they were getting ready to leave. I could already feel her gaze, a gaze like hot coals, hot enough to burn a hole in my skull. There was the rage in her eyes—blistering, focused rage—and I knew that this time she was right. She said nothing. She didn't yell at me, but I knew that I would probably receive a beating later. But this time she was right. I deserved whatever I got, but Sarah was the one who really had to pay.

The hospital admitted Sarah with third-degree burns, and my punishment was that I couldn't visit or have any contact with her.

Finally, when everything had more or less settled down, my mother got around to yelling at me and blaming me for the accident. Then she gave me the silent treatment, which was even worse. The rejection was unbearable, and it left me feeling invisible, as though I didn't matter. And, again, she refused to take any responsibility herself for leaving a child like me, a child not responsible enough to handle minor situations, to care for a younger sibling while she was out having fun.

Of course, when she'd talked to the paramedics, she convinced them it was no one's fault. I'm sure it crossed their minds that someone older than an eleven-year-old should have been babysitting *both* Sarah and me, but they said nothing. And they must have thought she could afford it too, because she dressed well and she had had her hair done and her nails freshly polished. To me, it just meant that all you had to do to avoid unnecessary attention was to dress nicely. People might suspect there was something wrong, but if you dressed nice and held a good job, you could thwart the investigation.

Eventually, Sarah recovered and came home. I was so relieved because I was beating myself up with guilt and fear.

In the fall, my mother got sick. The doctor said she had breast cancer. We were all sitting around the kitchen table when she told us she might die because there was no cure. I cried, and my sisters cried, but the dead man just sat there with a weird smirk on his face. I don't think my mother noticed it—I hoped not—but I did, and it gave me the creeps. Then I saw his face turn into a wolf, and he started ripping my mother to pieces with his razor-sharp fangs.

She had to go to the hospital to get one of her breasts removed. With all the horrible things I had imagined happening to her, I never imagined a disease wiping her out. One might have thought I'd feel overjoyed by her devastating news. But I felt compassion for her. She had always taken great pride in her looks, in being so perfect, in being beautiful and sexy, and now there was a risk of losing it all. I didn't see her cry even once, but I knew she had to hurt. I saw her as a vulnerable human being for the first time in my life. I felt pity for her and perhaps even a certain respect because she put on such a brave front. But I worried that she might eventually die even if they took a breast and that I would be at the dead man's mercy. It would also mean no more opportunity to get the love I so desperately needed from my mother.

While my mother was in the hospital, the dead man kept close tabs on me. He asked about my every movement, whether I was just getting a glass of milk or closing my bedroom door. He seemed to be everywhere that I was, and it made me nervous. Even when my mother called us from the hospital, he'd stand near me, listening. I cried on the phone because I was so afraid that she was going to die. I told her I loved her best, but she would twist it around and tell me to stop my blubbering because she was the one who was dying. She was right, but why couldn't she see how it was affecting me too. I tried hard to stop crying, but I just couldn't get a grip on my emotions at a time like that.

Several times she warned me to stop crying or she would hang up, and because I couldn't stop, she did just that. I felt my only recourse was to lose myself in fantasies of self-importance. I spent hours alone in my bedroom, daydreaming about newly discovered missions in life. First, I was to be God's chosen one who would become the messenger to his children. Then I fantasized about saving the world from some mass destruction, and then I'd bounce back and forth between missions, not knowing which one to do first.

When she came home from the hospital, my mother was the same bitter woman she was before her cancer. I had hoped there would be a change in her since her bout with death. But she had experienced no re-birth, and it devastated me. Instead, she moped around the house, lost and detached, and I thought it was entirely my fault. I blamed myself for her brush with death because of the incident with Sarah. I needed to talk to someone about it. I had questions that desperately needed answering, but she refused. Eventually, I buried my feelings as deep within myself as I could go. It helped to further detach me from reality, but there was a part of me that hurt, and I couldn't deny it.

I became even more watchful of attempts by others who preyed upon my madness to exploit my vulnerabilities. I drifted through time, lost in my mystifying private journey. I was a wizard with magical powers. I became absorbed in studying the mundane like a magazine cover, a light fixture, a colour, hoping to attain some secret knowledge about who I was. In school, math bored me, the kids bored me, and the teachers threatened to break into my world by trying to contact me, so I had to focus on figuring out when they were going to attack and invade me. It was a simple matter of survival and very time-consuming. It didn't leave much time for learning.

I strained to have any social interactions with the other kids. Their simple games, the innocent colouring of maps or writing of stories. And I couldn't get over how much they trusted the adults. I knew I differed from them, but then again, I wasn't really that different because I knew they had their problems too, many of which weren't all that different from mine when it got right down to it. For instance, like me, they had to conform to their parents' expectations. I saw it as a farce because we all suffered from identity issues, not just me. Everyone was just trying to fit in. I struggled with these questions daily.

I didn't really see the teachers as individuals. I saw them more like a group with the authority to fashion little minds into puppets like themselves. That's what the actual world offered, and so I couldn't trust it. I knew something wasn't right in my mind, but I had no direction, no way out. I saw others getting at least *some* of their needs met, and it crushed my spirit for I had needs too. But I was invisible. I tried, in a variety of ways, to get someone to hear and notice me. A sudden inappropriate laugh and the weird language I used should have been a clue to something not being right in my world. I was waiting and hoping somehow someone would try to contact me. Terrified as I was, I wanted someone to reach out to me. I wanted the opportunity to be normal, to be just like everybody else.

However, I found a group of kids who had accepted the way I was. They had chips on their shoulders and, like me, all came from troubled homes. They dressed in faded jeans with the knees purposely ripped out and baseball hats turned backward. Cigarettes dangled from the side of their mouths, and they swore like truckers. Therefore, I felt some kind of attraction to them. Though I didn't particularly like them, I was desperate for friends. Even though I knew nothing would ever fill the emptiness I felt inside, I used them as a convenient distraction from my suffering. I suspected that all the kids experienced some kind of abuse. I guess that's what drew us together. We were all fighting against the world.

That's around the time I met Susan. We could have been sisters because we both had freckles, were skinny as rakes, and acted out in the same way. We were also both thieves, and that proved to be a fairly powerful bond. We both thought it was fun to steal from department stores, houses, even lockers at the local recreation centers. It seemed to fill the emptiness in our lives, distracting us from the realities of our tortured existence. The best times were when we'd meet in the morning before school started and rummaged through the garbage bins behind the shopping mall. We often found completely wrapped chocolate bars, and we ate them. We had a ball. The more junk food we ate, the more it seemed to take away my blues.

My mother let me sleepover at Susan's house one night without even talking to her parents. Susan's parents seemed weighed down with the burdens of poverty and alcoholism. Her mother's eyes had big dark circles around them, and she wore oversized clothing to disguise her heaviness. Susan's father slumped in a La-Z-Boy chair reading a newspaper and looked up only once to see who I was. He was wearing dirty blue jeans, a torn white T-shirt, and brown vinyl slippers, and I was sure he hadn't shaved in a week.

Empty beer bottles littered the kitchen counter, and the floors were sticky from dropped food. It looked like the floor needed a good wash. Magazines and newspapers cluttered the living room. The unkempt house reflected their shattered lives. At least my mother was smart enough to hide our troubled lives by keeping a clean house.

Susan took me into her room and the stench of urine in the air startled me. There were books and toys scattered across the dirty hardwood floors. Susan acted like it was normal, but even I knew it wasn't. We jumped up on the bed and it squeaked. I pretended to listen to her ramble on about how she had hurt someone or another and manipulated someone else into giving her money. She showed me a fistful of money to prove her point.

They were poor, and so we both had to sleep in Susan's bed. When she thought I was asleep, she took my hand and put it in between her legs. I was shocked but continued to pretend to be sleep. But how could anyone sleep in a bed reeking of urine? I could have drawn my hand back or told her not to do that, but I froze. I couldn't move my legs or my hand. They began to tingle, and a creepy feeling washed over me.

Although I continued to play with Susan, I never slept there again.

When I got home the next day, I went directly to my bedroom. I carved out a new direction for myself based on my most recent experience. I would cut off even the slightest contact with other kids on an emotional level.

As I lay on my bed, deep in thought, Martha came in with a pack of cigarettes. She quietly urged me to try smoking one. Curious, I jumped off my bed. I had enjoyed smoking the dead man's Colt cigars, so maybe I would like regular smokes. She was standing next to my white dresser, and it made me notice how creamy her face was and how beautifully rich was her auburn hair.

I watched as she took one out of its package. She lit it, took a long drag, and then passed it to me. I followed suit, then blew the smoke out slowly and coughed till I was dizzy. Then Martha showed me how to smoke properly. It annoyed me because I hated being told what to do. I thought about rearranging her hair, but I knew she would scream and we'd both be in trouble.

At twelve, Martha looked like a porcelain doll on the outside, but if I said something that hit a nerve, she'd go nuts. She acted like a little Barbie doll, always fixing her hair, straightening out the wrinkles in her skirt, polishing her shoes, and brushing her teeth. We were only eleven months apart, but she seemed so much more mature. My mother had moulded her into somewhat of a miniature version of herself, and Martha seemed to enjoy the importance of her position. She was so unlike me, and I was jealous of her. I was afraid to even pick up a comb and glance into a mirror because I knew all I would see was ugliness. But Martha seemed so perfect, so prissy, and so together, no matter what was going on.

Anyway, I learned from Martha how to hold a cigarette between my fingers and to inhale and exhale effectively. I tried to do as she said, but I still ended up coughing. But it was gratifying just the same. Before she left my room, she put some cigarettes in my top dresser drawer and covered them with my underwear, warning me not to tell mother our secret. I never figured out why she got me started.

Now that I'd started smoking, I needed cigarettes but had no money to buy them. Therefore, I had to steal them from my mother and the dead man. When my mother wasn't looking, I'd steal some out of her pack of cigarettes or just take butts from an ashtray. Then I had to steal matches to light them with, so I took them from the kitchen drawer and went into the attic in my bedroom to smoke.

Sometimes, when my mother was in a terrible mood, I didn't dare steal her cigarettes, so I go looking for them in the street. And I really enjoyed it. Smoking was a very effective distraction, and it seemed to settle my nerves. It was like a new hobby. I spent hours collecting them, putting them in my pockets, and smoking them whenever I felt like it. Sometimes I laughed out loud when I was puffing away because it reminded me of a little steam engine in a kid's book. It wasn't really funny, but I somehow had the impulse to laugh at everything and anything.

One day, I walked to school dragging my left leg behind me like a pirate escaping from a shipwreck. The next day, I pretended I had a stiff shoulder from a steel pipe falling on me. I even took a handful of dirt and smeared it on my face for special effects. Another time, I used some of my mother's foundation and rubbed it all over my face, put a towel on my head, and pretended to be Pakistani. When the kids saw me, they laughed so hard I thought they were going to have a heart attack. The teachers didn't laugh, though. They thought I was just a spoiled brat who would do anything for attention. Well, they had half of it right, anyway.

When winter came, the roads became covered with about five inches of snow, and on my way to school, I watched the snow blowers working. I found the snow very fascinating. I stuck my tongue out and let the snowflakes land on it and felt them melt. I put my arms out straight and twirled around with my eyes closed, enjoying the feeling of freedom. It comforted me to know that the snow that touched me was pure, that nobody else had touched it. The snow was so shiny and bright, so perfect, and it was all around me. It somehow made me feel alive and pure myself. I felt, somehow, connected to it, as though I understood all about it and that it was a part of me and I a part of it.

Sometimes, I pretended to be a black panther stalking its prey, only my prey was the next car that came up over the hill near the school. I would wait until just the right moment when the rear bumper was in just the right position, and then I'd reach over and grab it, and enjoy the free ride. It was another kind of freedom. After a while, other kids joined, and that was okay by me, I could still do as I pleased.

That was the healthy part of my existence, the spark of life that couldn't be extinguished. But no matter where it went, I had to drag my best friend around—my friend schizophrenia. It would not abandon me nor hurt me and would protect me like no other friend I had ever known. Separating us was out of the question. If anyone tried to get too close, I would act so crazy they'd have to run to escape the harm I could do. If I felt threatened, I would resort to violence in a heartbeat. So mostly, people left me alone. They were afraid of me. They didn't know how to act around me, nor did they know what to say.

There were often long awkward pauses and uncomfortable silences when I felt uneasy, and so I'd speak my schizophrenic language in order to be left alone. Sometimes, I didn't even know they had gone, and I'd be still talking as though they were there. It was spooky. It scared the hell out of me, and eventually, I avoided entering into conversations whenever I could get away with it. It was a very lonely way to live, but the embarrassment that came with schizophrenia was worse. I remember times when I was playing by myself and talking out loud because I was conversing with the voices in my head. I didn't really get along with the voices because they were always putting me down or trying to get me to kill myself. But I had no control over the voices. They were part of my strange world.

# THIRTY-NINE

# OCTOBER 1991

In October, we packed up and moved into a new townhouse on Upper Wentworth across from the Limeridge Mall. The townhouse was quite spacious, with three large bedrooms, a decent sized living room, and a basement. It was spotless, and I didn't have to do a thing to it. Jeff bought us a new dining room set and a coffee with matching end tables. It felt like a new start again. And everything was going fine. Aaron was in elementary school by then. So while Jeff took off to work, I would walk Aaron to school with April in her baby carriage. It was feeling like I had a normal family.

At the end of the month, I received my phone bill, and when I read it, I found a slew of 1-900 numbers. I wasn't sure what they were for, so I dialled one number. It turned out it was a sex chat line. I hadn't heard of them before, but as soon as I realized Jeff was making them, I felt a surge of anger inside of me erupt. I waited for him to get in the door from work, waited patiently until he was through with his shower, and then grilled him about the phone calls. He didn't deny making the calls.

"Most men do it, nothing to worry about," he said. "I will pay you for them, but I don't have the money right now."

I didn't know what to say, so I just found something else to do and ignored him for the next few days. I never got the money he had promised me.

Jeff's daughter, Maria, came every other weekend. Most times the dates didn't line up with when my kids were at their dads, so I lost my free weekends away from my kids. His daughter was sweet, well-mannered, but acted older than most eight-year-olds. She reminded me of one those girls who took part in beauty contests. Her brown hair hung past her waist, and when she spoke, she would push it over her shoulders with her hands. I had a hard time warming up to her because she was a smarty pants, knew everything, and Jeff encouraged it by insisting she was a genius "just like her daddy."

If that's what genius looks like, I thought, then I'm a Rhodes Scholar. I hid my genuine feelings about her and treated her well. Over time, I came to like her and didn't mind her around. She was just a child.

There was one thing that really bothered me about Jeff and his daughter's relationship—Jeff was calling her sexy. I thought it was weird. Why was he sexualizing his daughter? Why was he treating his daughter as if she were eighteen years old? Instead of dwelling on it and driving myself crazy, I just ignored it.

Jeff and I were lying in bed one night talking about how this and that. Suddenly he sat upright and made a confession to me. I imagined a pop-up confession booth in the room. I wasn't a priest, and my back went stiff because I wasn't in the mood to listen to him.

He proceeded to tell me about the time when he was jacked up on cocaine and found two eleven-year-olds hanging out in the front lobby of his apartment building. He started joking with them and dared them to go with him to the back of the building to give him a blowjob. One of the small girls did in fact give him a blowjob, but when he got back the other girl had taken off somewhere. I could hear the disappointment in his voice, the sadness. Then a loud fire alarm went off in my head. I imagined four police cruisers rolling up in front of the building to an invisible crime scene.

A few weeks later, he confessed to me once again. While lying in bed together late at night, he told me when he was in the grocery store that day the produce manager brushed his arm against his. He got so turned on that he had to go to the washroom and jerk off on the stall wall. I didn't know whether to throw holy water on him or run like hell. The boxes in my head were shaking and my palms were sweaty. Finally, I told him to stop talking like that. Then I rolled over to my other side to face the white wall. I couldn't sleep. I tried to detach from the present situation, but I tossed and turned like a fish out of water.

The following morning, I woke up, got dressed quickly, and put on the coffee. I was so tired, I could barely keep my eyes open, and I had a severe case of bad nerves. I couldn't wait for Jeff to go out. After he left, I went over everything he had told me. I was in shock. I didn't know what to do about it. I felt like changing the locks, but he was on the lease, and I didn't know my rights. From that day forward, I watched him like a hawk and never allowed him alone with my kids. Soon, I forgot all about it and went deep into denial. It never dawned on me I had a child molester in my house because that kind of behaviour seemed normal to me, so I wasn't aware of the seriousness of it, even though I was being triggered like crazy.

There was a police choir in my head singing: Were coming to get you!

# FORTY

# APRIL 1977

I got my period at thirteen years old, and the cramps were unbearable. Thank God I was at home and in the bathroom when it happened. I yelled for my mother to come and help me, but when I told her I was bleeding she said nothing, just turned and left. A few minutes later she came back with a box of sanitary napkins and threw them into my lap, quickly explained what to do with them, and left again. I was shocked. I wanted her to sit down and explain things to me, to have a mother–daughter moment where she would tell me what was happening to my body. I shouldn't have been shocked by her behaviour considering her actions in the past, but she could still leave me feeling alone, embarrassed, and scared.

Afterward, I went to see where she was and found her sitting on the end of her bed staring at the floor. Her eyes looked wet, as though she'd been crying. I guess it had thrown her for a loop too. I didn't know how to respond, so I went to my bedroom and sat on the end of my bed, put my hands in my lap, crossed my legs, and stared at the wall. And there we were, both in our separate rooms, separate worlds, staring at the wall or the floor.

There was now a new distance between me and my stepfather as well. His physical attention and advances withdrew. He spied on me, instead. I'd catch him looking at me through the crack in my door. He'd watch while I changed into my panties and bra. And I saw the devil there too.

He would make lame excuses to come into my bedroom while I was getting dressed.

"Is your room clean?" he'd ask or, "Done your homework?"

But he wanted to know my every move. I noticed a change in his voice too. He sounded nice sometimes, but I knew he was still a wolf behind his sheep's mask. I was alert; my nerves strung tight, just waiting for him to attack me at any moment. I did not understand how long it might be before his sick impulses would get the better of him. And he wasn't the only one who had a special radar system anymore. No, I had developed an uncanny talent for spotting perverts and creeps who were attracted to little girls. I could swear that if I walked into a room with fifty people in it, there would be at least one blip on my radar.

And my mother didn't help any. One night she told me to come downstairs and pose for The dead man in my new bra and panties. They sat on the couch as I shyly descended the stairs, feeling like a fool. It seemed to amuse my mother as I slowly came into the dead man's view. I stood in front of them like a village idiot—light-headed, shoulders hunched, one leg crossed over the other, toes curled with tension and peering at them through my bangs. I imagined myself going over and slapping my mother hard across the face and then poking the dead man's eyes out with a stick. Finally, she dismissed me, and I turned and ran to my room, this time imaging that the devil had gathered me up in his large hands and was whispering in my ear.

*"Die bitch..."*

The dead man began harping to my mother about me being on the loose in the neighborhood all the time. He got on her case about her limited parenting skills and lousy housecleaning, and I knew he was out of control. He started drinking more, becoming increasingly drunk most of the time, falling and bumping into furniture and then accusing my mother of setting a trap so he would fall on his face. He moved with the unsteadiness of a toddler just learning to walk, and the comparison helped me to put things into perspective because he was looking weak to me, and I noticed the crow's feet around his eyes, the dark circles under them, his poor posture, a sunken jawline, and his childish ways. Now I saw him as a little boy that used tantrums to get his way, manipulating everyone by talking loud, throwing things, pouting, and even the silent treatment to keep everyone in line.

Once he stopped preying on me, I started to see him as a pathetic human being, but I also felt like he had withdrawn his love. I had sex and love all mixed up, and being so desperate for the one, I used the other to get it by trying to garner his attention by posing provocatively, mimicking the ways my mother had used so successfully in attracting the opposite sex. If he were sitting at the kitchen table, I would boldly throw my arms around his neck, and he would get angry and tell me to leave him alone. The rejection was devastating. It was bad enough that my own mother had been rejecting me for so long, but now the dead man was doing it too, and I felt the impact of the sting, so I dived into my world of hallucinations and voices and felt protected and comforted by something those around me could not give.

In August, we moved from our place to a house on South Service Road in the Lakeview area of Mississauga not far from the Dixie Outlet Mall. The road was busy, nowhere near as treed and residential as our place in the Elms, and our house faced a concrete sound barrier that that hid the Queen Elizabeth Way from view.

As much as it hurt to move from that neighbourhood and the Humber River Ravine where I had spent so much time, the house on Hadrian drive held a lot of ghosts, a lot of memories just beyond the periphery of my conscious mind. When the green curtains that had helped define my mother's room on Hadrian came down, I felt the boxes in my head shift then settle.

In the new place, I shared a room with Martha, while Billy and Sarah had their own rooms. My mother and Robert had a room across the hall from Martha and me, near the top of the stairs.

In the house on South Service Road, my senses intensified. The tiniest of details caught my attention no matter what I was doing. I felt like an outsider, a detective in search of clues to a case I didn't understand. The case of how things changed. Hard to make sense of events which your mind has boxed up. I started wondering how the light fixtures worked or how the toilet flushed, and with even greater interest, why people did the things they did. I especially noticed my two sisters and my little brother.

Martha reminded me of a box because of her square face. It reminded me of my grandmother's features, but unlike Grandma, Martha had beautiful auburn hair, dreamy almond eyes, and beautiful tanned skin. She seemed so grown-up, walking around the house with an aura of power and dominance surrounding her. I didn't like her, though, because she had too much power over me, power my mother had given her. But she was my surrogate mother, and she told me how to dress and how to act and disciplined me, occasionally shaking a tiny accusing finger in my face.

Sometimes she would get mad at me and tell me to stop acting crazy because it was upsetting the family. I saw her as a fraud, pretending to be perfect all the time, but I guess it was the only role she knew. I resented her because she had a pleasant room, and she had friends, and she was popular at school and got good grades, and the boys were always calling her. She was the person I wanted to be. She was well dressed, and in the morning, I'd find her ironing her clothes and putting on makeup. She also looked like the Golden Child to me.

My sister Sarah was a different story. She hid in her bedroom a lot, like a wallflower, as though her role was just decorative. Or she'd be at her best friend Lori's house. She didn't talk much, and I liked her shy ways and her ability to shut out noises going on in the house. She coped rather well considering the circumstances, but I noticed that she seemed to eat to suppress her emotions. Nobody could be that hungry unless she had a hollow leg.

When she wasn't home, I'd search through her room and find half-eaten bricks of cheese and packages of crackers under her bed or in a drawer? She remained trim. Her face reminded me of a moon, and she had almond eyes like Martha, but she represented hope to me, rather than authority like Martha. I found her easier to look at, too, because she didn't pose a threat to me. She was like a clown. She didn't seem to have a clue to what was going on. But she was playful. I didn't dare make contact with her, though, because I think she knew I was the craziest member of the family, and I must have made her uncomfortable because she seemed to avoid me whenever she could.

I noticed one way in which all of us girls were the same—we all tiptoed around the house.

We all knew we had to be quiet so we wouldn't trigger our mother's rage. It was like we were all maneuvering around her moods or the dead man's scrutiny as though crawling under a radar screen. Billy, though, was allowed to make all the noise he wanted as he played with his trucks, smashing them against the walls, or vrooming them on the floor. He was our mother's favourite, and every time I turned around, he was in her arms, talking and cuddling, with my mother hanging onto his every word. He got so much attention not just because he was the dead man's son, but also because my mother was fond of boys, whether adults or children. Seeing the two of them together all the time made me so mad that I'd throw him down the stairs every chance I got by pretending to be wrestling with him. I'd squeeze his arms and pull his hair until he started whining, and then the dead man or my mother would come and break us apart. Then the dead man would yell at my mother to keep me away from his son.

The family dynamics were changing, and I could feel it. I saw things more clearly and showed my mother how I felt. I wasn't a baby anymore, so I questioned her behaviour, bringing up incidents like when she'd made me pick up the lint on the carpet with my fingers. It made her nervous, even angry, and she responded by accusing me of focusing on the negative and conveniently forgetting about the good times we had. I couldn't recall any good times, so I'd press her for the kind of answers I wanted to hear. I questioned her relentlessly, but never about *some* things—things I had boxed up. I was searching for something. My intuition told me I needed to know something, but I couldn't pinpoint it, couldn't identify the true focus of my temporary obsession.

She became so agitated with my frankness and afraid that I might penetrate her secret world that she grew very defensive and said that I had always been a glutton for punishment.

I stopped asking questions and went back into my delusional world with never another thought. Every so often, I felt I had known insights into the truth about the family, and it disturbed me. I wanted nothing more than to be accepted by them and have the right to speak about what I believed to be the truth. I also realized that I was the black sheep of the family and that my mother was using me as a scapegoat.

I turned fourteen in the house on South Service Road. Then in February, came an unexpected hammer blow that reduced a fantasy of mine—one that I'd clung to since I was four years old—to rubble.

It came in the form of a phone call. My mother picked it up, and I happened to be there when she got the news. My father was dead in snowmobile accident, a collision with a tree that had killed him on the spot. It felt like part of the ground beneath my feet fell away. I had been waiting for him to come and rescue me since the day he dropped me off at the orphanage, and now it was never going to happen.

I was devastated and caught so entirely off-guard that I was inconsolable. I don't remember my mother's reaction to the news, only her reaction to my grief.

She laughed at my tears and told me I was being melodramatic.

# FORTY-ONE

# NOVEMBER 1991

It was a Saturday night, and Maria came to sleep over. Her mother had already made plans for her on Sunday, so we had to have her back by ten o'clock Sunday morning.

After dinner, we watched a movie together, some made-for-TV special. As usual, I couldn't stay focused on the show because I was too busy fantasizing about playing the lead role. It was a two-hour movie, but I drifted off at the twenty-minute mark. I couldn't shut off my mind, so I tried switching my sitting position, but it was no use. When I looked over at Maria, she appeared glued to the TV screen and was stuffing popcorn into her mouth.

As soon as she finished eating, she went and lay beside her father on the couch. Jeff was playing with her hair, and when he glanced over at me, he smiled, which made my heart melt. I enjoyed watching them express their love for each other. They were two peas in a pod. Jeff rarely called her by her proper name; he called her his little princess most times. And when he said it, with that soft voice of his, Maria's face lit up like a Christmas tree.

After the movie, Jeff took Maria up to bed and tucked her in. She slept in Aaron's bed when he wasn't there. I was getting ready to get into bed when I went in to say goodnight to Maria. I found her lying on Aaron's bed, nude with her legs spread wide open. Jeff was putting some kind of ointment between her legs. I asked him what it was, and he told me that Maria got vaginal infections from time to time, and he had to put the cream on her before she went to sleep. While he was putting it on, he turned to me.

"Look at her," he said. "She likes it."

When I looked, Jeff was touching her sexually, as if he were trying to arouse her. Maria's eyes looked glazed over, like she was enjoying herself. I could see her body react with pleasure. It was not normal. It wasn't normal for me to see that. I had to get out of there right away.

Maria was eight years old.

I quickly got out of the room. I shut the door behind me and went down to the living room and sat on the loveseat, dumbfounded. My mind was spitting out a thousand images like a machine gun firing rapidly with no target in sight. I couldn't process what had happened. My mind wouldn't let me. I didn't know what to do with myself, so after I settled down a bit I went back upstairs and got into bed and didn't say a word about it to Jeff who was now lying beside me. I turned my back to him. Then I felt his creepy hand on my shoulder, making its way down my side. I rolled over and told him I had a booming headache and was going to take a blanket and fall asleep on the couch.

As I lay on the couch, with my eyes staring off into the darkness, I went over and over in mind how I was going to handle the situation. Finally, I decided that the following morning I would write a letter to Jeff, but make it look like a note to myself, and leave it somewhere I knew he'd find it, and craft it in such a way as to convince him to leave.

It was a long, quiet drive back to Maria's house. Jeff had the tunes cranked up, so I was happy to rule out any conversation that could have taken place. Maria was content in the backseat playing with one of her dolls. I watched her as she talked to her doll, and a heavy sadness washed over me. I couldn't help but think about her future and how she'd turn out with a dad like that. I knew it was going to be the last time I would see her. I promised myself that I would try to help her by calling her mother and telling her what I had witnessed. I just hoped that she would believe me and do something about it. I wouldn't put it past Jeff to twist the story around to make him come out looking like a shining star. I am sure he'd lay on the charm.

On Sunday, Jeff was cleaning out the basement. Before he got started, I sent him out on a few errands, which gave me time to craft a note out on scrap paper. I can't remember exactly what I wrote but the gist of it was I was actually *using* him, and once he bought another piece of furniture, I was planning to throw him out of the house. Again, I made it seem like a note to myself, and I put it on top of a box in the basement—one I knew he'd go through.

Later, Jeff came up from the basement with heavy feet. He had the note in his hand, and I imagined fire coming out of his nostrils. He hadn't laid a finger on me so far, but I feared things would escalate. But nothing happened. He just told me he would never buy a single damn thing for the house ever again. I felt so uncomfortable because it was an awkward situation, something I had engineered myself. I turned on my heel and headed to the kitchen to pour a cup of coffee. The next thing I knew, he was upstairs collecting up all his clothes from the closet racks and bringing them downstairs to the hall closet. I asked him what he was doing, and he said he didn't want to wake me up in the morning because he had to go into work early. Just as I was about to say something, there was a knock on the door.

The kids were back.

When I woke up the next morning, Jeff was still there. He was fidgeting around with his tie in the bathroom and fixing his hair just right. I could smell his cologne. I said nothing to him. I got Aaron ready for school and put April in the baby carriage, and off we went out the door. When I got back, Jeff was gone. All his clothes from the hall closet were gone too. There was not one reminder of him in the house except for a dirty coffee cup on the kitchen counter.

It was over.

I thought I would feel relief once he was out of my life, but I didn't. I was already missing him. I guess it would take some time to break the spell he had put on me.

In the meantime, I was having horrible dreams. I kept seeing a green curtain, but I didn't know what it meant, and every time I thought about it, the voices in my head got louder. They were shouting obscenities at me, the same as usual. But this one time, the voices seemed closer, as if two ladies were sitting next to me having a chat on a train ride. I could pick out a few words here and there, something about a little girl hiding somewhere.

The voice was scaring me, so I made an appointment with a therapist because I knew I needed help. I had found in the telephone book. I saw a therapist instead of a psychiatrist because shrinks just give out drugs, and therapists got trained to listen and play a more active role in figuring stuff out.

Three days later, I walked in my therapist's office. The first visit was just to introduce ourselves and go over a plan that would work best for me. The therapist's name was Karen, and she had long dark hair, and could stand to lose a few pounds. She wore an unflattering baggy green skirt that reached her toes and a sweater two sizes too big. Stacks of files and loose paper cluttered her desk. Behind it, there was a bookcase full of psychology books and plants galore.

When I looked at the floor, I could see that the carpet was old, and the stitch work was coming apart in certain areas. First thing we went over was the cost of each session. I told her I was on welfare with two kids and had little money. She offered me a sliding-scale fee of ten dollars per session, so I took it. Those ten dollars would have covered the cost of milk and bread, though. It was hard parting with the money, but I made it okay in my mind by telling myself if I had to go without a meal then so be it. I couldn't believe that I so damned poor I couldn't even afford therapy. Social services wouldn't foot the bill. It was such a tragedy. It always felt like they designed the welfare system to keep anyone from getting off it, especially someone like me.

On the second visit, I brought up my schizophrenia and watched Karen squirm in her chair. That reaction devastated me. It took so much courage to get there in the first place, and now she was afraid of me. There was a long pause between us, and the silence was killing me. Then Karen started with my family history. I told her I remember little of anything except my mother was mean. I also told her about the time I was in the hospital and then under the care of Children's Aid Society. After I finished talking, Karen looked up from her notes.

"Did anyone ever sexually abuse you as a child, ritual abuse maybe?"

I didn't know what to say to that, so I just told her I could've been. I didn't know. I couldn't remember. Since I remembered nothing, Karen told me that the further we got into therapy, the more things might come up for me, so I should prepare for it. She wrote out a list of books I could read until I saw her again.

A few days later, I found myself at the local library. I was in the psychology section and came across a book called *The Courage to Heal: A Guide for Women Survivors of Child Sexual Abuse* by Laura Davis. It looked interesting, so I tucked it under my arm and grabbed a couple more books that Karen had recommended.

As soon as I got home, I stuffed the Laura Davis book into my socks and underwear drawer. I took the other two and put them on my coffee table. Then I fed April, changed her diaper, and put her on the couch beside me as I read. I scanned through the books and couldn't find anything worth reading. They were more geared to people who knew they had been sexually abused and were looking for ways to deal with it. I hadn't opened that can of worms yet, so I thought the book didn't apply to me.

On my third session with Karen, I told her about Jeff and his daughter and how I had walked in the bedroom while Jeff was touching his daughter inappropriately. I told her how I felt I had witnessed a girl being molested, but I wasn't sure. After I described the story in great detail, Karen said I had to report the incident to social services, and if I didn't feel up to it, she would do for me because it was her legal duty to report it to a welfare worker. I sat there for a few minutes and told her I would call Maria's mother and report it to her, and then she could take action. Before I left her office, I told her Jeff's secrets: the two girls and the incident at the grocery store.

By the time I finished, I couldn't wait to get out the door. My head was spinning, and on my way back home, it felt like someone was watching me, so every few metres I looked behind me to see if anyone was following me. It wasn't the first time I felt that way. I was always checking for cameras on hydro poles or inside stores for cameras. Wherever I went, it felt like I had a million eyes on me. The only place I felt safe was inside my home. But then again, I was always afraid someone was going to break in and do horrible things to me.

When I got home, I got the telephone book out and searched for Maria's mother's number. I couldn't find it, but I knew she had a sister, so I looked up her number and found it. On the third ring, a woman answered. I asked her if she was Maria's aunt and if she knew Jeff? She said yes. I told her who I was and that my therapist told me to call her before she called the welfare department. Then I told her the entire story, but before I could finish, she interrupted me.

She and her sister, Maria's mother, had suspected as much of Jeff for a while. She thanked me for calling.

I hung up and felt a sense of relief that I had made the call. I hoped Maria's aunt had taken the call seriously. I think she did. Of course, she did.

The following week I got a call from Jeff, and he was livid.

"How could you do this to me? We were friends."

With that, I hung up on him. As if I could have any empathy for a child molester. Good riddance, as far as I was concerned.

He could rot in hell.

## FORTY-TWO

# AUGUST 1978

It had been a year since we moved to South Service Road. A year where I spent a great deal of time lost in the hallucinatory world of my own head. A year putting Hadrian Drive behind me.

It was a Sunday morning. I was on my way downstairs for breakfast and had to pass my mother's bedroom. This morning I heard Sarah's voice in there. She was in there with Robert... with *the dead man*. My stomach lurched, and a question that had been frantically buzzing around inside my skull for the twelve months landed long enough for me to ask it.

*Why was it that Sarah now had her own room?*

I stopped halfway down the stairs, weak at the knees. I knew the answer.

The dead man had moved on to Sarah, who didn't deserve his attention any more than I had. She was harmless, just like I was. But I hadn't thought of myself that way until that very moment. Until then, I'd always felt, deep down, that I'd deserved it. I must have deserved it because my own mother made me feel that way. My own mother had been party to it. The realization of what was happening to my sister became overwhelming, and I had to run, run from the truth, run from the perversions all around me.

I turned and crept back upstairs and returned to the bedroom I shared with Martha. The bed we shared was already made. Martha was downstairs, probably watching Sunday morning cartoons with Billy and waiting to go over to a friend's house. I went to her jewelry box because I knew she kept money in there. It was just loose change, but I grabbed it anyway because I knew, even before I had a plan, that I would need it to survive. I was going to have to buy my food and clothing. How I was going to be able to do that with a couple of dollars I didn't know. I was shaking.

I grabbed my Garfield book bag from beneath the bed where it had lay all summer long. It was empty save for a spoon and some crumpled homework assignments and notes from teachers never delivered. I knew I should take clothes. But a weird paralysis was closing in around me, and so I slung the bag over my shoulders and went back downstairs.

I didn't hear anything from my mother's room.

I started to go to the kitchen to grab some food, but Martha was there waiting at the toaster. She saw the backpack and asked where I was going. I just turned and walked down the hall and out the front door.

My mother's car was gone, and I guessed she must have been out shopping, or maybe she had a hair appointment. I didn't know. But I knew if she was out, she could come back. Suddenly I just wanted to be as far away as possible. I went to the garage and grabbed Sarah's bicycle because the other one had a busted chain—plus it felt like I needed a part of her with me so I could pretend that I had become her guardian angel. I felt guilty knowing that I was leaving poor Sarah behind to fend for herself, so I used my magical powers to send a message through telepathy to tell her that none of it was real.

I glanced up at the window to my mother's room—the dead man's room—but the curtains were closed. It felt like the whole neighbourhood was holding its breath. That's when I noticed Martha looking at me from the living room window. I turned to go but she ran out of the front door.

By the time I had the bike turned around she was right there and grabbed at the handlebars. I pushed her and managed to get my foot on a peddle, but she chased me to the end of the driveway, and I had to swerve. Martha grabbed at the backpack and pulled me off balance.

She was saying something, but I could make out what it was. It sounded like questions. I was afraid to look at her face, scared of what I might see there. It felt like the world was closing in around me. Then I was standing again, and Martha was picking the bike up off the ground. I ran, while Martha yelled after me.

I didn't turn back. I just ran.

# FORTY-THREE

# THE GIRL ON THE BRIDGE

I was still staggering from the Jeff situation. I was upset in ways I didn't understand or appreciate and having crying spells daily. I couldn't figure out what was bringing it on. I didn't realize what Jeff had triggered in me or just what he was setting into motion. I would just be putting groceries away and would find myself doubled over on the kitchen floor in a fetal position sobbing like a baby. When the tears stopped, I'd go back to what I was doing as if nothing had happened. But something was happening. Jeff had triggered something deep inside me, a memory, but it was cloudy.

Soon, every day was like that, crying and trying to get some rest in between my tears. It got so bad that I couldn't even eat or sleep at night. I was incapable of looking after my kids. I kept seeing that green curtain in my mind.

When I got into see Karen, I explained to her what was going on for me. She said that's the way things are supposed to go, and it was going to get worse before it got better. She reassured me that things would get better, eventually. The last thing I wanted to do was come undone, especially when I had two children to look after.

Once again, I told her I wasn't feeling good, that she wasn't getting it. I was so upset I started crying, and my body was shaking. I told her I didn't know if I could do this. I told her I had a bad feeling about it. But something was rattling around in my head, and I couldn't make it stop. I got up from my chair and said I had to go.

"Before you go, Tracey, let's make another appointment. I think it's important."

"No, I have to go. I'll call you this week sometime to make another appointment."

It was a Wednesday night, and the weekend coming up was one I had the kids home with me. I was in such rough shape I was having a hard time keeping my tears at bay. I had a big decision to make. I was toying with the idea to put my kids in foster care for a couple of weeks until I got my shit together. I had stayed up all night thinking about what to do. I didn't want my kids to see me that way. I had to protect them from me. I was really concerned about Aaron and how he would feel. He had spent his entire life with me, and now I was putting distance between us because I saw myself as unfit to care for him and his little sister. But deep down, I knew they would be safer with a foster mom than with me. I knew it was the best thing for them—and for me—and I had put a two-week timeline on it.

Thursday morning, after I got Aaron to school, I came home and grabbed the phonebook. I dialed Children's Services and told them I had a family emergency. The lady on the line said she could send someone out to see me in the afternoon that same day. The social worker arrived with a briefcase in her hand, and I was pleasantly surprised that she didn't give me the stink eye. She didn't make any assumptions or judge me. She was very mindful of my situation. She told me that most parents wouldn't do what I was doing and that they'd keep their kids with them at a significant cost to their children's wellbeing. She made me feel like I wasn't a horrible person for doing what I was about to do. I was very grateful towards her for being kind and not shaming me. My kids were being picked up the next day in the afternoon—I would keep Aaron home from school to give me a chance to explain things to me. As for April, at two years old, she was too young to understand what was going on. I was more worried about Aaron.

After dinner, I let Aaron play for a while and then I gave him a bath with his sister. I let them sleep in my bed for the night, one of them on either side of me. It was story time, but instead of reading them a story from a book, I made up my story. It was about love and honour. I made Aaron the hero and his sister his sidekick. There were some bad guys coming into town, and it was their job to protect the town. I even threw in one of the Ninja Turtles weapons, which seemed to go over well with Aaron. When I finished the story, Aaron asked for one more story, so I grabbed a children's book from his closet and read that to them. I had mixed feelings about the next day. I didn't want to put them in foster care. I didn't want to let them go. I loved them so much. To me, they were the greatest gift I had ever received. They made up for all the things that had gone wrong in my life. They were my miracle.

I felt sad in the morning. I looked over at Aaron eating his cereal. Six years old and utterly innocent. I told him I had something important to tell him after breakfast and to meet me in the living room when he finished eating. The first thing I told him was that he wasn't going to school today, a very special lady was coming to see him in the afternoon, and he'd be staying at a mom's house for a couple of weeks. I promised him he would be okay and to think of it as a rest from school. I told him he would be with his sister and that I would call him every day at four o'clock sharp. To cheer him up, I told him he could bring all the toys he wanted, and I'd help him back. As I watched him, Aaron didn't seem too put off by the idea. He said he really didn't want to go. He wanted to stay with me. Once again, I reassured him, while hugging him tight while telling him how much I loved him. I asked him if he could help me put a bag together for him and for him to choose his favourite toys he wanted to take with him. I ended up packing a large suitcase with all their stuff in it.

It was a different social worker picking the kids up that day, and the one who came to get them was in a hurry. I remember her long coat flying open as she slammed the back car door. She wasn't at my house long. She had long dark hair and almond-shaped eyes. That's all I can remember.

I watched the car drive out of the complex with my two children in it. I waved at Aaron, and he waved back from the back window of the car. As soon as the car was out of sight, I went inside, locked the front door, and collapsed on the floor and began bawling my eyes out.

I stayed there for a good hour, soaked in tears. I started thinking about Jeff and how he turned out to be a child molester and how I didn't catch on to it during our relationship. I went over it in my head so many times. How could he harm that little girl in the lobby? How could he touch his daughter like that? It could have been my little girl. It could have been April. Then I turned my attention to my mother and hated her a little more. I hated her more than ever that day as I sat on the floor releasing raw emotion. I got up and tried to eat, but the only thing I could keep down was a piece of bread and a glass of water.

At four o'clock sharp, I called Aaron as promised. He told me was okay. We talked a bit about his day and then, before I got choked up, we said our goodbyes.

"I love you, Aaron," I said. "I'll call you tomorrow, okay?"

When I put the phone back on the receiver, I let out a sigh of relief in knowing that the kids were safe.

Two days later, I called my therapist's office to make an appointment, but she wasn't available for two weeks. It's not like she was doing much for me, anyway. I don't think she knew how to help me. But she pointed me in the right direction by suggesting a few books to read. I figured it was good enough for me. I wasn't expecting much from her, and the ten dollars I was giving her wasn't getting me anywhere. I think I was just paying her to listen to me, and it didn't sit well with me. It felt like a waste of time, especially when I had to pay bus fare.

Things got worse for me. I was having haunting dreams of faceless naked people. I remember pulling *The Courage to Heal* out of my dresser drawer one night. I did a quick scan of the book and then checked the table of contents for something interesting. I read the part about writing things down and use a plastic bat to unleash anger.

First thing in the morning, I went to Toys "R" Us and bought a jumbo plastic bat. Then I went to another store and picked out a blue typewriter to work on because I didn't like my handwriting. Besides, I had learned to type in high school, so I knew I could probably bang out more words on a typewriter than by hand.

That night I woke and sat bolt upright in bed. A box had tumbled over in my mind and lay open for the first time since my childhood.

*...I was nine years old, in the house on Hadrian drive, my mother's room downstairs behind the green curtains. She'd woken me in the night and brought me down to the dead man and told me to take off my nightgown. I'd been there before, naked and afraid with the two of them in the deep shadows [another box yet unopened]. But this was different.*

*I lay on the bed but this time my mother turned me over and put pillows under my knees. Face down, I could not look into her eyes as the dead man forced himself on me. The pain as my anus tore was intense, and at that moment I felt something snap.*

*The terror I felt was paralyzing. Transformative. My mind was in shock. I imagined my body thrashing back and forth, desperate for something to hang onto. Sights and smells became deadened, and the need to escape overwhelmed me. But where can a nine-year-old girl who's just got shattered in every way imaginable go—except into the safety and privacy of her mind?*

*I bled of course. And when the ordeal was over, my mother wiped the blood off me with a face cloth and then went out to the kitchen and put it into the garbage. I heard the lid slam down. When she came back in, she told me to go back to bed.*

The reality of that moment had been so disturbing, that I'd detached immediately, which triggered a state of mind that sought solace in becoming base, like an animal. Even afterward, I never cried. Nor did I respond outwardly in any other way to the trauma. I became as quiet and remote as the moon. I felt like a tiny mite—invisible to the human eye—in a world where everything else seemed unbelievably gigantic.

That was the night I felt the impact of my mind shattering into a million pieces. That was the night I was born into another world, a world I had been preparing for unwittingly all along, a world that would prove to be my saviour, a world that would protect me from the terrors of what others call the real world. For a while, I felt safe within the confines of my mind because I had finally gone mad. I didn't know it at the time, but that was when I developed a condition I would later know as paranoid schizophrenia. It was a natural response to the trauma, the only way out of it.

I was stunned.

I didn't know what to do. So I just sat there and watched the scene play out. The shocking and disturbing realization of what had happened to me brought me to my knees. I sobbed uncontrollably, so I moved to the floor and rocked myself to bring my anxiety down. Then I went to the closet and retrieved the plastic bat. I pounded the bat on my bed as hard as I could. I did it until I had no strength left in me. I was so exhausted. After that, I just lay on my bed, numb and disoriented. It was so quiet in the house. I felt so alone and exposed. I turned on the bedroom light because I didn't want to be in the dark alone.

I thought the worst was over, but it wasn't. It was only the beginning of unleashing my suppressed emotions and opening more boxes. There were too many of them. Then another round of crying took a hold of me. And I cried some more. My body was taking a beating.

At one point, I thought I was going to have a heart attack, so I made an appointment to go see my family physician. By the time I got to her office, I was a mess. I went to open my mouth to speak, but I collapsed on the floor and started hyperventilating. I couldn't get my words out. After I settled down, I told her a little about what was going on with me. I don't think I had to explain too much. It looked like I was having a breakdown, but what I was really having was a *breakthrough*. Without asking me questions, she reached for her prescription pad. She wrote it out for Ativan, and I was to take two a day. It was the kind you put under your tongue.

When I got back home, my intuition told me to throw out the pills. I had to do my recovery drug-free instead of using the drugs to siphon off my hard-to-deal with emotions. I needed to explore those feelings. I needed to express them. The pills would only prolong the emotional work I needed to do. It felt right to me. But in hindsight, I could have used some medication to take the edge off (and if I had taken the pills like the doctor told me to, she wouldn't have fired me as her patient a week later).

The next day, I sat at the kitchen table with my typewriter and pounded away at the keys. To an outside observer, my writings would have looked like some kind of secret code or some newly discovered language. But within that text, fragments of forgotten memories from my childhood had emerged. I suppose my mind could only handle a little at a time. So I bounced back and forth from reality to writing in my schizophrenic language.

The more I wrote, the more pieces of the puzzle I could put together. I could see that once I wrote about an incident and cried or raged the whole thing out, another memory would surface. Then I would release another round of emotions surrounding what happened in my mother's bedroom. The more emotions I let out, the more the symptoms of my schizophrenia faded until they ceased to exist. They were losing their power over me.

What looked like a mental breakdown was actually a breakthrough from schizophrenia. I figured if I would have gone to see a psychiatrist during my recovery, they would have locked me up. Mental health practitioners would probably not have recognized what I was going though as a breakthrough—they'd label my experience as a nervous breakdown and drug me into passivity. I was all too familiar with what went on in psychiatric hospitals. My experience in the hospital had taught me it wasn't a good place to show feelings or talk about personal problems.

I'd even read stories in books where people got locked up against their will just for having problems in living. I also knew that some patients who used psychotic drugs for a long time risked developing tardive dyskinesia, which causes damage to the muscles in the face.

I knew drugs were not the way to go for me. The last thing I wanted was to lose my kids to the authorities and spend my time confined to an institution against my will. I didn't want to be forced to take medication that could turn me into a zombie, a shell of a person.

As I was sobbing, the phone rang.

It was my Sarah. I burst out in tears. The truth of our mother and Robert (the dead man) and what they had done to me slipped easily out of my mouth. As soon as it escaped, I started crying hysterically. My sister told me she'd stay on the phone with me as long as I needed. I cried while she listened. After a good hour, my tears dried up, and I felt somewhat stable. Before she let me off the line Sarah told me to call her back if I needed anything. I was grateful for her being on my side. Just to hear her voice was a godsend.

## FORTY-FOUR

# MEMORIES

*...I was still eight years old, and it was within a month of our move to Hadrian Drive. When my mother nudged me awake and told me to follow her downstairs, I had no idea what was going on, but something about the look on her face made me nervous. She told me to be quiet as she led me out of my room.*

*Behind the green curtain of her room, the dead man was waiting on the bed, naked. I went numb and everything felt dreamlike. I was moving slowly, and though they were talking, I couldn't understand what they were saying.*

*The next thing I remember, I was naked and getting up onto the bed with my nightgown lying on the floor. Fear silenced me. Another part of me had shut down because I had become mute. My mother held me down by the shoulders and spread my legs.*

*A deep sadness swept through me like a gloomy shadow. I started to detach and further shut down. I felt my mouth open to scream. But she quickly put her hand over it so the scream went backward into my being and screamed futilely somewhere deep inside. I didn't really feel the force of her hand on my mouth because my whole face had gone numb.*

*But the dead man wanted to enter me from behind. My mother looked directly into my eyes, and I believe she saw the pain and fear in there. Maybe it moved her. I silently told her, by my body language and through my eyes, not to do what she planned to do.*

*Suddenly, inexplicably, she released me and told me to get out of her room. I just remember reaching down and picking up my nightgown and, without looking back, sauntered out of her room and back to my own. I felt humiliated knowing they had both seen me naked. I hung my head in shame. It was the worst feeling I had ever felt in my entire life. It was so degrading that it made me feel invisible, like I was nothing.*

*When I got to my bedroom I didn't reach for the knife because I knew, deep down in my heart, that there were some things my mother would never do to me. She had just proved that, hadn't she?*

*I stayed up throughout that entire night wondering if, perhaps, my mother had made some kind of connection with me at last. I wondered if that was what they called compassion. I hoped that—finally—she had recognized my vulnerability as a small child, and hers. I fantasized that, somehow, she had finally identified with me.*

*That night I wept openly for the first time that I could remember. I allowed the tears to flow until it saturated my pillow. Afterward, I felt a strange calmness. I suspected that crying, perhaps, was a good thing. I felt connected in mind, body, and spirit. I was alive, and I even wanted to stay that way.*

—

*...I was six years old, and we were living in the place on Rexdale Boulevard. My mother was pregnant with Billy, and perhaps as a result, the dead man's sick fascination with me was simmering. One night the he came into my room as I was trying to go to sleep. He didn't turn on a light but sat on the side of the bed. I remember the creak of the soft bedsprings.*

*"Your momma's a cold fish, Tracey. Do you know she kicked me out of our bed? She won't sleep with me."*

*I'd been holding my breath I think. The room started to swim. I remember him talking and talking but being unable to follow what he was saying.*

*Then he started running his fingers over my chest, and he was telling me he hated touching my mother. He positioned his body to press against my leg, then leaned down and kissed my lips. I could almost hear my heart explode, my breathing quickened, and something in the dead man's eyes stirred. A cold, dead look penetrated my nerves.*

*I looked away, went within myself, and was already putting the incident into its box on the shelf in my mind. There was just enough room to store my fear and the dead man's stare. His voice became very distant, and imaginary clowns suddenly jumped onto my shoulders, pinning me down with imaginary nails. It was as though the dead man had entered my heart and left little gift boxes with nothing in them. I didn't feel a thing, I was numb. I just had the weird sensation of the dead man's black hair touching my tonsils. But I also felt as though I was replacing my mother as his new lover.*

---

*...I was still six years old and had just started school. Billy was sleeping in my mother's room and he cried most of the night. The dead man had taken to sleeping on the couch. On this particular night, I was asleep when he crept into my room and awoke with him lying beside me on the edge of my bed.*

*"I'm lonely," he said and reached under the blanket and took my hand.*

*I lay there stiffly without replying. I kept my eyes wide open, hoping he would just say what he had to say and leave. But he didn't. He guided my hand and rubbed it against his private parts. I heard his breathing get louder and then he turned and whispered in my ear.*

*"You're doing a great job, babe."*

*My mind started pulsating out hundreds of tiny thoughts a minute. I remember the heat from his body and how it seemed to keep pulling me back to the present. Finally, there was sticky stuff all over my hand. He had ejaculated. Then he disappeared.*

*When I knew it was safe to do so, I quietly got up and ripped the sheets off the bed, throwing them on the floor. My heart was thudding against my ribs. I lay down on the mattress and brought my knees up close to my chest. I let my hand hang over the side of the bed. I didn't know what else to do with it, so I got back up and wiped the mess on the sheets and then lay down on the mattress again. I was so overwhelmed with fear that I believed it was going to kill me. That night I lay naked on the mattress all night long, wide awake, thinking only about the morning when it would be safe to get up and go to the bathroom and wash my hand.*

*In the morning I broke out of the paralysis I'd fallen into and got up to go to the bathroom. I moved in slow motion. I was dizzy and frightened and paranoid. I had to walk by the dead man, and he just smiled. As soon as I got to the bathroom, I turned the water on and scrubbed my hands fiercely with the soap, thinking the soap could also wash away the way I felt inside.*

*At the breakfast table, I was eating my cereal, so numb I could barely taste it. My mother was at the sink doing dishes. It was just the two of us.*

*"Did you have fun last night?" she asked without turning around.*

*Suddenly I couldn't swallow. I had a mouthful of cereal and I thought I would choke, but I dared not spit it out. When I didn't say anything, my mother turned around and the look on her face scared me.*

*She dropped the dishcloth in the sink and left the room.*

—

*...I was nine years old and had just started Grade 3. We were at Hadrian drive by now, and school was right across the street. It was a Monday morning, and I was eating breakfast. The dead man was sitting beside me for some reason. He was talking low, but I was so lost and dissociated that I couldn't make out what he was saying.*

*"Come with me!"*

*It was loud and startled me out of my reverie. He hauled me out of the chair, spinning me slightly off balance. His hand on my shoulder, he walked me to the bathroom and closed the door behind us.*

*He sat on the edge of the bathtub. He didn't have to tell me what to do, I already knew. It was just a regular routine. The only thing I didn't know was when he was coming to get me. Sometimes he even took me into his work van to do his thing. Anywhere he could get me alone, he'd make me do the dirty thing.*

*When he had finished, he told me to get up and go to school. He closed the bathroom door behind me as I left. I remember staggering down the hall and out the front door and crossing Hadrian Drive and starting my school day.*

---

*...I was five years old, and it was the first morning at Rexdale Boulevard. My mother called for me to come to her bedroom. When I got there, I stood reluctantly by the door and noticed the outlines of their flesh through the bed sheets. There was a funny odour in the room too.*

*It made me turn to ice inside, and I backed away, but my mother's soft voice pulled me in and told me to come over and kiss "Robert"—the dead man. The room spun. I knew I could not refuse, so I kept my body as stiff as possible and my emotions in check. I became lightheaded. I slowly crept like a mouse across the wooden floor, leaving my soul behind. It would not be me kissing his lips. No way! I obeyed my mother as always, but I could only do it by being controlled, moulded, a little plastic figurine. The figurine felt the wetness of his lips. It wasn't me because I had left my soul standing in the doorway.*

*I glanced up into the dead man's eyes, and in a flash, I saw the lust. It the same look I had seen in my mother's eyes whenever she talked to the bad boys. Then I glanced at her, and a sense of real danger almost overwhelmed me because it seemed like she was enjoying the experience too. She had changed into something hateful, furious, an envious green monster. That was the last time I purposely looked into the dead man's eyes.*

*She insisted that I touch his private parts. I was horrified, yet too terrified to protest. I slowly reached out and placed my little hand on top of the sheet that covered him. I felt the hardness. My hand felt so small and tiny, like a ladybug against him. Suddenly, she laughed. It was a sick broken laugh.*

*"Get lost."*

*I left.*

*Somehow, I found my way out of the bedroom with my mother's laughter ringing in my ears. I was just introduced to a dirty little secret, and it made me sick to my stomach. I headed directly to the bathroom, lightheaded and afraid, but got to the toilet bowl in time. I tried to vomit, but only a watery fluid came out, dripping warmly from my mouth, and in my mind, I saw the drops fall and turn into the shape of cut-out paper monsters. The bathroom became alive, the walls breathed, the tiles moved, and I saw tiny demons run across the floor. I thought they were trying to trap me. Then I realized that it wasn't the room becoming alive. It was me dying. It wasn't the tiles moving—it was my fear moving around and around and around inside me.*

## Forty-Five

# November 1991

The phone rang. It was my mother. She said Sarah had called her and told her what I had said about her and Robert. I could hear the coldness in my mother's voice as I listened to her on the phone.

"Do you want me to call the police?" she said.

I couldn't believe what I was hearing. In fact, it took me a few seconds to even form a response.

"The *police*?" I hissed at her. "You were part of what happened. It wasn't Robert on his own."

"I can't remember," she said. "You know that I am on medications now. A lot happened to me when I was a kid too. You have no idea." Then she took a deep breath, and what she said next sounded sinister. "You can do anything to children, they always survive. Nobody gets into my past. You—"

I hung up on her.

Our relationship was over for good. I never saw her again, nor did I attempt to find out anything about her through my family members. If anybody asked about my mother, I'd just say she was dead. I considered that only half a lie.

I ran upstairs, grabbed the porcelain dolls off the top of my dresser, the ones my mother had given me, and smashed them as hard as I could onto the floor while screaming how much I hated her. The doll pieces flew everywhere. Then I fell to the floor and wept uncontrollably until I had no more tears to shed. I was so tired that I fell asleep on the floor. When I woke up in the morning, I picked up all the broken doll pieces from the floor and put them in a green garbage bag. Later on, I took the bag to the dumpster in the parking lot. It was my way of letting go of my mother and all the horrible things she had done to me.

Things were making sense to me. I was figuring things out about my schizophrenia. The more I dug into my past, the more I understood how my schizophrenia developed. Even though the pain of it was all-consuming, I was making progress. Things were becoming a little easier, a little clearer. I was embarking on a new adventure, full recovery from schizophrenia, and it was going to be one hell of a ride.

I was supposed to get my kids back the next day, but I called the social worker to tell her I needed one more week to myself.

"Whatever you need," she said, "your children are okay."

I called Aaron at four o'clock and told him he was coming home in one week and that I couldn't wait to see him and his sister.

"Why can't I come home now?"

I told him I was really sick and couldn't look after him or his sister, but the gracious lady would. I knew he didn't like my answer, but I told him he could ask the lady to mark off the days on a calendar and it would make the time go by faster. My heart broke for him. But I knew it was for the best for the both my kids. I didn't want them to witness their mother in that kind of mental state because they were counting on me. Besides, I couldn't look after them.

I took a brief break from typing, grabbed a fresh cup of coffee and went outside to sit on the front step. The fresh air and the sun on my shoulders felt good. It felt like I had just come out of a war zone. I was just sitting there quietly, reflecting on my childhood, when suddenly the birds chirping on a tree branch got my attention. I looked over, trying to find them in the trees. Then I saw some of them perched on a branch. I thought about how lucky they were to be free. I wanted that kind of freedom more than anything. At first it didn't dawn on me, but the voices in my head were gone. The schizophrenia was gone. It was as if it were never there. I felt somewhat normal, yet my entire body was ready to collapse. I felt like I had just gone through an exorcism, minus the priests, of course.

I went and put the coffee cup in the kitchen sink, and then I headed up to my bedroom to lie down. But before doing so, I went into the bathroom. I stood in front of the mirror and looked at myself, and it was as if I were seeing myself for the very first time. I didn't see that ugly little girl staring back at me anymore. I saw a beautiful young woman who had been to hell and back.

I was twenty-eight or soon approaching it.

I touched my face with my hand and ran my fingers through my hair. It was soft. Then I ran my fingers over my lips like I was finding my voice for the very first time. I had lost so many years of my life to schizophrenia, but now I wanted to experience joy. I wanted a good life, so I made that my goal. I don't know why my mother did those things to me, but I suspect that she never survived her own childhood trauma, and in some sick way—to ease her own pain—she projected it onto me. She had hurt me on purpose. I knew that for sure. She stripped me of my humanity, but the fight was over. I was taking my life back.

The hard part was over. I had confronted my schizophrenia head-on, but I soon realized I had lots of psychological work ahead of me. Beneath my schizophrenia there was a group of conditions I had to deal with still. I had PTSD, agoraphobia, anxiety, and panic disorder. At least those were the ones I was aware of. I don't like labels, especially the label schizophrenia. The stigma alone ruins lives. People who know nothing about it assume that everything they hear on TV is true. There is the stigma that people with schizophrenia are maniacs going around killing people.

Most psychiatrists believe schizophrenia is an incurable brain disease. I guess that's what they learn in medical schools. And because of poor training, sufferers don't get a chance at full recovery. I read somewhere that most mental health conditions are automatic responses to trauma. What kinds of trauma? It doesn't always come out of one's childhood. I know that for sure.

A week later, there was a knock at the front door. It was the social worker with my kids. I took one look at Aaron, grabbed him, and hugged him as hard as I could while I whispered in his ear how much I loved and missed him. Then I did the same to April. I hugged her tight and then removed her little coat and threw it to the side. I was so grateful to social services for helping me and understanding my situation. I thanked the social worker as she was going out the door.

That night, Aaron and April piled up on the bed with me. I told my usual silly stories. Aaron looked over at me smiling.

"I love you, Mom."

"I love you too."

I turned to April and gave her a peck on cheek and told her I loved her too. The next thing, Aaron was standing up on the bed with a pillow in his hand. That was my cue to grab one and do battle with him. In between gentle blows, we laughed like crazy. I had my little family with me, and I was happy. When they finally fell asleep in my bed, I stayed awake and watched them sleep peacefully. Sometimes, it is hard to put a mother's love into words, but I know in my heart that I will love them forever.

I wasn't yet stable (and I wouldn't be for a long time), but I had some tools to help me get through the tough times. Music had always been a big part of my life, so I listened to it as much as I could. Sometimes I would play the same tune repeatedly for hours. I loved music, the kind that reached into my soul and soothed it. I am sure my kids got sick and tired of me playing the same song repeatedly. But it was what I needed. Sometimes I'd go down in the basement and crank the music up and dance all over the floor like nobody was watching. I'd spread my arms out and twirled around like a ballerina while snatching the little freedom I could catch in the air. I had my kids who meant the world to me, and that's all that mattered.

I knew I had a lot of self-work to do. I wasn't looking forward to it. It scared me. But I knew the worst was over. The road ahead of me would have all kinds of curves and bumps. I would make plenty of mistakes. I really looked forward to fixing my unhealthy behaviours in the next few months, but I knew that was unrealistic. There was just way too much damage for me to correct in such a short time. It didn't help that I was living in poverty while trying to sort through the mess in my head. It was a constant stress. I would have loved to go see a psychologist to help me correct my problems I had in living, but the health care system didn't—and still doesn't—pay for it, so I was stuck in between a rock and a hard place. The strain of helping myself and putting food on the table was wearing me down too. But I kept trying, and I kept typing. When I finally had everything typed out on paper, I had over three-hundred pages.

A couple of months later, the kids' father disappeared. I had tried to call him, but Paul had disconnected his number. I remember Sandra saying that Paul wasn't taking care of kids when they came over, so I suspect she had given him an ultimatum—it was either her or the kids.

I called Paul's mother to see what was up. Susan told me that Paul loved Sandra, and they were trying to make their relationship work, and the kids couldn't go there anymore. I begged her for his new number, but she said she couldn't give it to me. It floored me. When I got off the phone, I was feeling shaky. I had no idea how I was going to tell Aaron. It would break his heart. He and his sister were about to grow up without a father, just like I had. I was so mad at myself for repeating the cycle. I never expected Paul to give up his children for a woman. But he did, and I had to deal with it and clean up his ugly mess.

A few weeks later, Aaron asked about his dad's whereabouts.

"When am I going to see him, Mom?"

I could see the concern on his face. I grabbed him by the hand and got him to sit on the couch beside me. The only thing I could think to say was that his father couldn't be a dad and that it had nothing to do with him, it was all about his father. How do you really explain to a kid that their father wasn't coming back? I didn't bash his father at all. I knew it would leave a permanent scar. I tried best to play both father and mother, but it was impossible. It made me mad that I had to do the disciplining and try to be a loving mother at the same time. I could barely be a proper mother because of my own personal problems. But I gave it my all. Oh, I tried so hard, but my own issues kept coming up. Most of the stuff I learned about being a parent was through reading books. If I wasn't reading a parenting book, I was reading a self-help book. It was never ending.

I felt so bad that I couldn't fill the hole in the hearts of my children that their father had left. It's something kids never get over, I knew that. I did the best I could do with the tools I had, which wasn't much.

When Aaron turned seven, I bought him a cake and gifts to celebrate his special day. I can't remember what I got him, but if I was to guess, it would be more action figures.

I had another problem, once Paul was out of the picture, I wasn't get any breaks from Aaron and April. As my stress mounted, I would catch myself taking it out on the kids, so I decided to put April in daycare to give myself some regular downtime—she was three. My doctor filled out the forms and I took them down to social services. I got approved for funding right away. I wouldn't have to pay a cent.

Four weeks later, at eight in the morning, a brown minivan pulled into my driveway. It was the daycare driver. I helped put April in the backseat, put the seatbelt on her, and kissed her goodbye. Then I walked Aaron to school. When I got back home, I got my typewriter out and begun writing again. Come lunchtime I'd break and have a piece of toast or something else, sometimes I took a quick nap before the kids came home.

Having April in daycare helped me a lot. It gave me plenty of mental space during the day to work through my issues. I continued to type every day. When my kids got home, I'd slap on a smile. But behind that smile, I felt a great sadness. I was grieving all the years I had lost.

# Epilogue

My mother died in 2016. The last time I talked to her was in November of 1991, when I finally confronted her with her role in my abuse. Sarah left my mother too. But she too had a complicated relationship with her right up to her death. There was no contact between them for many years before my mother's death. My mother tossed Sarah aside like garbage. My mother took her money and threw her out of the house she helped pay for.

Robert died in Vancouver from lung complications. He was an alcoholic. When he moved there with Billy years ago, he was terrified of being arrested for what he had done to me (and I suspect, Sarah). I found out about Robert's death in 2017 from Billy, and while I'm not sure when he died, I know he was dead before my mother.

I have a relationship with Billy but we don't talk about the hard stuff, and Martha and I have cut each other out of our lives entirely.

I moved to British Columbia with Aaron and April in 1995, and in 2002, I met the love of my life, a man who taught me how to love and trust. He's a gentleman, kind, loving and very supportive. We take care of each other. We are best friends. He is the one who encouraged me to publish my book this time around. I will always be grateful for him and for all that he has done for me and my children, and for loving me unconditionally. I can honestly say he is my one true love.

Both Aaron and April grew up to be wonderful adults. I am astounded by their sense of responsibility for their own lives. They are kind, caring, and well-rounded adults. I take no credit for their accomplishments or who they have become today. I know it hasn't been easy for them growing up without extended family and not knowing their biological father. I haven't always been the best parent. I have made tons of mistakes. I wish it could have been different for them. I will always carry a sense of guilt over that.

I love my children with all my heart. It is an absolute joy to have them in life. My family might be small, but it is perfect for me. I always say if you can find one person to love you, then consider yourself lucky.

Over the course of my recovery, I would surf the net, looking for other survivors of schizophrenia. I also wanted to gauge current psychiatry for shifts that started exploring trauma as a contributing factor of schizophrenia. In 1998, I stumbled onto Jack Rosberg's website. I started reading his work. It floored me. He was talking about what I had experienced. He talked about the human process in the development of schizophrenia and the language. I knew right away that his findings were correct. Jack Rosberg founded the Anne Sippi Clinic in California (annesippiclinic.com) and trained many professionals around the world to work with people with schizophrenia.

I sent Jack an email right away telling him who I was and about my recovery. He responded immediately. Over the next eight years, we talked extensively about my case and his experiences. I even sent him a copy of my writings by mail. After he read them, he cried. My writings confirmed his findings on how schizophrenia develops.

When the topic of my writing a memoir came up, I will admit I felt a little ambivalent at first, but Jack felt I had an obligation to tell it. I felt obligated, but I wasn't sure if I was up to it, especially when I had so much work to do on myself still. The stigmas were also affecting me. There would be non-believers. But Jack said not to worry about that because I was just telling my story, and if I wanted him to, he would join me. I felt, at times, like he was pushing me too hard. And the thought of going up against big pharma and airing the dirty laundry of clinical psychiatry felt daunting.

Furthermore, my sister Sarah told me at the time that if I tried to publish one word, my mother had threatened that she was going to sue for libel. Her response scared the hell out of me. Even though I was a grown woman, I didn't know how to stand up to my mother or people like her. I didn't believe I was strong enough to challenge her. Just hearing her name was enough to make me freeze and send shivers up and down my spine.

After a while, I started pulling away from Jack. I only replied to a few of his emails, and when I did, I kept my replies short. Then finally, I came right out and told him I was going to college. Besides, I still had a lot of work to do on myself before I could talk confidently about my recovery. I had to wait till I had the courage to do it. I just didn't have it in me back then. I was preparing for it, though, and knew the day would come. I just didn't know when.

In 2015, Jack passed away, and his son, Michael Rosberg, took over the Anne Sippi Clinics. He is now the director. Unfortunately, Jack will never see my book in print. However, I am grateful for the time I got to spend with him. He taught me a lot and gave me a big-picture perspective when it came to the role of the pharmaceutical industry in the peddling of hypotheses that helped secure them billions of dollars in profit.

Most of all, he listened.

If there was ever a great man, it was Jack. When I look back on my journey through schizophrenia, I wish I could have had someone like Jack to help me from the very beginning. It was such a great honour to know him. I will always remember him fondly and am grateful for all that he did for me. And I can still hear his booming voice that demanded attention and sometimes intimidated me.

When I first came across Jack's work over twenty years ago, his was something of a voice in the wilderness. Not so today, but a great deal of work remains to be done. There are still too many practicing psychiatrists relying on their prescription pads and not enough resources put into proper psychotherapeutic approaches.

Looking back, I'm glad Jack pushed me as hard as he did.

Here's to you, Jack. I finally did it.

## AFTERWORD BY JACK ROSBERG PHD

I consider it a privilege to write about this book and its author, Tracey Higgins.

It's not about treatment; it's not just about schizophrenia. It's about one person's experience with schizophrenia and her subsequent recovery. It's also an exquisite, sensitive, and painful rendition of a struggle against almost impossible odds. It says very much about the human spirit and how a person with determination can overcome what is commonly referred to as 'an incurable brain disease.'

In my forty-six years of practice, as a psychologist, psychotherapist, and researcher dealing with this difficult condition on a daily basis, I have never ever heard such a unique story of full recovery from schizophrenia without medication.

This is not a book about psychotherapy or medication or psychosocial rehabilitation. This is about courage, determination and an attitude that becomes a self-fulfilling prophecy. Tracey Higgins did it all by herself. Research that has been replicated in several countries around the world shows that patients with long histories of this condition can make good social recoveries, given the opportunity. Why is then, that treatment is very poor? Is it because it is so difficult to treat this population? Certainly, it is difficult. Is it true that everyone has some madness in them they are afraid of discovering and therefore reject treatment as being a useless alternative? In order to be effective, therapists need to overcome their own insanity. There is no question in my mind that everyone carries the seeds of craziness, and if there is a lack of synthesis and integration that certainly does stir up the fear of madness.

To understand schizophrenia, we need to know about the process rather than the end result, the environment and culture that surround them and to have some understanding of the professionals who treat them. To quote Thomas McGlashan, the well-regarded psychiatrist and researcher, "Current treatment modalities for schizophrenia are extracting diminishing returns." And then there is the eminent Karl Menninger who wrote in 1957, "The psychology of schizophrenia is, in my opinion, as much in the minds of the observers as in the mind of the patient. We must change before he can change. He has long been incurable because we have been hopeless."

Tracey Higgins did not receive medication, she did not undergo psychotherapy, and she was not in a psychosocial rehabilitation program. She wandered the world as it was, her world, frightened, even terrified, and concerned with her very survival every minute of every day. She had completely lost her identity and did not, for many years, have any idea what direction to take. Yet she recovered completely. However, many people, professionals, and laypersons alike will doubt the accuracy of her diagnosis simply because they have no faith in an individual's capacity to overcome the most difficult condition alone. When you read her book and see through her eyes, the pain of her everyday existence, you will not doubt that she was most certainly a schizophrenic? Yet, there are professionals in the mental health field, whose perception of schizophrenia is so totally negative, that they will deny the possibility that anyone can recover from it and, therefore, will claim that the patient was simply misdiagnosed. And there are many who have recovered from schizophrenia that are unwilling to present their selves because few will accept their recovery as a result.

*The Girl on the Bridge* is unique in that Tracey Higgins has recovered without the aid of drugs or any kind of therapy. She was deprived of such treatment, and it appears, to her benefit. What she had in her favour was an incredible will to conquer an illness without help. One can only imagine what a monumental battle it was.

Tracey Higgins was schizophrenic. She no longer is. This vividly points out that we do not know enough about the human condition to limit a person's potential even under the worst of circumstances. She not only is a stimulus for our need to review our efforts, but also encourages those individuals who feel so very hopeless.

I think that it is critically important to ask ourselves this question. What is schizophrenia? There are many myths about this condition that need to be dispelled in order for us to have a better understanding of this human process. *Schizophrenia is a brain disease*; this is a myth. *There are no psychological causes of schizophrenia*; this is a myth. *Schizophrenia is a virus*: this is a myth. *Schizophrenia is caused by a genetic factor*; this is a myth.

But what is schizophrenia? Can we understand it as a delusional system? Do we understand it as being those afflicted with auditory hallucinations? Can we understand it as a paranoid system? Can we understand it as weird thoughts? Is this what schizophrenia is? In the DSM codes of the American Psychiatric Association, the symptoms and characteristics are classified. But nowhere do you see anything about the human process. Schizophrenia, its early onset of the acute phase, is a state of terror. These human beings whose great fear makes them suffer a loss of identity and a disintegration of the self. People undergoing this terrifying experience feel like they hang between life and death, and there has to some way of reaching a state of survival in the face of this enormous fear. When they are treated in this acute phase, they are treated primarily with medication that pushes them back to a pre-morbid state, which in itself is a very disturbing condition. Tragically, this form of treatment is woefully inadequate and is very often followed by repeated acute exacerbations that often ends up to be a terminal condition. To treat the individual successfully, we also need to understand the logic and language of this condition.

Tracey Higgins suffered an acute onset. Her life was like a nightmare for many years. She had fantasies of annihilation and destruction. There was no great sense of relief from these fears. She did not make peace with her condition. It never did, in fact, become a survival system. It never did, in fact, become and remain her identity. With whatever tools she had at her disposal, she struggled, incredibly, to find a solution to this intolerably painful condition. Gradually the recovery process began to emerge, which gave her the encouragement that she required to go further and to conquer her enemy that controlled her life for such a long period of time.

Currently, she is free of schizophrenia, and her life is normal. The future is good for her. Today, her search for herself as turned into a deep desire to educate both professionals and the lay public and promote the realization that there is hope for this condition we call schizophrenia. We must continue our struggles to develop better treatment methods and fund alternative treatment centers that will offer to those individuals with the opportunity to recover. This need for her to discover this has become her mission, and we must come to believe that her successful efforts at recovery will influence many people to help them understand there is no one beyond hope.

Jack Rosberg PhD

2000

# Acknowledgements

I would like to thank my husband and two adult children for bringing so much joy into my life. It is a privilege and an honour to have them in my life. I am eternally grateful for them.

I thank my editor, Warren Layberry of Darkwater Editing, for making my book the best it can be with his remarkable writing skill set. It was a joy to work with him. I am grateful to him for his expertise.

I also want to thank Jack Rosberg, founder of the Anne Sippi Clinic, for believing in my story and me. He will live on in my memory forever.

# RECOMMENDED READING

Davis, Laura. *The Courage to Heal: A guide for women survivors of child sexual abuse.* New York: Harper & Row, 1988.

Hahn, Patrick D. *Madness and Genetic Determinism: Is mental illness in our genes?* New York: Palgrave Macmillan, 2019.

———. *Prescription for Sorrow: Antidepressants, suicide and violence.* Samizdat Health Writer's Co-operative Inc., 2020.

Harrington, Anne. *Mind Fixers: Psychiatry's troubled search for the biology of mental illness.* New York: WW Norton, 2019.

Kusters, Wouter. *A Philosophy of Madness: The experience of psychotic thinking.* Boston: MIT Press, 2020.

Lynch, Terry. *The Systematic Corruption of Global Mental Health: Prescribed drug dependence.* Limerick, Ireland: Mental Health Publishing, 2018.

Whitely, Martin. *Overprescribing Madness: What's driving Australia's mental illness epidemic?* Melbourne, Australia: Wilkinson Publishing, 2021.

McCarthy Jones, Simon. "The concept of schizophrenia is coming to an end – here's why." *The Conversation.*

theconversation.com/the-concept-of-schizophrenia-is-coming-to-an-end-heres-why-82775.

Moncrieff, Joanna. *The Myth of the Chemical Cure: A critique of psychiatric drug treatment*. New York: Palgrave Macmillan, 2008.

Pies, Ronald W. "Debunking the Two Chemical Imbalance Myths, again." *Psychiatric Times.*

www.psychiatrictimes.com/view/debunking-two-chemical-imbalance-myths-again.

Ruby, Chuck. *Smoke and Mirrors: How you are being fooled about mental illness*. Welcome, MD: Clear Publishing, 2020.